RMED
S GUIDE
IAL
TIONS

ing Stocks, Bonds,
tual Funds, Futures,
and Options

Howard M. Berlin

IRWIN
Professional Publishing
Burr Ridge, Illinois
New York, New York

© RICHARD D. IRWIN, INC., 1994

Senior sponsoring editor: Amy Hollands Gaber
Project editor: Beth Yates
Production manager: Bob Lange
Interior designer: Mercedes Santos
Cover designer: Tim Kaage
Art coordinator: Mark Malloy
Compositor: TCSystems, Inc.
Typeface: 11/13 Palatino
Printer: Arcata Graphics/Kingsport

Library of Congress Cataloging–in–Publication Data

Berlin, Howard M.
   The informed investor's guide to financial quotations :
evaluating stocks, bonds, mutual funds, futures, and options /
Howard M. Berlin.
      p.   cm.
   Includes index.
   ISBN 1-55623-954-8
   1. Financial quotations.   2. Newspapers—Sections, columns, etc.—
Finance.   I. Title.
HG4521.B439   1994
332.63'2042—dc20   93–38864

Printed in the United States of America
2 3 4 5 6 7 8 9 0 AGK 1 0 9 8 7 6 5 4

Preface

This book describes and illustrates as simply and clearly as possible how to read, understand, and interpret financial market quotations that appear in the financial press as well as in many local newspapers for a wide range of markets. In nine chapters, the coverage includes stocks, bonds, Treasury securities, agencies, futures, options, mutual funds, and foreign currency exchange. This book was not written to help you find the next super stock, or how to make a million by trading pork bellies or Japanese yen. Many books have been written that claim to be able to do these things, and there are also many books that explain in greater depth the underlying basics for the types of investments discussed here.

This sourcebook should be extremely helpful to people whose work brings them into contact with financial markets. Many of these will be beginning investors or students who are taking courses in economics and finance, in which it is necessary to be able to follow financial markets from newspaper accounts and to perform several necessary and meaningful calculations to verify values.

Several features add to the usefulness and clarity of this book. All quotation formats are explained, column by column, term by term. All major formulas are presented in boxes, to emphasize their importance. Many numerical examples are presented to illustrate the use of the formulas and the interpretation of the results. These examples also are presented in boxes. In addition, calculations refer to equations by number. Terms appearing in boldfaced type are explained in the book's glossary.

As one who has always been interested in numbers, I wrote this book as a companion to one of my earlier books, *The Handbook of Financial Market Indexes, Averages, and Indicators*, which is another helpful sourcebook of financial information. While I have spared no effort in my attempts to make this book as complete as possible, any comments concerning omissions are welcomed. Naturally, I as the author bear full responsibility for any errors. I can be reached via E-mail on the Internet at berlin@apache.dtcc.edu or by conventional mail at P.O. Box 9431, Wilmington, DE 19809.

Finally, I am grateful to the following sources for their permission to reproduce the copyrighted material used in the illustrative exhibits.

Associated Press

Barron's

Chicago Sun Times

Investor's Business Daily

Morningstar Mutual Funds

The New York Times

Standard & Poor's Corporation

USA Today

Value Line Publishing, Inc.

The Wall Street Journal

Howard M. Berlin

Contents

Chapter One

Stocks

INTRODUCTION

Stocks are referred to as *equity instruments,* because the stockholder has equity, or ownership, in a corporation. The percentage of ownership is proportional to the number of shares owned in comparison to the total number sold by the corporation (i.e., outstanding shares). For the individual investor, **stocks** are the most popular form of investment. This is primarily because they are **liquid,** or easily marketable. In addition, plenty of information is available about the companies that issue them. Stock market information appears nightly on television news shows and on radio news broadcasts during trading hours. Information can also be found on several cable channels in the form of ticker tapes at the bottom of television screens and in virtually every local newspaper in the country.

TYPES OF STOCK

As explained previously, owning stock means having part ownership in a company.[1] However, not all stocks are created equal; some types of stock give their owners certain rights and privileges not afforded to owners of others.

Common Stock

The most prevalent form of stock available is **common stock.** Yet in fact, common stock is considered the riskiest form of stock: owners of it are often referred to as *residual claimants.* This is

---

[1] The terms *corporation* and *company* are interchangeable.

because these owners are entitled to the corporate assets and earnings remaining after all prior claims against the company have been satisfied. Those having prior claims are bond holders, loan holders, and owners of preferred stock. On the positive side, common stockholders can share in the corporate dividends that may be declared from periodic profits as well as in any capital appreciation (or loss) in the stock's value.

Preferred Stock

The other major form of stock is **preferred stock,** which has some of the characteristics of both common shares and corporate bonds (see Chapter 2). Like bonds, preferred stocks have a stated rate of return on the face value, but they do not have the security generally associated with bonds. On the other hand, like common stocks, preferred shares also represent ownership in a corporation. Preferred stock owners do not benefit from increased earnings and do not participate in management to the same extent as common stockholders do.

In return for some restrictions, owners of preferred shares have a preference over owners of common shares to the dividends and assets in the event the company is liquidated. If cash dividends are declared by the corporation's board of directors, then the preferred stockholders have to be paid before common stockholders are paid. If, however, the board decides not to pay cash dividends when such payments are due, the stock is said to be in **arrears.** Almost all preferred stocks are issued with a cumulative dividend feature, and are called *cumulative preferreds,* as opposed to *noncumulative preferred stocks.* For the former, the unpaid dividends accumulate for future payment and, when paid, must be paid before any dividends are paid to common shareholders.

Rights

Rights are **instruments** issued to common stockholders when a corporation sells additional shares of common stock to the public. The purpose of rights is to permit common shareholders to buy additional shares in the company in order to maintain their proportionate share of ownership. In effect, a right is an **option** (but not an obligation) that is given to common stockholders, permitting them to buy additional shares of common stock within a given time frame.

Like other forms of stock, rights have value and are actively traded during their short lifetimes, typically 90 days or less. They can be either exercised or sold. It is the New York Stock Exchange's policy to trade stocks with rights, known as **cum-rights.** Until the rights are mailed to the stockholders, they are traded on a **when-issued (WI)** basis. The trading of WI rights usually begins on the day the stock goes **ex-rights.** As soon as the rights are mailed to the stockholders, the company's stock is traded in the conventional manner.

Warrants

As opposed to rights, which are a form of short-term option, **warrants** are long-term options to buy a specified number of shares at a specified price. Some warrants expire in one or two years, while some never expire; these are said to be perpetual. Like rights and stocks, warrants are traded. The value at which the option is exercised is fixed above the current market price of the stock at the time the warrant is issued.

In the language of stock options, a warrant is basically a call on a stock. Its owner has no voting rights, the warrant pays no dividends, and the owner is not entitled to any claims on the assets of the corporation. In short, warrants are speculative.

STOCK EXCHANGES

Because stocks are marketable securities, they are traded in organized markets such as stock exchanges or **over-the-counter (OTC) markets.** The two major US "national" stock exchanges are the **New York Stock Exchange (NYSE)** and the **American Stock Exchange (AMEX),** both of which are located in New York City. Of these two, the NYSE is the most dominant. Besides these two national exchanges, there are smaller regional stock exchanges, such as the Boston, Chicago, Pacific (San Francisco and Los Angeles), and Philadelphia stock exchanges. Major Canadian exchanges are the ones in Montreal and Toronto. The Toronto Stock Exchange is the larger.

Unlike stock exchanges where the traders are face to face, the OTC market consists of thousands of dealers and brokers who communicate with each other via telephone, computer, or some other means. Unlike the formal national and regional exchanges, there is no formal organization for OTC markets, although traders are regulated by the **National Association of Securities Dealers (NASD)** and the **Securities and Exchange Commission (SEC)**.

THE ANATOMY OF THE STOCK TICKER SYMBOL

Each security that is traded on an exchange is assigned a unique ticker symbol. Besides stocks, ticker symbols are also assigned for other tradable securities such as stock options, tradable indexes, **bonds, futures contracts,** and options on futures contracts.

The stock ticker symbol is a unique abbreviation used to represent a stock. It should not be confused with a commonplace abbreviation for a given company used in newspaper stock tables, although in some instances the two may be the same. For example, Capital Holdings is usually abbreviated in newspaper stock tables as CapHldg, but its ticker symbol is CPH. On the other hand, International Business Machines is abbreviated as IBM and its ticker symbol is also IBM.

The ticker symbol is assigned by the particular exchange on which the stock is traded, although the company itself may have a hand in its selection. In practice, the ticker symbol should be as short as possible—it can be a single letter or as long as five letters—and should be distinctive enough to be identified with the company. Only the following 22 companies currently have the distinction of a single-letter ticker symbol:

A	Atwoods PLC (ADR)[2]	N	Inco Ltd.
B	Barnes Group	P	Phillips Petroleum

---

[2] An **American Depository Receipt (ADR)** is a US security representing ownership of a specified number of ordinary shares of a foreign company traded on the NYSE, AMEX, or OTC. The physical shares are held by an agent or a foreign branch of an American bank (an ADR bank). The custodian bank is usually an office of the American bank in the country of the company whose ADR is issued. If not, the custodian bank is the bank closest to the foreign company.

C	Chrysler Corporation	R	Ryder System
D	Dominion Resources	S	Sears Roebuck & Company
E	Transco Energy	T	American Telephone & Telegraph
F	Ford Motor	U	US Air Group
G	Gillette	V	Vivra Inc.
H	Helm Resources	W	Westvaco Corporation
I	First Interstate Bancorp	X	USX Corporation
J	Jackpot Enterprises	Y	Alleghany Corporation
K	Kellogg Company	Z	F.W. Woolworth Corporation

All these companies are listed on the NYSE, with the exception of Helm Resources (H), which is listed on the AMEX.

The ticker symbol is often viewed as a company's personal moniker. To answer the question of "What's in a name?" ticker symbols appear to fall into one of several categories, as follows:

- Ticker symbols that consist of the company's initials

IBM	International Business Machines
JCP	JC Penney
KLM	KLM (Koninklijke Luchtvaart Maatschappij)
MMM	Minnesota Mining and Manufacturing
WGL	Washington Gas & Light

- Ticker symbols that closely approximate the company's name or initials

AAPL	Apple Computer
CHF	Chock Full o'Nuts
MRK	Merck & Company
SLE	Sara Lee
XLNX	Xilinx

- Ticker symbols that are exactly the same as the company's name

  BETZ   Betz Laboratories Inc.
  CULP   Culp Inc.
  GREY   Grey Advertising
  LUND   Lund International
  ZEOS   Zeos International

- Ticker symbols that appear to have nothing in common with the company's name

  HFOX   Ultra Bancorp
  LLB   Computrac
  LUV   Southwest Airlines
  RVR   Cruise America

- Ticker symbols that do not have their first letter in common with the company's name but are designed to identify the company's industry or promote one of its products

BUD	Anheuser-Busch	NUT	Mauna Loa Macadamia
FOTO	Seattle Film	OIL	Triton Energy
FLY	Airlease	SODA	A&W Brands
HAMS	Smithfield Companies	VO	Seagram

- Ticker symbols that are novel enough to gain attention and to easily remember

COOL	Cooper Development	HEAL	Healthwatch
EAT	Brinker International	TOY	Toys ''R'' Us
FUN	Cedar Fair	ZAP	Helionetics

NYSE and AMEX Ticker Symbols

With the exception of 22 companies, stocks that are traded on the NYSE use two- or three-letter ticker symbols, while AMEX-listed stocks use two-, three-, or four-letter ticker symbols. When an

AMEX ticker symbol has four letters, the last letter is frequently used to signify the class of stock. Examples are:

FCEB   Forest City, Class B
GFSA   Giant Food, Class A
IMOA   Imperial Oil, Class A
NYTA   New York Times, Class A
TBSB   Turner Broadcasting, Class B

OTC and NASDAQ Ticker Symbols

All stocks traded OTC and listed on the **National Association of Securities Dealers Automated Quotations (NASDAQ)** system have four- or five-letter ticker symbols. When a fifth letter is used, it signifies that the stock issues are not common or capital shares, or are subject to special conditions, as summarized in Exhibit 1–1. The following symbols are examples:

BHAGB   BHA Group (Class B stock)
CANNY   Canon (ADR)
INDHK   Independent Insurance (non voting stock)
LWNGF   Loewen Group (foreign company)
VLANS   Land (shares of beneficial interest)

READING U.S. STOCK QUOTATIONS

Domestic stocks are traded on the NYSE, on the AMEX, in regional stock exchanges, and over the counter. Virtually all local newspapers publish stock quotations in one form or another. As there are progressively fewer "afternoon" newspapers being published these days, stock quotations tend to be summaries of the previous day's trading.

NYSE Issues

Apart from preferred stocks, warrants, rights, and other classes of stocks, the NYSE has approximately 2,600 companies listed on its exchange. The quote format for stocks traded on the NYSE is

EXHIBIT 1–1
NASDAQ 5th Letter Stock Identification System.

A	Class A stock
B	Class B stock
C	Exempt from NASDAQ listing qualifications for a limited period
D	New issue of an existing stock
E	Delinquent in required filings with the SEC
F	Foreign company
G	First convertible bond
H	Second convertible bond, same company
I	Third convertible bond, same company
J	Voting stock
K	Nonvoting stock
L	Miscellaneous situations, including second-class units, third-class warrants, or sixth-class preferred stock
M	Fourth preferred, same company
N	Third preferred, same company
O	Second preferred, same company
P	First preferred, same company
Q	In bankruptcy proceedings
R	Rights
S	Shares of beneficial interest
T	With warrants or rights
U	Units
V	When issued and when distributed
W	Warrants
Y	American Depository Receipt (ADR)
Z	Miscellaneous situations, including second-class warrants; fifth-class preferred stock; and any unit, receipt, or certificate representing a limited partnership interest.

Source: National Association of Security Dealers.

generally the same in virtually all local papers, such as the *News Journal* (Wilmington, Delaware), as well as in national papers, such as *USA Today, The Wall Street Journal, Investor's Business Daily,* and *The New York Times.*

EXHIBIT 1–2
***NYSE Stock Quotations from* The Wall Street Journal.**

Quotations as of 5 p.m. Eastern Time
Thursday, June 24, 1993

	52 Weeks Hi	Lo	Stock	Sym	Div	Yld %	PE	Vol 100s	Hi	Lo	Close	Net Chg
			-A-A-A-									
	14⅝	10¾	AAR	AIR	.48	3.6	...	237	13½	13	13⅜	+ ⅜
	11¾	10¾	ACM Gvt Fd	ACG	.96e	8.3	...	462	11⅝	11½	11½	– ⅛
	10	9	ACM OppFd	AOF	.80	8.3	...	92	9¾	9⅝	9⅝	...
	11⅞	9⅞	ACM SecFd	GSF	.96	8.7	...	553	11⅛	11	11	– ⅛
	9¾	8⅝	ACM SpctmFd	SI	.80	8.4	...	485	9½	9⅜	9½	+ ⅛
	11	9¼	ACM MgdIncFd	AMF	1.08	9.8	...	605	11	10¾	11	+ ⅛
	11⅝	8⅝	ACM MgdMultFd	MMF	.85e	9.4	...	159	9⅛	9	9	...
n	15⅛	14½	ACM MuniSec	AMU		...	...	141	14⅝	14½	14⅝	...
	9⅞	6⅜	ADT	ADT		...	...	500	9	8⅞	9	...
	2⅛	⅞	ADT wt			...	...	60	1½	1⅜	1⅜	...
s	32⅛	22⅞	AFLAC	AFL		...	15	1093	29⅛	28⅝	28⅞	– ¼
	29⅜	18	AL Labs A	BMD	.18	.7	33	690	26⅜	26⅛	26¼	– ½
	65⅞	52⅝	AMP	AMP	1.60	2.6	22	3154	62¾	61¾	62⅜	– ⅞
	72⅞	54⅜	AMR	AMR		...	dd	6377	63	60½	62⅝	+1⅜
	47¼	39¼	ARCO Chm	RCM	2.50	5.7	23	28	44	43¾	43¾	– ⅛
	2¼	1⅜	ARX	ARX		...	13	4	2⅛	2⅛	2⅛	...
	51½	29¾	ASA	ASA	2.00	4.3	...	1530	46⅞	45⅛	46¾	+1⅜
	33	22⅝	AbbotLab	ABT	.68	2.6	17	8851	26⅛	25¾	26	+ ⅜
n	9⅞	3⅝	Abex	ABE		...	dd	186	4¼	4⅛	4¼	+ ⅛
	13½	10¼	Abitibi g	ABY	.38j	...	...	14	11⅜	11¼	11¼	...
s	15	6	AcceptIns	AIF		...	dd	107	12⅝	12½	12⅝	+ ⅛
n	4⅝	2¼	AcceptIns wt			...	...	56	3⅜	3¼	3¼	...
nx	32	25½	ACE Ltd	ACL	.10p	.4	...	1531	27¾	27⅜	27¾	+ ⅜
	11⅛	4¾	AcmeCleve	AMT	.40	4.1	13	493	10	9½	9⅞	– ⅛
	9¼	3¾	AcmeElec	ACE		...	dd	12	8⅝	8⅝	8⅝	+ ⅛
n	24¾	15⅛	Acordia	ACO	.29e	1.4	...	6	21⅜	21¼	21¼	– ¼
	20⅞	10⅜	Acuson	ACN		...	13	1228	12	11⅞	11⅞	– ⅛
	22¼	18⅜	AdamsExp	ADX	1.62e	8.0	...	44	20⅜	20⅛	20¼	+ ⅛
	32⅞	7⅜	AdvMicro	AMD		...	9	8398	21¼	20½	21¼	+ ⅛
	66	30⅜	AdvMicro pf		3.00	6.1	...	119	49¾	48¾	49	– ¼
	7¾	4⅞	Advest	ADV		...	dd	16	5¾	5¾	5¾	– ⅛
s	24¾	12⅜	Advo	AD	.04e	.2	22	689	21⅛	20¾	21	+ ¼

As illustrated by the NYSE issues of Exhibit 1–2, which appeared in *The Wall Street Journal,* NYSE stock quotes are given in the following format:

❶		❷	❸	❹	❺	❻	❼		❽		❾
52-weeks					**Yld**		**Vol**				**Net**
Hi	**Lo**	**Stock**	**Sym**	**Div**	**%**	**PE**	**100s**	**Hi**	**Lo**	**Close**	**Chg**

The columns used in the format are described below.

❶ 52-week high and low.   The stock's highest and lowest closing prices for the last 52-week period. This trading range will generally indicate the stock's volatility, at least for the last year. Prices are generally expressed in whole dollars and eighths. For *The Wall Street Journal* stock tables, letter codes are often used preceding the 52-week high price to indicate various situations such as that the stock is trading ex-dividend (x), the stock is a new issue of less than 52 weeks (n), or the stock has split (s). In this case, the 52-week high and low prices are adjusted to account for the split in shares. Examples are:

52-weeks					Yld		Vol				Net
Hi	Lo	Stock	Sym	Div	%	PE	100s	Hi	Lo	Close	Chg
x $27^3/_4$	$13^1/_4$	FreMontGen	FMT	.72	3.2	8	562	$23^3/_4$	$22^1/_8$	$22^3/_4$	+ $^1/_4$
n 23	$22^1/_8$	Holly Resdntl	HLY		. . .	. . .	438	$22^3/_8$	$22^1/_4$	$22^1/_4$	. . .
s $22^1/_8$	$16^3/_8$	Service Cp	SRV	.40	2.0	18	2611	$21^1/_8$	$20^1/_2$	$20^1/_2$	− $^1/_2$

❷ Stock.   The name of the company issuing the stock. Companies are listed in alphabetical order, and the company name is often abbreviated. Furthermore, the abbreviation used by one newspaper may not be exactly the same as that used by another. For example, *The Wall Street Journal* uses the abbreviation AmBrand for American Brands (AMB); *The New York Times* and *USA Today* use ABrand; and *Investor's Business Daily* uses AmerBrands.

Unless noted otherwise, all stocks listed are assumed to be common shares. Preferred stocks have the letters pf following the stock name and are listed on the next line immediately following the corporation's common shares. Rights are usually indicated by rt and warrants by wt. "When issued" stock is indicated by WI following the company name.

❸ Ticker symbol.   The unique ticker symbol assigned by the exchange on which the stock is traded. For preferred stocks, ticker symbols are not given. For companies issuing more than one class of stock, the symbol omits the customary period between the ticker abbreviation for the stock and the stock class. For example, the following quotation is for Crawford Class B stock.

52-weeks					Yld		Vol				Net
Hi	Lo	Stock	Sym	Div	%	PE	100s	Hi	Lo	Close	Chg
25	15⁷/₈	Crawfrd B	CRDB	.52	2.6	15	56	17¹/₂	17¹/₄	17¹/₄	. . .

The listed symbol here is given as CRDB instead of CRD∎B (or CRD.B) as it would appear on the ticker tape. Many newspapers, such as *The New York Times* and *USA Today*, omit this column to save space.

④ Dividend. The current annual cash dividend per share, expressed in dollars and cents, effective with the last dividend payment. Generally dividends are paid quarterly, so that each dividend payment will be one-fourth that indicated in the tables unless the declared dividend has changed from one of the previous values. For example,

52-week					Yld		Vol				Net
Hi	Lo	Stock	Sym	Div	%	PE	100s	Hi	Lo	Close	Chg
47¹/₄	39¹/₄	ARCO Chem	RCM	2.50	5.8	22	59	43³/₄	43³/₈	43³/₈	− ¹/₄

shows that ARCO Chemical Company (RCM) pays an annual dividend of $2.50 per share. Any letter following the dividend refers to changes in the annual rate, etc. Qualifying footnotes are explained either at the beginning or at the end of the tables. If a company, on the other hand, does not pay dividends, then this column is blank, as follows:

52-weeks					Yld		Vol				Net
Hi	Lo	Stock	Sym	Div	%	PE	100s	Hi	Lo	Close	Chg
16200	8875	BerkHathwy	BRK		. . .	42	z110	16075	15950	15950	−25

Stocks trading **ex-dividend** (or ex-rights) are usually indicated by the letter x, either as part of the 52-week high and low prices (as in *The Wall Street Journal*) or following the stock name, as shown below.

52-weeks		Stock	Sym	Div	Yld %	PE	Vol 100s	Hi	Lo	Close	Net Chg
Hi	Lo										
x$27^3/_4$	$13^1/_4$	FreMontGen	FMT	.72	3.2	8	562	$23^3/_4$	$22^1/_8$	$22^3/_4$	$+^1/_4$

⑤ Percent yield. The percentage return on the investment, based on the cash dividend per share and the current market (closing) price. The formula is:

$$\% \text{ Yield} = \frac{AD}{SP} \cdot 100 \qquad\qquad (1\text{--}1)$$

where:

AD = Annual dividends (in dollars)

SP = Current stock price (in dollars)

An example is:

52-weeks		Stock	Sym	Div	Yld %	PE	Vol 100s	Hi	Lo	Close	Net Chg
Hi	Lo										
$47^1/_4$	$39^1/_4$	ARCO Chem	RCM	2.50	5.8	22	59	$43^3/_4$	$43^3/_8$	$43^3/_8$	$-^1/_4$

such that ARCO Chemical Company currently has a return on the investment of 5.8 percent, based on an annual dividend of $2.50 a share when the stock is priced at $43^3/_8$ a share. If a company does not pay dividends, the percent yield cannot be computed.

⑥ Price/earnings (P/E) ratio. The **price/earnings (P/E) ratio** refers to the relationship between the stock's current price and the annual earnings per share of the company. Earnings are the profits a corporation earns during the year, and are frequently stated as dollar value per share. This data is obtained from quarterly or annual reports. The P/E (sometimes written P-E) ratio is an important barometer that investors look at in evaluating a stock, as it expresses the value of a stock in terms of company earnings and current stock prices. Some investors avoid stocks having P/E ratios greater than 10. Since earnings are not given in the quotations, the P/E ratio cannot be readily calculated.

If a corporation has experienced a loss in the most recent four quarters, the P/E ratio is not calculated, and a letter symbol is given in its place to note that fact. In the quotation below, the letters dd denote that Champion International Corporation (CHA) had a loss in the most recent four quarters and the P/E ratio is not calculated.

| 52-weeks | | | | | Yld | | Vol | | | | Net |
Hi	Lo	Stock	Sym	Div	%	PE	100s	Hi	Lo	Close	Chg
$34^5/_8$	$23^3/_4$	Champlnt	CHA	.20	.6	dd	2653	$32^5/_8$	$32^3/_8$	$32^3/_8$	$-^1/_8$

Some newspapers simply leave this column blank if there are no earnings.

⑦ Volume. The number of shares traded on a given day, expressed in 100s. The actual number of shares traded is obtained by multiplying this number by 100, as follows:

| 52-weeks | | | | | Yld | | Vol | | | | Net |
Hi	Lo	Stock	Sym	Div	%	PE	100s	Hi	Lo	Close	Chg
$47^1/_4$	$39^1/_4$	ARCO Chem	RCM	2.50	5.8	22	59	$43^3/_4$	$43^3/_8$	$43^3/_8$	$-^1/_4$

The 59 means that 5,900 shares of ARCO Chemical Company were traded.

On occasion, a letter code is added to indicate that the number listed is the actual number of shares. *USA Today*, *The New York Times*, and *The Wall Street Journal* use the letter z to indicate that the volume represents actual shares. In the following example for Berkshire Hathaway (BRK), z110 means that 110 shares were traded that day, not 11,000 shares. This is undoubtedly due to the extremely high per share price ($15,950 at the close).

52-week					Yld		Vol				Net
Hi	Lo	Stock	Sym	Div	%	PE	100s	Hi	Lo	Close	Chg
16200	8875	BerkHathwy	BRK		. . .	42	z110	16075	15950	15950	−25

Volume is a measure of the trading activity of a particular stock issue but may not be indicative of large price changes on a given day.

❽ Day's high, low, and close. A stock's highest, lowest, and closing trading prices for the given day. These figures are a measure of how widely the stock's price fluctuated during the day. Like the 52-week high and low prices, these prices are also generally expressed in dollars and eighths. In some newspapers, "last" is sometimes used as the column heading for the closing price.

As an example, the following quotation shows that Allen Group's stock traded within a $1/2$-point range from $42^7/8$ to $43^3/8$, and the last trade for that day was at $43^1/8$:

52-week					Yld		Vol				Net
Hi	Lo	Stock	Sym	Div	%	PE	100s	Hi	Lo	Close	Chg
$43^5/8$	$18^7/8$	AllenGp	ALN	.24	.6	24	457	$43^3/8$	$42^7/8$	$43^1/8$	$+^1/8$

❾ Net change. The change in the stock's closing price with the closing price of the previous trading day.

Example: Calculating Earnings and Percent Yield

For Friday, June 18, 1993, the quotation for ARCO Chemical Company appeared as follows:

52-week					Yld		Vol				Net
Hi	Lo	Stock	Sym	Div	%	PE	100s	Hi	Lo	Close	Chg
$47^{1}/_{4}$	$39^{1}/_{4}$	ARCO Chem	RCM	2.50	5.8	22	59	$43^{3}/_{4}$	$43^{3}/_{8}$	$43^{3}/_{8}$	$-^{1}/_{4}$

With a P/E ratio of 22 and a closing stock price of $43.375 a share, the company earned $43.375/22, or $1.97 a share. If the total number of shares outstanding were known, it would be possible to calculate the total earnings for the period.

The percent yield is determined from the annual dividends and the closing price for the day (Equation 1–1):

$$\% \text{ Yield} = \frac{\$2.50}{\$43.375} \cdot 100$$

$$= 5.76\%$$

and it agrees with the published yield when rounded off to the first decimal place.

AMEX Issues

The AMEX currently lists over 800 companies. Despite the smaller size of the AMEX, both *The Wall Street Journal* and *The New York Times* use the same format for AMEX issues as for NYSE issues. Other papers, such as *USA Today*, greatly abridge the information concerning AMEX-traded stocks, as illustrated in Exhibit 1–3, while others choose not to list AMEX issues at all.

USA Today's abridged format is as follows:

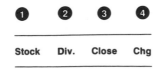

| ❶ | ❷ | ❸ | ❹ |
| Stock | Div. | Close | Chg |

EXHIBIT 1–3
AMEX Stock Quotations from **USA Today.**

AMEX

AMERICAN EXCHANGE CLOSING
STOCKS IN BOLDFACE ROSE OR FELL 3% OR MORE

Stock	Close	Chg		Stock	Close	Chg
AIM Str	.60 9	...		AMed	10	+ ⅛
				ARelian	.60 24⅜	+ ¼
ALC	6¾	+ ¼		ARestr	1.40 11¼	...
AMC	1.14e 5⅞	...		AScIE	5¼	− ⅛
AOI	5/16	− 1/16		AmShrd	4⅝	...
ARC	1	+ 1/16		ATechC	2⅛	...
ASR	.80 2⅞	− ⅛		A-axp	.95 21½	− ¼
ATT Fd	2.63e 59¼	+ ⅛		A-axp sc	1/128	...
Abiomd	10¾	− ¼		Ampal	5⅞	...
AckCom	2⅛	...		Amwest	.28 9¼	
Action	4⅝	...		**Andrea**	**8½**	**+ ⅜**
AdmRs n	4¾	− ⅛		Angel un	2.75 16½	+ ¼
AdvMag s	**11½**	**− ⅝**		AngMtg	2.00 17¼	...
AdvMed	8¼	...		AngPar	2.00 18½	...
AirWat	11⅛	− ⅜		ArrowA	7¼	...
AirExp s	.14 20⅞	+ ¼		Arhyth	5¾	...
Aircoa	**1**	**− ⅛**		**Astrotc**	**5¼**	**− ⅜**
Alafst s	.60 14⅞	...		Astrt wt	1	...
AlbaW	**7¾**	**− ⅜**		Astrot pf	1.20 24½	− ½
Alfin	1	...		**Atari**	**1¾**	**+ ⅛**
AllouH	6½	...		**Atlantis**	**3¼**	**− ⅛**
Alou wtB	**1¾**	**− ⅛**		**AtlsCM**	**9/16**	**− 1/16**
Alphaln	3	...		Atlas wt	2¼	...
AlpinGr	7⅜	...		Audvox	3½	...
Alza wt s	32⅞	− ¾		**B&H Mr**	**.05j 2¼**	**− ⅛**
Amdhl	.10 13⅛	+ ⅛		**B&HO**	**.10j 3⅛**	**− ⅛**
Amhhth	**15/16**	**− 1/16**		BAT ln	.93e 14¼	+ 1/16
AFstP2	1.64 16¼	+ ⅜		BHC	60¾	+ 1
ABkCT	1.32 19⅜	+ ⅛		BSN	.72 6¼	...
AmBilt	.15 14½	− ¼		Baker s	12¾	− ¼
AExpl	2⅞	...		Baldw	3⅞	...
AExpl wt	11/16	...		BanFd	1.33e 20½	...
AFruc A	.48 19¼	+ ⅛		BanyHI	3/16	...
AFruc B	.48 18¼	+ ⅛		**BanymSh**	**1⅜**	**+ ⅛**
AHltMg	4⅝	+ ⅛		Barnwl	.30 13¾	− ¼
AIM 84	.62e 4⅜	...		**BarrLb**	**7½**	**+ ¼**
AIM 85	1.02e 12⅜	...		BaryRG	7	− ⅛
AmList	1.00e 15⅜	+ ⅛		BayMea	.80e 13¾	− ⅜
AMzeA	.64 23⅜	+ ⅛		Bayou	2½	...
				Beard	**13/16**	**+ 1/16**

The columns used in the format are now described.

❶ **Stock.** The name of the company issuing the stock, listed in alphabetical order. The company name is often abbreviated. Furthermore, the abbreviation used by one newspaper may not be exactly the same as that used by another. All stocks listed are assumed to be common shares, unless otherwise indicated. Preferred stocks have the letters pf following the stock name.

② Dividend. The current annual cash dividend per share, expressed in dollars and cents effective with the last dividend payment. Although there is no specific column heading, the annual dividend in dollars and cents follows the stock name. As an example, the quotation below indicates that Air Express pays an annual dividend of $0.14 per share.

Stock		Close	Chg
AirExp	.14	$20^7/_8$	$-^1/_4$

In many cases no dividend is listed, as there are many AMEX-listed stocks that do not pay dividends.

③ Close. The stock's closing trading price for the day.

④ Change. The change in the stock's closing price with the closing price of the previous trading day.

OTC Issues

Stocks traded OTC are usually listed under a number of major headings, including:

OTC Stocks
Over-the-Counter Market
NASDAQ
NASDAQ Supplemental List
National Market System

and their variations.

Quotations for OTC stocks are published in several formats. The one used by *The Wall Street Journal* is for "NASDAQ National

Market Issues" and is arranged in the same columnar format as the one used for NYSE and AMEX quotations, as shown below.

52-week					Yld		Vol				Net
Hi	Lo	Stock	Sym	Div	%	PE	100s	Hi	Lo	Close	Chg

However, the format is abridged for listing "NASDAQ Small-Cap" (i.e., small capitalization) issues to the following:

		Vol		
Stock	Div.	100s	Last	Chg

The OTC quotations published in the *Chicago Tribune* have only four columns (Exhibit 1–5). The format is:

Stock	Sales	Close	Chg

Here the column for dividends is omitted, since the majority of OTC stocks do not pay dividends.

The final format for quoting OTC stocks is the *bid-asked* format, which is similar to that used for bonds. Many newspapers used to publish OTC stocks with this format, but most have dropped it in favor of the format used in Exhibit 1–5. The bid-asked format is as follows:

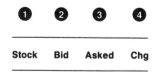

Stock	Bid	Asked	Chg

The columns used in the format are described in the following:

❶ **Stock.** The name of the company issuing the stock. The companies are listed in alphabetical order.

EXHIBIT 1–4
NASDAQ Small-Cap Quotations from The Wall Street Journal.

NASDAQ SMALL-CAP ISSUES

Issue	Div	Vol 100s	Last	Chg
Caprck		225	1/4	– 1/16
Capucin		770	7/16	– 1/16
CarMrt		120	6 3/8	...
CarMt wt		182	2 5/8	– 1/4
CareCon		39	2 1/2	...
Caretnd		149	1 13/16	+ 1/16
CaroFt pf	2.08	3	30	...
CarolB		488	6 1/4	...
Cavco		2	7 1/4	– 1/8
viCedrG		800	11/32	+ 1/4
Cellex		810	15/16	+ 1/16
Cellex un		105	7 1/4	+ 1/8
CellCm		29	5	...
CellrTc		252	7	– 1/4
CelTel		3	2 1/8	...
Celox		50	2 1/8	...
CnBkSy		31	7/8	...
CtrlVA		107	13 1/4	+ 3/4
CntMne		3927	2 1/8	+ 7/32
Cerprbe		1	5 3/4	– 1/4
Certron		3	1 5/16	...
ChalInt		55	2 7/8	+ 1/16
ChmpSpt		463	3/4	...
ChpSp pf		7	4	– 1/2
Chantal		116	1 1/16	+ 1/32
ChtBnc	.20	6	12 3/4	...
ChrtFdl		20	3 1/4	+ 1/8
ChkExp s		232	1 3/8	– 3/8
ChefInt s		510	6 1/4	...
Chemex		57	2 3/8	+ 3/16
Cherokee		290	5 1/4	– 1/2
Chrk wtA		17	1/4	– 1/2
Chrk wtB		22	3/16	– 5/16
Chrk wtC		118	1/4	– 1/4
ChldBrd		1010	6 1/2	– 1/4
ChromCS		80	6 1/8	– 1/4
ChmCS wt		122	2 5/8	– 1/16
ChrchllD		11	52	...
ChchTc s		6	7/8	+ 1/32
CtzFBk pf		145	24 1/2	– 1/4
CtyLTr		10	5/8	...
CluckWd		188	9 1/4	+ 1/4
Cluck wt		138	4 3/8	+ 5/8
CoastFla		200	5/32	– 3/32
Codenol		355	1 3/4	+ 3/8
ComCent		24	3 3/4	– 1/16
Comtek		50	1/8	+ 1/32
CmndCr s		2428	15/32	– 1/32
ComndAr		90	9 7/8	...
CwlthAs		255	10	+ 3/4
CmtyBTn	.24	1	9	+ 3/8
Comprt		1610	1/32	– 1/32
Complnk		1059	7	+ 1/8
CmpMed		212	1/4	+ 1/32
Cmpflt s		5	1 3/8	...
CptConc		1103	7 1/8	...
CptMkt		1921	7 1/2	...
CptM wtA		724	3 3/8	...
FUtBG pf	2.12	x3		...
FUtdSv	.20e	222	14 7/8	+ 3/8
FstLI	.66	5	32 1/2	+ 1 1/2
FtFdKY	.40	110	23 1/4	+ 1 1/4
FFFn pfA	1.75	2	36	+ 1
FschWt		70	7/16	+ 1/32
FocusEn		202	3 7/8	...
Focus wt		155	1 13/32	– 1/8
Fonar		954	1 9/32	+ 1/32
Fonic		241	4 1/8	...
ForeInd		509	4 5/16	+ 5/16
Forum		31	3 3/8	– 1/4
FountP		190	27/32	– 1/32
FtnPh un		6	6 1/2	– 1 1/2
Foxmor		65	2 1/8	– 1/4
FrkSB wt		1	3 1/4	...
FrkCon		2646	5/16	+ 1/32
FrJuice		195	2 1/2	...
FrntDir		27	3/4	+ 1/8
FutureHlt		67	12	...
FutMed		4691	1 11/32	+ 9/32
GB Fds		276	13 3/4	+ 5/8
GTEC 45pf	.90	22	14 1/2	+ 1/4
GTEC 56pf	.90	20	14 1/8	+ 1/4
GTEC 5pf	1.00	6	15 3/8	...
GamngCp		1600	12 1/2	...
Gamng wt		58	6 3/4	+ 1/8
Gamng un		27	15 1/4	– 1/4
Gamaln		301	4 5/8	– 1/8
Gaml wt		405	1 15/16	– 1/16
GnCom		43	4	...
GnPrcl		65	5 3/4	...
Genertn5		156	11/32	...
Gentnr		702	1 1/2	...
Gentnr wt		100	3/8	– 1/16
GeoWste		3	7/8	...
GeoTek		10080	8	+ 1/8
GeoTk pf		46	8	+ 3/8
Gerant		17824	7/32	– 1/32
GlacH wt		69	1 1/8	...
GlcrHd		207	5	+ 1/4
GlbEnv		201	1	...
GlbSpl		156	6 5/8	– 3/8
Globlink		104	6	– 1/4
Glblnk wt		8	1 1/4	– 1/4
Glblnk un		60	13 1/4	– 1/2
GldStd		360	1 3/8	...
GldEagl		68	4 1/2	...
GldEg wt		15		...
GoldPac		139	5 1/8	+ 5/32
GldQual		1037	1/2	+ 1/16
GoldTr		680	3/32	...
Goldex		35	2 1/4	– 1/4
GoodTm		18	1 9/16	– 1/16
Gotham		4	4 5/8	...
GrcHlth		60	4 3/8	...
GrcHlt wt		15	1	...
GrcHl un		10	9 3/8	...
GrntSt		80	9/32	+ 1/32
KLH Eng		1485	1	– 1/8
KSB Bc		447	13	...
KeithG		100	21/32	+ 1/8
KdyWils		48	4 1/2	– 1/2
KentFn		1	6 5/8	...
KngsRd		25	3/8	...
Kinross s		1404	1 3/4	+ 1/16
KooKR		211	2 1/16	– 1/16
L Rex		30	2 3/4	– 1/2
LDB		1	3 1/4	– 1/4
LF Bcp		1	16	– 2
LaTeko		94	1 13/16	...
Lancit		223	10 3/4	+ 1/4
Lanc wt94		16	8 1/2	+ 1/2
Lanc wt96		222	6 7/16	– 1/16
LarDav		418	3 3/16	+ 1/16
LasVEnt		4530	6 3/16	+ 9/16
LasVE wtA		321	5 1/4	+ 5/8
LasVEE wtB		72	2 3/4	+ 1/4
LaserMd		2	1 3/8	+ 1/16
LaserP		100	2 7/16	...
LsrSght s		101	7 5/8	– 3/8
Lasrtch		398	1 1/4	...
LsrVide		508	5 3/8	+ 1/8
LsrV wtA		1	1 13/16	– 1/8
LsrVd un		100	13 1/4	+ 1/4
LsrVis		414	6	...
LatexRs		562	4 3/16	+ 3/16
Latex wt		356	13/16	– 1/8
Latex un		27	6	– 7/16
Leadvle		10	1 7/16	...
LeakX		160	3 3/8	...
Leak X wt		10	2 1/4	...
LehTH		2	1 1/8	– 11/32
LeisMkt		1	5/8	...
LibNBk	.80	10	7 1/8	+ 1/8
Licon		510	1 5/16	– 1/4
Licon wt		10	2	...
Lidak		897	2 25/32	– 3/32
Lidak wt		509	7/8	– 3/32
Lidak wtC		20	1 13/16	– 3/16
LfeMed		102	7 7/8	+ 1/4
LfMd wtA		75	3 1/4	– 1/4
LfMd wtB		50	1 5/8	+ 5/16
LfeMd un		31	12	...
Lifecell		41	10 1/4	– 1/2
Lifeway		11	1 1/2	– 1/2
LoJack		488	5 9/16	+ 1/16
LneStar		897	5 3/4	+ 3/8
LouG 5pf	1.25	x9	18 1/4	– 3/8
LouG pf	1.86	x2	28	+ 1/4
LukMed		268	3 1/2	...
Lunnl		25	6 1/4	– 1/2
LuthMed		8	2 1/2	...
Luxcel		161	3	...
Luxtec		3	2	– 1/4
M-SysFD		294	14	– 1/4
M-Sys wt		20	6	– 1/8
MBF		412	1 5/16	– 1/16
OmegaEn		1088	5 5/8	– 1/16
Omnicp		73	7/16	...
OnGrdSy		74	5 1/8	...
OnGrd wt		80	1 3/16	– 5/16
OpthImg		252	3 7/8	– 1/8
Opticm		42	8 1/2	– 1/2
Optima		516	5 9/16	– 1/16
Orthlog		83	3 1/4	+ 5/16
OrthopT		328	7 3/4	– 1/2
OutTake		691	5 1/8	– 3/8
OutT wtA		5	1 1/2	...
OutT wtB		176	1 1/16	+ 1/4
OutTk un		5	7 1/2	...
OxboroM		2	2 1/4	...
OxfrdC		1	3 3/4	...
P&F pf	1.00	29	7 3/4	...
PAM		404	3 3/4	– 3/4
PCC Gp		12	2 3/4	– 1/2
PDG En		145	3	...
PVC	.05e	85	1 7/16	...
PacTec		44	1 1/8	– 1/8
PceOstr		114	3 7/16	– 1/16
PacSen		24	3 5/8	+ 5/32
PalmrMd		209	3 1/2	– 5/8
PalMd wt		255	1 3/8	– 1/16
Panthen s		517	5 3/8	– 1/4
Parclsn		31	2 1/2	+ 3/8
ParMtg		145	1 9/16	– 1/8
ParPet		308	1 13/16	...
Parlux		5	3 3/4	+ 1/4
PartchHd		1466	1 7/16	– 1/16
PatPtr pf	.12e	40	9 1/8	...
Paulson		150	1 1/4	...
PeachFb		50	1 5/8	...
PchFb wt		65	5/16	...
PenG pf	2.25	30	25 1/4	...
Percptr		25	5 7/8	...
Perfdta		45	1 1/2	– 1/32
PermFix		134	7 3/4	+ 1/8
PermF wt		386	7/8	+ 1/8
PersCpt		1888	1 7/32	– 1/16
PerDia		12	2 1/4	+ 3/16
PetPrd		98	5 3/4	– 1/8
PetPd wt		100	1 5/16	...
PetroUn		429	2 5/8	+ 1/2
PtHel vtg	.04	7	18	...
Petromt		50	3 31/32	+ 1/4
Pharmos		225	2 1/2	...
Phrmlnc h		10	1	...
Phrmhse		125	5 7/8	– 1/8
PhnxA wt		89	1 9/16	– 3/16
PhnxA		170	4 11/16	– 3/16
PhxNet		3018	4 17/32	+ 9/32
Photcm		140	1 1/4	– 1/8
PhylnMl		5	13	...
PiedMn		15	2 1/8	...
PlntT		931	7/8	+ 5/32
PlasmT	†	30	5/8	
PolutRs				

Reprinted by permission of *The Wall Street Journal,*

❷ **Bid.** The per share price at which a dealer (i.e., a buyer) has offered to buy this stock. In the following quotation,

EXHIBIT 1–5
NASDAQ Stock Quotations Appearing in the **Chicago Tribune** *(August 27, 1992).*

Nasdaq

Wednesday, August 26, 1992

	Sales	Last	Chng
A&W Bd	1353	35 7/8	− 1/8
ATS Med	154	6 3/4	+ 1/2
Abaxis	225	4 3/4	− 3/4
AbbyHlth	389	13	+ 1/4
ABS	20	13 3/4	− 1/4
ACC Cp	95	15 1/2	......
Accel	22	4 5/8	+ 1/8
Aclaim	363	8 7/8	+ 3/8
Acetob	61	15 1/4	......
AcmeSt	609	13 1/2	− 2 1/4
Acxiom	33	18	......
AdacLb	1387	3 5/16	+ 1/16
Adage s	33	5	......
Adapts	4678	23 1/4	+ 5/8
ADC	779	35 7/8	+ 5/8
Adingt	226	11	+ 1/4
Adesa	1182	5 5/8	− 1 5/8
↓**AdobeS**	22333	32 1/8	− 3 3/4
AdvCre	383	9 3/4	+ 1/2
AdvCirs	347	5 3/8	− 3/8
AdvRos	111	10 1/2	− 3/8
AdvInt	18	4	− 1/4
AdvLog	292	4 5/8	− 1/8
AdvPoly	1305	9 5/8	......
AdvPro	246	5 5/8	+ 1/8
AdvSem	23	1 5/8	......
AdvLab	360	17 1/4	......
AdvTel	111	25 1/4	......
AdvTis	1089	8 7/8	+ 1/4
Advanta	1206	18 3/4	+ 3/8
Advanta B	620	17	− 1/2
AdvBcp	62	16 3/8	− 3/8
AdHlth	67	15 1/2	......
AdvoSy	1133	21 1/2	......
AEP	18	11 1/4	......
Aequtrn	406	2 1/4	+ 1/4
Aerovx	9	4 3/8	− 1/4
AESCp	394	19	......
AfintyBio	200	4 1/4	+ 1/4
Afymax	124	18 1/4	− 1/4
AgSvcs	20	10 3/4	− 1/8
Agco	9	6 7/8	− 1/8
AgncyR	260	8 3/4	− 1/4
Agnico	89	4 5/8	......
Agourn	288	11 3/8	+ 1

	Sales	Last	Chng
Autodk	2870	45 3/8	+ 1/2
AutoInd	663	15 3/4	− 1/8
Autote	9	10	......
AW AE	199	3	+ 1/8
Aztar	1844	5 3/4	+ 1/4
BI Inc	195	7 3/4	− 1/8
BF Ent	10	4 3/4	− 3/8
Babage	257	15 3/4	− 1/2
BachInf	72	7 1/2	......
BackBay	90	14	− 3/4
BadgrP	8	21 1/2	− 1
BHugh wt	637	2 1/4	......
BakerJ	521	14	+ 1/4
Balchms	65	8 1/2	+ 1/4
BaldPia	11	13 3/4	+ 5/8
Balard s	142	25 1/2	+ 1/2
BllyGamg	1337	14 7/8	+ 7/8
BncOnpfC	106	62 3/4	− 1/4
BcpNJ x	10	13 3/4	+ 1/8
BcMiss	35	28	− 3/4
Banctec	63	25 1/4	+ 1/4
BandoM	31	13	......
BnkNH	106	9 1/4	− 1/2
BkSou	751	10	......
BkWorc	202	13 1/8	......
BankAfl	7	4 1/2	− 1/4
Bankrs	14	24	......
BnkFst	405	8 1/2	+ 3/4
Bknth	10	13	......
BanPnc s	237	25 3/8	− 3/8
Banta a	33	35 1/4	+ 1/2
BanySL2	70	15/16	− 1/16
BanySv	458	12	+ 1/2
Banya	18	5/32	......
BanyaIII	37	7/16	......
BanyaII	1467	1/8	......
BanySL	148	4 3/4	− 1/8
BareFt	21	13 1/2	− 1/8
Barra	25	7 1/4	+ 3/4
BaretRs	162	5	− 1/2
BsTn A	102	3 1/2	......
BsetF s	519	35 3/4	− 3/4
BayVw	77	16 1/8	− 3/8
BayBks	1382	30 3/8	+ 5/8
Bayprt	180	13/32	+ 1/32

a dealer has offered to buy shares of Coors Brewing from a seller at 19 5/8 a share.

Stock	Bid	Asked	Chg
Coors B	19 5/8	19 7/8	+3/8

❸ **Asked.** The **asked price** is the per share price that a dealer (i.e., a seller) would like the buyer to accept. The asked price is always higher than the bid price. The difference between bid and asked prices is known as the **spread** and must not be considered the same as the difference between the daily low and high prices for NYSE-traded stocks. In the Coors Brewing quotation, shares are quoted as being purchased by an investor from a dealer for 19⅞ a share.

The quoted bid and asked prices are generally averages of the many trading quotes made during the day. Unlike stock exchanges on which stock buy and sell trade prices are auctioned through a single specialist, OTC stocks are arrived at by many dealers, each competing for the best bid and asked prices. The spread is where the profits are made, and it generally moves in the direction opposite to that of the trading volume. A large spread is usually caused by low trading volume. In the Coors Brewing quote, the spread is from 19⅞ to 19⅝, or ¼ point.

❹ Change.   The change in the stock's average **bid** price from the previous day. In newspapers that still use the bid-asked format, this column is often omitted.

STOCK TABLE QUALIFIER CODES

Stock tables are full of various pieces of information in addition to the basic quotation summaries of trading volume; high, low, and close prices; and so forth. Some of these additional items, such as stock splits, new issues, and stocks trading ex-dividend, have already been noted. However, a vast number of qualifier codes use letters and symbols to indicate additional information. The explanation of these codes usually appears as "explanatory notes" or footnotes to the tables, such as that illustrated in Exhibit 1–6, from *The New York Times*.

Exhibit 1–7 summarizes the many qualifier codes that are commonly found. Most newspapers, including *USA Today*, *The New York Times*, and *Investor's Business Daily*, use most of the same codes as *The Wall Street Journal*.

EXHIBIT 1–6
Explanatory Notes Explaining Stock Qualifier Codes from **The New York Times.**

N.Y.S.E. and Amex Tables Explained

Sales figures are unofficial.

The 52-Week High and Low columns show the highest and the lowest price of the stock in consolidated trading during the preceding 52 weeks plus the current week, but not the current trading day.

u—Indicates a new 52-week high. d—Indicates a new 52-week low.

g—Dividend or earnings in Canadian money. Stock trades in U.S. dollars. No yield or P/E shown unless stated in U.S. money. n— New issue in the past 52 weeks. The high-low range begins with the start of trading and does not cover the entire 52-week period. s—Split or stock dividend of 25 percent or more in the past 52 weeks: The high-low range is adjusted from the old stock. Dividend begins with the date of split or stock dividend. v—Trading halted on primary market.

Unless otherwise noted, rates of dividends in the foregoing table are annual disbursements based on the last quarterly or semiannual declaration. Special or extra dividends or payments not designated as regular are identified in the following footnotes.

a—Also extra or extras. b—Annual rate plus stock dividend. c—Liquidating dividend. e—Declared or paid in preceding 12 months. i—Declared or paid after stock dividend or split-up. j— Paid this year, dividend omitted, deferred or no action taken at last dividend meeting. k—Declared or paid this year, an accumulative issue with dividends in arrears. r—Declared or paid in preceding 12 months plus stock dividend. t—Paid in stock in preceding 12 months, estimated cash value on ex-dividend or ex-distribution date.

x—Ex-dividend or ex-rights. y—Ex-dividend and sales in full. z—Sales in full.

pf—Preferred. pp—Holder owes installment(s) of purchase price. rt—Rights. un—Units. wd—When distributed. wi— When issued. wt—Warrants. ww—With warrants. xw—Without warrants.

vi—In bankruptcy or receivership or being reorganized under the Bankruptcy Act, or securities assumed by such companies.

Besides letter and symbol codes, major newspapers often use boldface type and underlining as visual aids to indicate certain performance levels achieved on the day's trades, as follows:

The Wall Street Journal

Boldfaced   Price change greater than 3 percent from previous day

EXHIBIT 1–7
Summary of Stock Table Stock Qualifier Codes and Symbols.

Meaning	WSJ	USA and NYT	IBD
New 52-week high.	▲	u	
New 52-week low.	▼	d	
Extra dividend or extra in addition to regular dividend.	a	a	
Liquidating dividend.	c	c	l
Loss in the most recent four quarters.	dd		
Dividend was declared or paid in preceding 12 months, but there is no regular dividend rate.	e		e
•Annual dividend rate, increased on latest declaration.	f		
Dividends and earnings are in Canadian dollars; stock trades are in U.S. dollars.	g	g	g
Dividend was declared or paid on cumulative issues, with dividends in arrears.	k	k	
Earnings due in next four weeks.			k
Annual dividend rate, reduced on latest declaration.	m		
New issue in last 52 weeks.	n	n	n
Initial dividend.	p		
Preferred stock.	pf	pf	pf
Cash dividend was declared or paid in preceding 12 months, plus a stock dividend.	r	r	
Rights.	rt	rt	rt
Stock split or dividend greater than 10% in last 52 weeks.	s	s	
Trading of stock halted on primary market.	v	v	
In bankruptcy, receivership, or being reorganized.	vi	vi	b
Units.	un	un	un
When distributed.	wd	wd	
When issued (WI).	wi	wi	wi
Warrants.	wt	wt	wt
Ex-dividend or ex-rights.	x	x	x
Traded without warrants.	xw	xw	
Ex-dividend and sales in full, not 100s.	y	y	y
Sales in full, not in 100s.	z	z	z

Sources: *The Wall Street Journal (WSJ)*, *USA Today (USA)*, *The New York Times (NYT)*, and *Investor's Business Daily (IBD)*.

Underlined   Large change in volume (40 largest NYSE issues; 20 largest NASD issues)

USA Today

Boldfaced   Price change greater than 3 percent from previous day

Underlined   Not used

Investor's Business Daily

Boldfaced   Price increase of 1 point or greater, or new 52-week high

Underlined   Price decrease of 1 point or greater, or new 52-week low

The New York Times also uses boldface or underlining to indicate performance levels reached on a day's trading.

READING FOREIGN STOCK QUOTATIONS

Foreign stocks are often of interest to investors who have investments in international-type mutual funds. A number of major foreign stocks, in the form of ADRs, are traded on U.S. stock exchanges, and their prices are quoted in U.S. dollars. With the possible exception of Canadian stocks, very few domestic newspapers carry quotations of foreign stocks that are traded on foreign exchanges.

Exhibit 1–8 shows the stock table from *The Wall Street Journal* for Canadian stocks traded on the Toronto Stock Exchange. Here, all prices are quoted in Canadian dollars. Otherwise there is very little that is different from quotations for domestic stocks.

The New York Times carries an extensive listing of foreign stocks under the heading "Other Foreign Stock Exchanges," as shown in Exhibit 1–9. The information given in these listings is the absolute minimum: stock name, current (closing) price, and the previous day's closing price, all quoted in the currencies of the respective countries. Current foreign exchange rates must be used to convert these prices to equivalent dollars (see Chapter 9). The only sources

EXHIBIT 1–8
Toronto Stock Exchange Quotations from **The Wall Street Journal.**

Quotations in Canadian Funds
Quotations in cents unless marked $
Tuesday, June 1, 1993

TORONTO

Sales	Stock	High	Low	Close	Chg.
11872	Abti Prce	$14⅞	14⅞	14⅞	
90820	Agnico E	$12⅝	11⅝	11⅝	− 1
47900	Air Canada	335	320	330	+10
71990	Alt Energy	$20¼	20⅛	20¼	+ ⅛
757000	Alta Nat	$15¾	15⅜	15¾	− ⅛
846450	A Barick	$29⅜	28	28	−1⅜
31200	Atco I f	$13½	13¼	13¼	− ⅛
10500	Aur Res o	430	415	420	− 5
464253	BCE Inc	$44⅝	44¼	44⅜	
24952	BC Gas	$15	14⅞	14⅞	
277210	Bank N S	$25¼	24¾	25	− ¼
3000	Baton	$6½	6⅜	6⅜	
18601	BCE Mobl	$37⅛	37	37	
562150	Bramalea	18½	16	18	+ 2
75777	BC Telcom	$21	20⅝	21	+ ⅛
39842	CAE	$5¼	5	5¼	+ ¼
3582	CCL B f	$8⅞	8⅝	8⅞	+ ⅛
12135	Cabre	$18	17½	18	+ ½
22475	Cambridg	$16¾	16½	16¾	+ ⅛
88	Camdev	290	290	290	+ 5
6750	Cameco	$20⅝	20½	20⅝	
244176	CI Bk Com	$30⅜	30⅛	30⅜	
24000	CP Forest	$20¾	20	20¾	+ ⅝
342390	CP Ltd	$21¼	20¾	20¾	− ⅜
33466	CTire A f	$13½	13¼	13⅜	
1600	C Util B	$22⅞	22⅝	22⅞	
123104	Canfor	$39⅞	38½	39	− 1
6500	Cara	430	420	420	
700	Celanese	$47½	47½	47½	+ ¼
83800	Cineplex	350	335	345	+10
1800	Co Steel f	$23⅝	23⅝	23⅝	− ⅛
88084	CocaCBev	465	455	460	− 5
700	Conwest A	$21½	21⅜	21½	+ ½
300	Crownx	$7½	7½	7½	
47112	Crownx A f	370	360	360	−10
27100	Corel	$20¼	19⅜	20⅛	+ ⅝

of more extensive quotation statistics for foreign stocks are the foreign newspapers of the respective countries.

READING THE TICKER TAPE

The **ticker tape** is a record of the continuous trade-by-trade transactions of a stock exchange. It is on a 15-minute delay from the time the actual trades were made. The modern ticker tape appears as

EXHIBIT 1–9
Foreign Stock Quotations from The New York Times.

TOKYO (In Japanese Yen)

Issue	Cur	Prev
Ajinomto	1140	1050
Alps	840	795
Amada	859	825
Anitsu	695	671
Asahi Chem	554	532
Asahi Glas	910	891
Bank of Tokyo	1130	1110
Banyu	762	732
Brigestone	1090	1070
Brother	360	343
Canon Cam	1230	1180
C. Itoh	365	345
Calpis	1230	1180
Casio	960	905
Dai Nippon	1300	1220
Daiei	761	720
Dai-ichi Kan	1380	1300
Daiwa House	1420	1350
Daiwa Sec	735	675
Descente	450	437
Eisai	1220	1150
Fanuc	3040	2860
Fuji Bank	1420	1340
Fuji Elec	478	463
Fuji Photo	2570	2440
Fujisawa	800	765
Fujitsu	534	532
Green Cross	880	780
Heiwa Real	683	640
Hitachi	760	729
Honda	1270	1230
Indus Bank	1860	1710
Isuzu	253	243
Ito-Yokado	3600	3550
Iwatsu	280	263
Jaccs	399	367
JAL	602	560
Jusco	1250	1270
Kajima	822	776
Kansai	2210	2190
KAO	1010	960
Kawasaki Hvy	346	338
Kawasaki Stl	225	238
Kirin	1050	1040
Kokusai	1440	1330
Komatsu	589	562
Kubota	470	435
Kyocera	3450	3350
Makino	482	450
Makita	1580	1500
Marubeni	335	309
Marui	1030	977
Matsushita	1170	1130
Mazda	426	405
Minebea	380	360
Mitsu Heavy	509	491
Mitsu Chem	375	361
Mitsu Elec	448	425
Mitsu Corp	865	858
Mitsu Bank	1900	1770
Mitsu Trust	861	827
Mitsu Estate	814	763
Mitsui	532	512
Mitsui Real	875	820
Mitsukoshi	716	702
NEC	760	720
NKK	215	205
Nikko	490	475
Nikkon	620	591
Nintendo	9900	9700
Nippon Exp	648	615
Nippon Oil	579	550
Nippon Seiko	480	460
Nippon Shimp	520	515
Nippon St	243	235
Nippondenso	1290	1280
Nissan	585	558
Niitsuko	425	410
Nomura Sec	1280	1170
NTN Toyo	470	441
NTT	493000	478000
Oki Elec	312	315
Okuma	709	665
Olympus	765	751

Issue	Cur	Prev
Tanabe Sei	720	695
TDK	3300	3140
Teijin	370	355
Tokio Mar	1050	1010
Tokyo Elec	2400	2320
Toppan	1020	990
Toray	555	540
Toshiba El	580	554
Toyoda Mach	512	516
Toyota	1390	1360
Yamaha M	645	600
Yamaichi	480	430
Yamanouchi	2360	2290
Yamoto	895	875
Yaskawa	330	310
Yasuda	683	661
Yokogowa	655	650

LONDON (In British Pence)

Issue	Cur	Prev
AA Corp	$26.87	$27.00
Abbey Nat	256.00	263.00
Allied Lyons	588.00	599.00
Argyll	333.00	331.00
Asc Brit Fds	398.00	399.00
BAA	665.00	671.00
Barclays	295.00	300.00
Bass	520.00	521.00
B.A.T.	744.00	740.00
BET	111.00	115.00
BICC	274.00	279.00
Blue Circle	176.00	179.00
Boc Group	618.00	625.00
Boots	452.00	443.00
Bowater	777.00	748.00
Bracken	$0.33	$0.33
Brit Aero	208.00	204.00
Brit Air	234.00	238.00
Brit Gas	236.50	235.50
Brit Pet	192.50	192.50
Brit Steel	53.00	53.50
Brit Telecom	351.50	349.00
BTR	419.00	424.00
Buffels	$5.12	$5.37
Burmah Cstrl	565.00	564.00
Cable	508.00	509.00
Caddy Schw	454.00	449.00
Charlr Cons	492.00	495.00
Coats Vi	160.00	163.00
Comm Union	472.00	472.00
Courlaulds	464.00	467.00
DeBeers	$15.00	$15.56
Deelkraal	$1.33	$1.23
Dixons	198.00	203.00
Doorns	$0.40	$0.40
Driefont	$9.81	$9.81
East Rd Gld	$0.98	$0.88
East Rd Prp	$2.12	$2.12
Elands	$4.12	$4.12
Elect Compon	279.00	280.00
Eng China	499.00	492.00
Eurotunnel	351.00	351.00
Fisons	170.00	179.00
Forte	130.00	131.00
Freegold	$7.00	$7.12
GEC	229.00	228.00
Gen Accid	429.00	428.00
Glaxo	729.00	728.00
GKN	370.00	365.00
Gold Fields	$15.25	$15.50
Granada	240.00	235.00
Grand Met	422.00	423.00
Groot	$1.10	$1.10
Guardian	129.00	128.00
Guiness	526.00	527.00
Gus A	1404	1412
Hanson	192.00	191.75
Harmony	$3.75	$3.65
Harties	$3.18	$3.08
Hillsdown	94.00	107.00

Issue	Cur	Prev
Marks	298.00	297.00
MEPC	239.00	243.00
Midland	453.00	458.00
Nat Power	234.00	233.00
Nt West Bk	321.00	328.00
Ofsil	$16.12	$16.50
Pearson	330.00	342.00
P & O	332.00	333.00
Pilkington	89.00	88.00
Powergen	254.50	253.00
Prudentl	236.00	235.00
Racal El	64.00	63.50
Randfont	$3.18	$3.18
Rank	527.00	528.00
Ranks Hovs	160.00	159.00
Reckit	583.00	589.00
Redland	410.00	419.00
Reed Intl	448.00	459.00
Reuters	1033.00	1026.0
RMC	469.00	472.00
Rolls Royce	139.00	138.00
Rothman	1040.00	1040.0
Royal Ins	168.00	173.00
RTZ	531.00	533.00
Rustenburg	$18.00	$17.75
Saatchi	137.00	138.00
Sainsbury	444.00	438.00
Sears	67.00	66.00
Sedgwick	113.00	115.00
Shell	463.00	461.00
Sime Darby	68.00	68.00
Smithkline	457.00	456.00
Smith	135.00	137.00
Southvall	$12.62	$12.87
Std & Ch Bk	379.00	385.00
Stilfontn	$0.55	$0.55
Storehouse	120.00	121.00
Sun Alliance	243.00	242.00
Tarmac	71.00	68.00
Tate & Lyle	309.00	307.00
Tesco	234.00	237.00
Thomson Cp	605.00	608.00
Thorn EMI	708.00	696.00
Ti Group	269.00	266.00
Trafalgar	48.50	52.00
TSB	127.50	128.00
Unilever	946.00	938.00
Unisel	$1.53	$1.53
United Bis	300.00	294.00
Vaal Reefs	$38.00	$39.50
Warburg	411.00	406.00
Welkom	$4.25	$4.31
Wellcome	802.00	792.00
West Areas	$0.78	$0.78
Whitbread	397.00	399.00
Winkels	$7.62	$7.62
WPP	37.00	37.00

JOHANNESBURG
(In South African Rand)

AMSTERDAM
(In Dutch Guilder)

Issue	Cur	Prev
ABN Amro	46.50	46.40
ACF Holding	31.80	31.70
Aegon	60.60	60.90
Ahold	78.80	79.60
Akzo	146.10	145.90
Amev	54.70	54.70
Bols	43.60	43.70
Boskalis	20.30	20.40
Buhrmn-Tetr	39.40	40.30
CSM	97.50	97.60
DSM	102.30	101.30
Elsevier	107.50	107.20
Fokker	20.20	20.90
Gist Brocads	35.40	36.10
Hagemeyer	128.00	131.00
Heineken	172.90	171.70

Copyright © 1992 by The New York Times Company. Reprinted by permission.

an electronic display on the wall in offices of many brokerage firms as well as at the bottom of the television screen on cable television channels such as CNN (on its *Headline News* program) and CNBC. These cable networks each display two ticker tapes that are of different colors. The top ticker represents trades on the NYSE, while the bottom ticker gives National Market System (NMS) trades.

Traditionally, the ticker tape has a two-line format:

Line 1   Name of stock traded as a ticker symbol, with any qualifier suffix or other special information

Line 2   Amount traded (volume), followed by the trade price

A typical section of ticker tape displayed in brokerage offices or on CNBC might appear as follows:

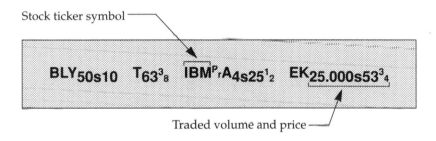

Stock ticker symbol

$$\text{BLY}_{50}\text{s}10 \quad \text{T}63^3{}_8 \quad \text{IBM}^p{}_r\text{A}4\text{s}25^1{}_2 \quad \text{EK}25.000\text{s}53^3{}_4$$

Traded volume and price

On the other hand, CNN's *Headline News* uses a one-line format for the same transactions as above, which might appear as follows:

$$\text{BLY}50\text{s}10 \quad \text{T}63^3{}_8 \quad \text{IBM}^p{}_r\text{A}4\text{s}25^1{}_2 \quad \text{EK}25.000.\text{s}.53^3{}_4$$

Stock Ticker Symbol and Qualifier Suffix

Every company is indicated by its ticker symbol. Unless more qualifier suffixes indicate otherwise, it is assumed that all transactions involve **common shares,** as opposed to warrants, rights, or preferred shares. For example, **DD** stands for ordinary common shares of DuPont, while **RDA∙B** stands for the Class B common shares of Reader's Digest. With the exception of preferred stocks, warrants, and rights, all qualifiers are separated from the company's ticker symbol by a square period (∎), although many electronic displays now tend to use the more conventional round period.

Preferred shares. Preferred shares are indicated by a ^P_r symbol immediately following the stock symbol. If a company has more than one class of preferred stock, then the ^P_r symbol is followed by the letter of the class of stock. Examples of this include **TA^P_r**, which represents the preferred shares of Transamerica Corporation, and **PPL^P_rA**, which represents the Class A preferred shares of Pennsylvania Power and Light.

Warrants and rights. Warrants and stock rights are represented by the symbols ∎**WS** and $\mathfrak{l}$ (respectively), which immediately follow the stock symbol. For example, **CHH∎WS** represents warrants for Carter Hawley Hale, while **MSF$\mathfrak{l}$** represents Morgan Stanley Market Fund stock rights.

When issued, when distributed, and ex-dividend trades. Stocks and their variants are often traded under various circumstances. Stocks (or rights) traded on their ex-dividend (or ex-rights) date have an ∎**XD** qualifier added. For example, **IBM∎XD** means that IBM is being traded ex-dividend. Qualifiers are also used to identify stocks trading on either a when-distributed or a WI basis. As examples, **ZTR∎WD** represents the shares of Zweig Total Return Fund when distributed, and **FG^w_i** represents the shares of USF&G WI. These qualifiers can then be combined with other qualifiers. For example, **IBM^P_rA∎XD** refers to Class A preferred shares of IBM that were traded on their ex-dividend date.

The qualifier symbols used on the ticker tape are summarized in Exhibit 1–10.

Trade Volume and Price

In addition to the stock ticker symbol, every transaction on the ticker tape includes information about how many shares were traded (volume) and at what price. In a two-line format such as that printed by the original ticker tape machines, the volume and

EXHIBIT 1–10
Stock Ticker Tape Qualifier Suffixes.

Qualifier Suffix	Example	Meaning
∎A, ∎B, ∎C, etc.	**RDA∎B**	Reader's Digest Class B stock.
Pr	**TA$_r^P$**	Transamerica Corporation preferred stock
∎**PrB**	**PPL$_r^P$A**	Pennsylvania Power and Light preferred stock, Class A
∎**XD**	**IBM∎XD**	IBM, traded ex-dividend
∎**WS**	**CHH∎WS**	Carter Hawley Hale warrants
∎**WD**	**ZTR∎WD**	Zweig Total Return Fund, when distributed
∎**CV**		Convertible shares
$_i^w$	**FG$_i^w$**	USF&G, WI
$_t^r$	**M SF$_t^r$**	Morgan Stanley Market Fund rights

price information appears on the second line immediately to the right of the stock ticker symbol. In the single-line format, it appears immediately after the ticker symbol.

Single trades.   For a single trade, the general format is that the volume is stated first and represents the number of **round lots** (multiples of 100 shares) traded, followed by the letter s, which stands for "shares," and then the price. For example,

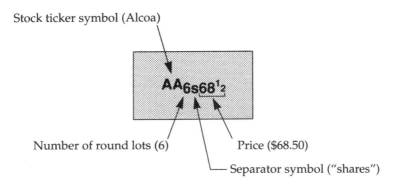

Stock ticker symbol (Alcoa)

Number of round lots (6)   Price ($68.50)

Separator symbol ("shares")

means that 600 shares (six round lots) of Alcoa were traded at $68.50 per share. One exception to this general format is that when only 100 shares (i.e., one round lot) are traded, the **1s** that would normally precede the price (using the rule cited previously) is omitted, as being redundant. For example,

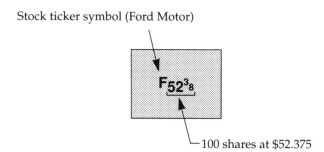

Stock ticker symbol (Ford Motor)

100 shares at $52.375

means that 100 shares of Ford Motor were traded at $52.375 per share. Contrary to the normal practice in mathematics, fractions of a dollar are written as fractions but without the bar separating the two numbers. Fractional dollars are written either as one number right over the other ($\frac{3}{8}$), as in the traditional ticker tape machine, or with the top number (numerator) more to the left than the bottom (denominator) number ($^3_8$), as in most electronic displays.

Another normal situation can occur when the volume is omitted. This occurs for the **closing prices** for each stock. After approximately 4:30 PM Eastern time, the exchanges (such as the NYSE) summarize the closing prices in alphabetical order of all the companies that are traded on the exchange. Since these are closing prices rather than transactions, no volume figures are given. As an example:

$$OFP_{15^1_4} \quad OG_{24^1_2} \quad OGE_{36} \quad OGE^P{}_rA_{14}$$

On the other hand, some ticker tapes include the change in the closing price from the previous day's close, as follows:

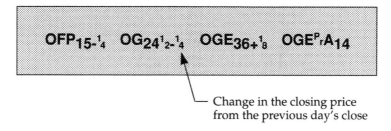

— Change in the closing price
from the previous day's close

When the volume of a transaction is more than 10,000 shares (100 round lots), the volume is then stated in full, and is followed by an s and the price per share.[3] For example,

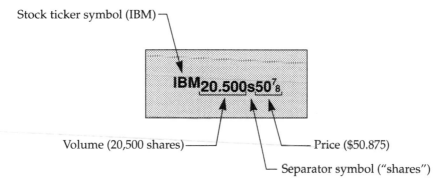

Stock ticker symbol (IBM)

Volume (20,500 shares) — Price ($50.875)

— Separator symbol ("shares")

This means that 20,500 shares of IBM were traded at $50.875 per share. Exhibit 1–11 summarizes the various representations for stock ticker volumes and prices.

Dollar fractions for sixteenths, thirty-seconds, and sixty-fourths. Fractional dollars involving sixteenths, thirty-seconds, and sixty-fourths are not printed in the conventional sense. Instead, they are printed as two numbers separated by a period.

---

[3] On some electronic tickers, such as on CNN's *Headline News*, full lot volume has a period on both sides of the letter s. For a trade representing 20,500 shares of IBM at $50.875, this would be represented as **IBM20∎500∎s∎50$^7_8$**.

EXHIBIT 1–11
Stock Ticker Tape Volume and Price Formats.

Volume and Price Example	Meaning
$25^3{}_8$	100 shares at $25.375 per share
$6s125^1{}_2$	600 shares at $125.50 per share
$20{.}500s18^7{}_8$	20,500 shares at $18.875 per share
$14s11{.}5s11{.}$	1400 shares at $11 per share, followed by 500 shares at $11 per share
$10^3{}_8{}^1{}_2$	100 shares at $10.375 per share, followed by 100 shares at $10.50 per share
$4s7^1{}_4{}^1{}_4$	400 shares at $7.25 per share, followed by 100 shares at $7.25 per share

For example,

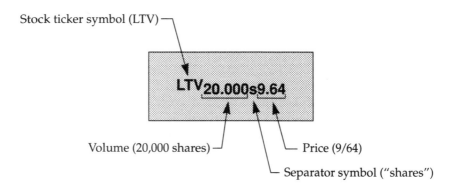

represents the trade of 20,000 shares of LTV at 9/64 of $1.

Combined trades. Very often, when there are two or more consecutive transactions involving the same company, the ticker tape will indicate these trades combined with a single stock ticker symbol. Following are some of the possibilities that can occur:

Consecutive trades at the same price but with different volumes. Consecutive trades of the same company can occur involving different volumes but at the same price. The following ticker transaction represents two consecutive trades of Goodyear Tire & Rubber at $41.125 per share.

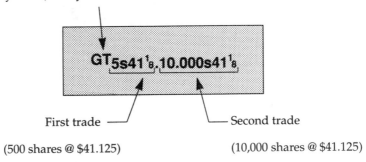

Stock ticker symbol (Goodyear Tire & Rubber)

First trade   Second trade

(500 shares @ $41.125)   (10,000 shares @ $41.125)

The first is for 500 shares; the second is for 10,000 shares. Here, the trades are separated by a period. If the volume of one trade is 100 shares, the 1s notation is always omitted. For example,

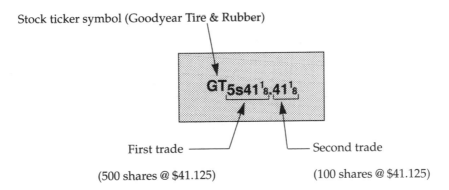

Stock ticker symbol (Goodyear Tire & Rubber)

First trade   Second trade

(500 shares @ $41.125)   (100 shares @ $41.125)

represents two consecutive trades of Goodyear Tire & Rubber at $41.125 per share. The first is for 500 shares; the second is for 100 shares.

Consecutive trades with different volumes and different prices. Consecutive trades of the same company can occur involving different volumes at different prices. The following ticker transaction represents two consecutive trades of JP Morgan.

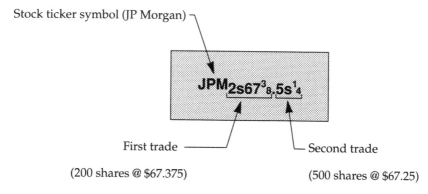

The first is for 200 shares at $67.375 per share; the second is for 500 shares at $67.25 per share. Here, the numbers representing whole dollars (i.e., 67) are omitted for the second trade, as they are the same in both trades.

Consecutive trades with same volume and price. Consecutive trades involving the same company and having the same volume and price appear as follows:

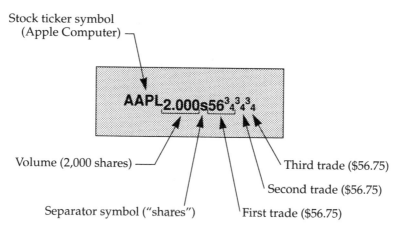

This represents three consecutive trades of Apple Computer, each for 2,000 shares at $56.75 per share. Notice that the whole dollars (i.e., 56) are omitted for all but the first trade. If, on the other hand, there were three consecutive 200-share trades of Apple

Computer at $57.00 per share, the price would contain only whole dollars and would then be shown on the ticker tape as:

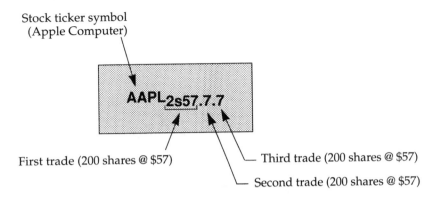

Stock ticker symbol
(Apple Computer)

First trade (200 shares @ $57)

Third trade (200 shares @ $57)

Second trade (200 shares @ $57)

Consecutive trades of 100 shares at different prices. The final situation is concerned with consecutive trades of the same volume but at different prices. The following ticker transaction represents two consecutive 100-share trades of Thiokol.

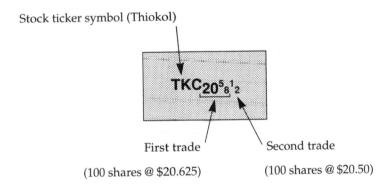

Stock ticker symbol (Thiokol)

First trade

Second trade

(100 shares @ $20.625)

(100 shares @ $20.50)

The first is at $20.625 per share; the second is at $20.50 per share.

Additional Items of Information

On occasion there are situations requiring information in addition to the stock ticker symbol, the volume, and the traded price. These situations can occur when there was a mistake in a previous trade, when a trade is canceled outright, when trading is halted, when the opening of trading is delayed, or when certain news items are displayed.

Correcting a previous trade. The quotation appearing on the ticker tape may be in error. The following transaction message indicates that the last trade of 3,000 shares of Nuveen Insured Quality Municipals (NQI) originally was traded at $17.25 a share, but is corrected to read a trade of 3,000 shares at $17.125 a share.

$$\text{CORR.1 \quad SALES.BACK.NQI.SLD}_{30s}17\tfrac{1}{8}$$

$$\text{WAS.NQI.SLD}_{30s}17\tfrac{1}{4}$$

Cancellation of a trade. On occasion a trade is canceled outright later in the trading day. The following message indicates that 5,000 shares of Bell Bank Corporation (BELL) were traded at $47.625 per share and that the previous trade was then canceled.

$$\text{BELL}_{50s}47\tfrac{5}{8} \quad \text{CXL.PREV} \quad \text{BELL}_{50s}47\tfrac{5}{8}$$

Here, the ticker symbol, volume, and price of the cancelled trade are repeated even though the trade is immediately reported as canceled by the next quotation. On the other hand, the following message indicates that the trade of 5,000 shares of BELL at $47.625 per share (eight trades back) is canceled.

$$\text{CXL.8 SALES. BACK} \quad \text{BELL}_{50s}47\tfrac{5}{8}$$

Market statistics. Periodically, the current market statistics are transmitted on the tape. These usually include the **Dow Jones Industrial Average (DJIA),** the **Dow Jones Transportation Average (DJTA),** the **Dow Jones Utilities Average (DJUA),** NYSE trading volume, and the AMEX and NASDAQ indexes. On television ticker tapes such as those used by CNN's *Headline News* and CNBC, this information occurs about every minute, and might appear as follows:

> **..AT 2:31 DJIA + 3474.84 + 24.91 NYSE VOL 194.992.800**

This gives the market summary for the DJIA at 2:31 PM. The average is up 24.91 points at 3474.84. The volume of shares traded at this point on the NYSE was 194,992,800 shares. At the conclusion of the market summary, continuous trade-by-trade transactions resume, as indicated by:

> **NYSE TRADES .. MGI$_{7s}$12$^5_8$ BMY$_{3s}$56$^1_4$**

Here, the ticker resumes with a trade of 700 shares of MGI Properties (MGI) followed by 300 shares of Bristol-Myers Squibb (BMY).

Example: Reading the Tape

The ticker tape for a sequence of seven continuous trade-by-trade transactions on June 15, 1993, might appear as follows

> **CMO^P.B.XD$_{14}$$^1_4$ AMD$_{15.000s}$22$^1_8$ HAN.WS$_{50s}$1$^1_8$**

$$LTV_{80s0\frac{7}{8}}\ CIC.SLD_{12s28\frac{1}{4}}\ BLY_{10}\ SWY^{w}_{i}10.000s3\frac{1}{8}$$

The tape would then be read as 100 preferred Class B shares of Capstead Mortgage (CMO) traded ex-dividend at $14.25 per share, followed by 15,000 shares of Advanced Micro Devices (AMD) at $22.125 per share, followed by 5,000 warrants of Hanson Trust PLC (HAN) at $1.125 each, followed by 8,000 shares of LTV (LTV) at $0.875, followed by 1,200 shares sold out of sequence at $28.25 per share, followed by 100 shares of Bally Manufacturing (BLY) at $10.00 per share, followed by 10,000 shares of Safeway (SWY), WI, at $3.125.

READING PUBLISHED ADVISORY REPORTS

Besides market information concerning stocks that is published in newspapers, a wealth of financial analyses on corporations is constantly done by several firms. These firms then make their information available to the public as advisory services on a sub-scription basis. These reports are very useful to investors and investment advisers, as much of the information is not readily available, especially to investors who are not stockholders of the company. Perhaps the two best-known stock investment publications are the Standard & Poor's Corporation's *S&P's Stock Reports* and the *Value Line Investment Survey*.[4] Other firms that publish investment information include Weisenberger Services and Vickers Associates.

Standard & Poor's Stock Reports

S&P's Stock Report Services publishes four weekly reports that cover a total of about 4,700 companies. The weekly reports are:

NYSE Stock Reports
ASE Stock Reports

---

[4] Standard & Poor's Corporation, 25 Broadway, New York, NY 10004. Value Line Publishing, Inc., 711 Third Avenue, New York, NY 10017.

OTC Stock Reports
OTC Profiles®

All of *S&P's Stock Reports* are published by S&P's Equity Research Department, which is operated independently of and has no access to information obtained by S&P's Corporate Bond Ratings Department.[5]

Each company is analyzed in two pages (Exhibits 1–12 and 1–13). Exhibit 1–12 illustrates the front page of a typical report summary for Hewlett-Packard. The top of the front page lists the official name of the corporation, followed by several major pieces of information, most of which are usually found in newspaper stock tables and many of which have already been discussed in this chapter.

This information includes:

• *The stock exchange where the stock is traded.* The trade could be made on the NYSE, on the AMEX, or over the counter.

• *The stock ticker symbol.* Each security that is traded on an exchange is assigned a unique ticker symbol.

• *Tradable options contracts (if any), the exchange on which they are traded, and their expiration dates.*[6]

• *S&P 500 Index Component.* This is a broad-based, capitalization-weighted market index of 500 companies with an average base level of 10 for the 1941–1943 base period. The components represent 400 industrial sector stocks, 40 financials, 40 utilities, and 20 transportation stocks. This index is widely considered to be representative of the stock market as a whole. Because of its breadth the *S&P 500* is the benchmark against which virtually all money managers compare the performance of their portfolios. The report indicates whether the particular stock is a component of the index.

• *The stock closing price and date.*

• *The trading range for the current year.* This range includes the high and low trading prices for the current year and provides some measure of the stock's price fluctuations.

---

[5] Corporate bond ratings are discussed further in Chapter 2.

[6] Quotations for tradable options are discussed in Chapter 7.

EXHIBIT 1–12

Front Page,* Standard NYSE Stock Report *Analysis for Hewlett-Packard.

Hewlett-Packard

1137

NYSE Symbol HWP Options on CBOE (Feb-May-Aug-Nov) In S&P 500

Price	Range	P–E Ratio	Dividend	Yield	S&P Ranking	Beta
Feb. 26'93	1993					
73¾	76–66½	22	0.80	1.1%	A	1.61

Summary

Hewlett-Packard manufactures a broad array of electronic instruments and computer systems. The company has been witnessing strong order growth in recent quarters, aided by the introduction of new products, which suggests good revenue growth in fiscal 1993. Coupled with controlled operating costs, higher revenues should lead to earnings gains for the balance of the year.

Current Outlook

Earnings for the fiscal year ending October 31, 1993, are estimated at $4.65 a share, up from fiscal 1992's $3.49, which excludes an accounting charge of $1.31.

Dividends should continue at $0.20 quarterly.

Results for the balance of fiscal 1993 should benefit from recent strong order rates which have been aided by strong acceptance of HWP's new products and the sharp rise in PC sales. HWP benefits not only from higher sales of its PCs but also increased sales of its peripherals, particularly laser printers. HWP's workstation business has also been growing, aided by the November 10 announcement of new products. However, revenues from multi-user systems were disappointing in the first quarter of fiscal 1993 and will probably not rise much for the balance of the year. Gross margins are not exected to improve because of increasing competition and a continuing shift in product mix. Earnings should rise due to the higher volumes; we are estimating a 16% increase in equipment sales, and well controlled operating costs.

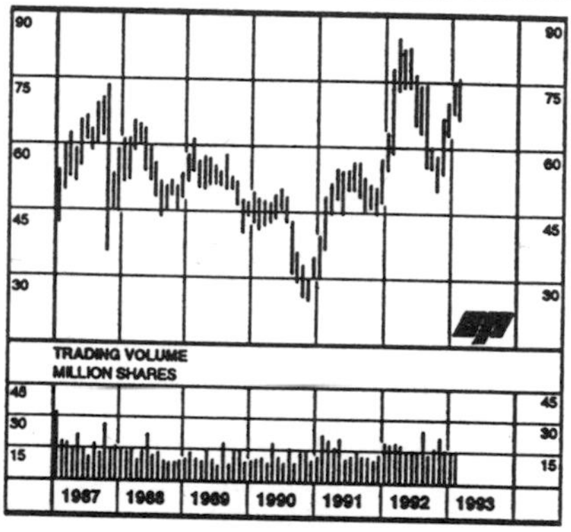

Net Sales (Billion $)

Quarter:	1992–93	1991–92	1990–91	1989–90
Jan.	4.57	3.86	3.41	3.10
Apr.	—	4.18	3.73	3.31
Jul.	—	4.04	3.52	3.24
Oct.	—	4.32	3.83	3.58
	—	16.41	14.49	13.23

Revenues for the quarter ended January 31, 1993, grew 18%, year to year, aided by a 23% gain in computer products and services. Gross margins narrowed, and although operating costs rose less rapidly than revenues, pretax income fell 11%. After taxes at 34.9%, versus 33.0%, net income was down 14%, to $261 million ($1.03 a share), from $302 million ($1.19). Results for the fiscal 1992 interim exclude a $1.31-a-share charge from an accounting change.

Common Share Earnings ($)

Quarter:	1992–93	1991–92	1990–91	1989–90
Jan.	1.03	1.19	0.83	0.72
Apr.	E1.25	1.27	0.93	0.78
Jul.	E1.11	0.75	0.76	0.73
Oct.	E1.25	0.28	0.50	0.83
	E4.65	3.49	3.02	3.06

Important Developments

Feb. '93— Orders in the first quarter of fiscal 1993 totaled $5.2 billion, up 24% from $4.2 billion in the year-earlier period. U.S. orders grew 18%, to $2.1 billion, while orders from outside the U.S. rose 28%, to $3.1 billion. Separately, the company announced that its PA-RISC-based HP 9000 server recorded the industry's highest results for online transaction processing for the new industry-standard benchmark, TPC-C.

Next earnings report expected in mid-May.

Per Share Data ($)

Yr. End Oct. 31	1992	1991	1990	[1]1989	1988	1987	1986	1985	[5]1984	1983
Tangible Bk. Val.	27.43	[2]28.90	[2]26.07	21.22	19.35	19.52	17.08	15.50	13.82	11.33
Cash Flow	6.15	5.24	5.08	5.37	4.81	3.83	3.27	3.07	3.52	2.44
Earnings[3]	3.49	3.02	3.06	3.52	3.36	2.50	2.02	1.91	2.59	1.69
Dividends	0.725	0.480	0.420	0.360	0.280	0.230	0.220	0.220	0.190	0.158
Payout Ratio	21%	16%	14%	10%	8%	9%	11%	12%	7%	9%
Prices[4]—High	85	57⅜	50⅜	61½	65½	73⅝	49⅝	38⅞	45½	48¼
Low	50¼	29⅞	24⅞	40¼	43¾	35¾	35¾	28¾	31⅛	34¼
P/E Ratio—	24–14	19–10	16–8	17–11	19–13	29–14	25–18	20–15	18–12	29–20

Data as orig. reptd. Adj. for stk. div. of 100% Aug. 1983. 1. Refl. merger or acq. 2. Incl. intangibles. 3. Bef. spec. item of -1.31 in 1992. 4. Cal. yr. 5. Refl. acctg. change. E-Estimated.

Standard NYSE Stock Reports
Vol. 60/No. 44/Sec. 14

March 5, 1993

Copyright © 1993 Standard & Poor's Corp. All Rights Reserved

Standard & Poor's Corp.
25 Broadway, NY, NY 10004

Published by Standard & Poor's Corporation. Reprinted by permission of Standard & Poor's. ALL RIGHTS RESERVED.

1137   Hewlett-Packard Company

Income Data (Million $)

Year Ended Oct. 31	Revs.	Oper. Inc.	% Oper. Inc. of Revs.	Cap. Exp.	Depr.	Int. Exp.	Net Bef. Taxes	Eff. Tax Rate	Net Inc.	% Net Inc. of Revs.	Cash Flow
1992	16,410	2,183	13.3	1,032	673	96	1,325	33.5%	[4]881	5.4	1,554
1991	14,494	1,890	13.0	862	555	130	1,127	33.0%	755	5.2	1,310
1990	13,233	1,650	12.5	955	488	172	1,056	30.0%	739	5.6	1,305
[1]1989	11,899	1,630	13.7	915	435	126	1,151	28.0%	829	7.0	1,264
1988	9,831	1,572	16.0	648	353	77	[3]1,142	28.5%	816	8.3	1,169
1987	8,090	1,354	16.7	507	342	50	[3]962	33.1%	[2]644	8.0	986
1986	7,102	1,101	15.5	499	321	NA	[3]780	33.8%	[2]516	7.3	837
1985	6,505	1,057	16.2	632	299	NA	[3]758	35.5%	489	7.5	788
[2]1984	6,044	1,097	18.2	661	237	NA	[3]860	22.7%	665	11.0	902
1983	4,710	919	19.5	466	191	NA	728	40.7%	432	9.2	623

Balance Sheet Data (Million $)

Oct. 31	Cash	Assets	Curr. Liab.	Ratio	Total Assets	% Ret. on Assets	Long Term Debt	Common Equity	Total Cap.	% LT Debt of Cap.	% Ret. on Equity
1992	1,035	7,679	5,094	1.5	13,700	6.9	425	7,499	7,973	5.3	11.9
1991	1,120	6,716	4,063	1.7	11,973	6.4	188	7,269	7,700	2.4	10.9
1990	1,106	6,510	4,443	1.5	11,395	6.8	139	6,363	6,763	2.1	12.4
1989	926	5,731	3,743	1.5	10,075	9.4	474	5,446	6,168	7.7	16.5
1988	918	4,420	2,570	1.7	7,497	11.0	61	4,533	4,770	1.3	17.9
1987	2,645	5,490	2,735	2.0	8,133	8.9	88	5,022	5,264	1.7	13.7
1986	1,372	3,814	1,518	2.5	6,287	8.6	110	4,374	4,635	2.4	12.4
1985	1,020	3,342	1,376	2.4	5,680	9.0	102	3,982	4,212	2.4	13.0
1984	938	3,201	1,322	2.4	5,153	14.2	81	3,545	3,738	2.2	20.6
1983	880	2,632	920	2.9	4,161	11.2	71	2,887	3,195	2.2	16.4

Data as orig. reptd. 1. Refl. merger or acq. 2. Refl. acctg. change. 3. Incl. equity in earns. of nonconsol. subs. 4. Bef.spec.items. NA-Not Available.

Business Summary

Hewlett-Packard produces a broad range of electronic instruments and syst ems for measurement, analysis and computation. The company derived 25% of fiscal 1992 revenues by providing service for its equipment, systems and peripherals. Orders originating outside of the U.S. accounted for 55% of total orders in fiscal 1992, down from 56% in fiscal 1991.

Key computer products, services and support (73% of fiscal 1992 revenues) include the HP 3000 series, which runs the proprietary MPE operating systems and is sold for business applications; the 9000 line of UNIX-based technical computers, including workstations; and the HP Vectra series of IBM-compatible personal computers. Both the 3000 and 9000 families are based on the company's Precision Architecture reduced instruction set computing (RISC) design. The company offers software programming services, network services, distributed systems services and data management services. Peripheral products include printers, such as the HP LaserJet and DeskJet families; plotters and page scanners; video display terminals; and disk and tape drives.

Electronic test and measurement instrumentation, systems and services (14%) include voltmeters and multimeters, counters, oscilloscopes and logic analyzers, signal generators and specialized communications test equipment.

Medical electronic equipment and services (6%) include continuous monitoring systems for critical care patients, medical data managment systems and fetal monitors.

Analytical instrumentation and service (4%) includes gas and liquid chromatographs, mass spectrometers and spectrophotometers.

Electronic components (3%) include microwave semiconductor and optoelectronic devices sold primarily to original equipment manufacturers.

Dividend Data

Dividends have been paid since 1965.

Amt of Divd. $	Date Decl.	Ex-divd. Date	Stock of Record	Payment Date
0.20	May 20	Jun. 18	Jun. 24	Jul. 15'92
0.20	Jul. 24	Sep. 17	Sep. 23	Oct. 14'92
0.20	Nov. 20	Dec. 17	Dec. 23	Jan. 13'93
0.20	Jan. 22	Mar. 18	Mar. 24	Apr. 14'93

Capitalization

Long Term Debt: $422,000,000 (1/93).

Common Stock: 252,824,000 shs. ($1 par).
Institutions hold about 54%; W.R. Hewlett and D. Packard families control 26% (in part held by institutions).
Shareholders of record: 73,394 (11/92).

Office—3000 Hanover St., Palo Alto, CA 94304. Tel—(415) 857-1501. Chrmn—D. Packard. Pres & CEO—L E. Platt. EVP-Fin—R. P. Wayman. Secy—D. C. Nordlund. Treas & Investor Contact—George F. Newman Jr. Dirs—T. E. Everhart, J. B. Fery, R. A. Hackborn, H. J. Haynes, W. B. Hewlett, S. M. Hufstedler, G. A. Keyworth II, P. F. Miller Jr., D. Packard, D. W. Packard, D. E. Petersen, L. E. Platt, C. Rice, W. E. Terry, H. P. Waldron, T. A. Wilson. Transfer Agent & Registrar—Harris Trust & Savings Bank, Chicago. Incorporated in California in 1947. Empl—92,600.

Information has been obtained from sources believed to be reliable, but its accuracy and completeness are not guaranteed.   Neeraj K. Vohra

• *Price/earnings (P/E) ratio.* This ratio refers to the relationship between the stock's current per share price and the annual earnings per share of the company, as follows:

$$P/E \text{ ratio} = \frac{\text{Current stock market price}}{\text{Earnings per share}} \qquad (1\text{--}2)$$

The P/E ratio is usually an important barometer that investors look at for evaluating stock prices, as it expresses the value of a stock in terms of company earnings instead of only its current stock prices. Some investors avoid stocks with P/E ratios greater than 10.

• *The annual dividend.* This is the total cash payment per share, based on a 12-month period.

• *The percent yield.* This is the same as calculated by Equation 1–1. As shown in Exhibit 1–12, Hewlett-Packard pays an annual dividend of $0.80 per share, at a closing price of 73³/₄. The percent yield is then 0.80/73.75, or 1.1 percent.

• *S&P corporate ranking.* The ranking system measures the historical growth of earnings and dividends on its most recent 10-year period. This should not be confused with the bond ratings scale used for corporate and municipal bonds (discussed in Chapter 2).

The scale has eight grades, as follows:

Above average	A+, A, and A−
Average	B+
Below average	B, B−, and C+
In reorganization	D

An NR (not rated) designation is given to companies that have common stocks with insufficient historical data, and to companies that have stock that is not amenable to the ranking process. Standard & Poor's, as a matter of policy, does not rank stocks of foreign companies, investment companies, and certain finance-oriented companies.

One item that should be noted is that the rankings do not take the stock's market price into consideration. A company can have an above-average ranking and yet the stock may be currently overpriced; a stock of a lower-ranked company may be undervalued.

• **Beta (β).** This statistic measures how responsive the stock is to a given market index and indicates the volatility of a stock's market price. In terms of least-squares regression coefficients, it is equivalent to the slope of the line. By definition, the beta of the comparison market (i.e., the *S&P 500*) is 1.00. If the stock moved exactly as the market moved (point for point, up or down), the stock would have a beta of 1.00. If a stock has a negative beta, this means the stock's price moves in a direction opposite to the index's price movements. If a stock has a beta of 1.50, it means that the stock is expected to perform 50 percent better than the market when the market is up and 50 percent worse than the market when it is down. Standard & Poor's computes beta values for the last 5-year period, using month-end prices. In addition, dividends are used in the calculations. For low **risk,** betas lower than 1.00 are usually preferred.

Each report's front page (Exhibit 1–12) is further broken down into the following sections:

"Summary" section.   This is the analyst's brief summary of the highlights of this report and is usually only two or three sentences in length. [The analyst's name is given at the bottom of the second page of the report (Exhibit 1–13).] The first sentence is normally a statement about the corporation's primary product line. The remainder of the summary highlights the past year's performance and provides an estimate of future performance.

"Current Outlook" section.   This section includes a statement concerning the corporation's earnings, along with any historical comparisons and a statement about the future course of dividend payments. The analyst amplifies on the statements made in the "Summary" section, focusing on what factors (positive and negative) have contributed to the company's performance. Finally, the section concludes with a quantitative estimate of future performance.

"Net Sales" table. This table summarizes the corporation's quarterly and yearly net sales for the current year and three previous years.

Graphs. In this section, two graphs are shown, with all data plotted on a monthly basis. The top graph is a high-low bar graph showing the stock price and its historical trend for the previous 6 years. The bottom graph is a vertical bar graph illustrating the monthly trading volume for the stock.

"Common Share Earnings" table. This table lists the corporation's common share earnings for the current year and the three previous years (the same as for net sales), broken down by quarters. Earnings, based on generally accepted accounting standards, are the profits a corporation earns during the year and are frequently stated as dollar value per share. For future quarters, estimates are given for per share earnings.

This data allows the computation of the stock's P/E ratio from the stock price and the earnings per share. For Hewlett-Packard's 1991–1992 earnings of $3.49 per share coupled with the high share price of $76.00 per share, the P/E ratio (Equation 1–2) is $76.00/$3.49, or 21.78 (22 when rounded off to the nearest whole number).

"Important Developments" section. This section highlights significant milestones, particularly those of new products or corporate acquisitions.

"Per Share Data" table. This table gives the statistics described below on a per share basis at the end of each fiscal year for the most recent 10-year period. Data in this section may be repetitive, having been cited elsewhere in the report.

Tangible book value. This line indicates the theoretical dollar amount per common share that an investor may expect to receive from a corporation's tangible "book" assets if the company undergoes liquidation. This is found by adding the paid-in capital and retained earnings to the value of the common stock. From this sum are subtracted intangible assets (i.e., excess cost over equity of acquired companies, goodwill, trademarks, copyrights, and patents), preferred stock valued at liquidation, and unamortized debt. This difference is then divided by the number of outstanding common shares.

Cash flow. This is the net income plus depreciation, depletion, and amortization, divided by the same number of shares used to calculate the company's common share earnings.

Earnings. This includes data from the "Common Share Earnings" table, for industrial companies. Insurance companies instead report operating earnings before gains (or losses) on securities transactions and earnings after such transactions.

Dividends. These generally are the total cash payments per share based on the ex-dividend dates over a 12-month period.

Payout ratio. This is the percentage of earnings paid out in dividends. It is calculated from:

$$\% \text{ Payout ratio} = \frac{\text{Annual dividend}}{\text{Earnings per share}} \cdot 100 \qquad (1\text{--}3)$$

From the viewpoint of a stockholder who is primarily interested in income, a high payout ratio is desirable. If growth is the prime objective, a lower payout ratio may be appropriate, as more money is retained by the company for investment in its operations and it may be hoped that the stock price will rise in time.

Example: Calculating the Percent Payout Ratio

The "Per Share Data" table for a Standard & Poor's report on Hewlett-Packard (Exhibit 1–12) in 1990 says that the company earned $3.06 per share and paid an annual dividend of $0.42 per share. The percent payout ratio is then (Equation 1–3):

$$\% \text{ Payout ratio} = \frac{\$0.42}{\$3.06} \cdot 100$$

$$= 14\%$$

rounded to the nearest whole number, which agrees with the published report's value for that year.

For insurance companies, the payout ratio instead uses earnings after gain and losses of securities transactions as the denominator in Equation 1–3.

Calendar year high and low stock prices.

P/E ratio. As discussed previously, the P/E ratio refers to the relationship between the stock's current per share price and the company's annual per share earnings (Equation 1–2).

Example: Calculating the P/E Ratio

The "Per Share Data" table for S&P's report on Hewlett-Packard (Exhibit 1–12) in 1991 says that the market price for the stock ranged from a low of $29.875 to a high of $57.375, and that the earnings were $3.02 a share. Based on the year's high price, the P/E ratio is (Equation 1–2):

$$\text{P/E ratio} = \frac{\$57.375}{\$3.02}$$

$$= 19.0$$

Based on the year's low price, it is:

$$P/E \text{ ratio} = \frac{\$29.875}{\$3.02}$$

$$= \mathbf{9.9}$$

When rounded off to the nearest whole number, the P/E ratio during 1991 varied from 10 to 19.

If the report summary instead is for an investment company, then the company's net asset value and portfolio turnover rate are also included as part of the "Per Share Data" table. These figures are a measure of the aggressiveness of the investment company's trading practices. The higher the ratio, the more aggressive the company's trading practices.

The back page of each report summary (Exhibit 1–13) is primarily an accounting summary of the corporation's statement of financial condition.

"Income Data" table and "Balance Sheet Data" table. These two tables (Exhibit 1–13) summarize the various components of the company's income statement and balance sheet (on a fiscal year basis). These data are for the same most recent 10-year period as used for the "Per Share Data" table on the report's front page (Exhibit 1–12). The specific components reported in the income statement and the balance sheet depend on the type of company being reported. The types include banks, industrial companies, insurance companies, investment companies, real estate trusts, savings and loans, and utilities.

The statistics, which may be repeated among company types, are generally used to gauge company performance. The major ones used in Standard & Poor's report summaries are listed on the following page.[7]

---

[7] All accounting measures used by Standard & Poor's in the "Income Data" and "Balance Sheet Data" tables are defined in a glossary of terms in *S&P's Stock Reports Index*.

Banks

1. *Percent return on assets.* A measure of use of assets.
2. *Percent equity to assets.* A measure of capital adequacy.
3. *Percent return on equity.* A general measure of performance and industry comparison.
4. *Deposits/capital funds ratio.* A measure of leverage.
5. *Percent equity to loans.* Reflects the degree of equity coverage to loans outstanding.

Industrial companies

1. *Percent operating income of revenues.* A measure of operating profitability.
2. *Current ratio.* A measure of liquidity. A very large current ratio designates a cash-rich company that could easily be a takeover target.
3. *Percent return on assets.*
4. *Percent long-term debt to invested capital.* A measure of how highly leveraged a company may be.
5. *Percent return on equity.*

Insurance companies

1. *Percent return on revenues.*
2. *Percent equity to assets.*
3. *Percent return on equity.*
4. *Percent investment yield.*

Investment companies

1. *Percent net investment income to net assets.*
2. *Percent expenses to net assets.*
3. *Percent expenses to investment income.*
4. *Percent change in net asset value.*

Real estate trusts, savings & loans

1. *Percent expenses to revenues.*
2. *Loss reserve.*
3. *Price times book value (high-low).*

Utilities

1. *Percent return on revenues.*
2. *Percent return on invested capital.*
3. *Percent earned on net property.* A measure of plant efficiency.

"Business Summary" section.   This summary provides a breakdown on the corporation's business sectors.

"Dividend Data" table.   In this section, there is a statement concerning when the corporation first started to pay dividends. Next, there is a table summarizing the corporation's last four dividend periods in the following format: amount of dividend, declaration date, ex-dividend date, date for stockholder of record, and the payment date. From this table, it is easy to analyze the corporation's payment history and the trend of dividend payments. This gives a measure of the stability of the corporation's profitability.

"Capitalization" section.   This section gives the amount of long-term debt owed by the corporation, as well as the number of shares of the corporation's common stock, its major stockholders (name and percentage), and the number of shareholders of record.

Operations data.   This section contains information about the corporation's organizational structure, including:

Address and telephone number of corporate headquarters
Names of corporate officers
Names of directors
Stock transfer agent and registrar
State and year of incorporation
Number of employees

At the very bottom of the page, there is a disclaimer indicating that information for the preparation of the report had been obtained from sources believed to be reliable (such as stockholder quarterly reports or periodic filings with the SEC) but that the accuracy and completeness of this information are not guaranteed. Following the disclaimer is the name of the analyst who prepared the report.

Value Line Investment Survey

The *Value Line Investment Survey* has many items and features in common with *S&P's Stock Reports* services, accomplishing virtually the same purpose. Each company is analyzed on a single page. The summary for Tandy Corporation in Exhibit 1–14 is an example.

The official name of the corporation is listed at the top of the page and is followed by several major pieces of information, most of which are found in newspaper stock tables and many of which have already been discussed in this chapter. This information includes:

*   *The stock exchange on which the stock is traded.*
*   *The stock ticker symbol.*
*   *A recent stock price* (as of 9 days prior to delivery).
*   *The P/E ratio.* This ratio is computed according to Equation 1–2, using the stock's most recent closing price and the latest 6-month earnings per share plus the earnings that are estimated for the next 6 months.
*   *The relative P/E ratio.* This is the stock's current P/E ratio divided by the median P/E ratio for all stocks that are under review by Value Line. As shown in Exhibit 1–14, the current P/E ratio for Tandy is 12.3, while the relative P/E ratio is 0.75, which is 75 percent of the median P/E ratio of 12.3/0.75 or 16.4 for all stocks under review by Value Line.
*   *The percent dividend yield.* This is computed according to Equation 1–1 using the estimate of the amount of cash dividends that will be declared in the next 12 months and the most recent closing market price. As shown in Exhibit 1–14, Tandy had been paying a constant quarterly dividend of $0.15 per share, or $0.60 annually, and was expected to continue this trend. At a closing price of 29, the percent yield is then 0.60/29, or 2.1 percent as published when rounded off to the nearest 0.1 percent.
*   *Value Line corporate rankings.* Three statistical measures are the focal point of Value Line's advisory, and two of these are

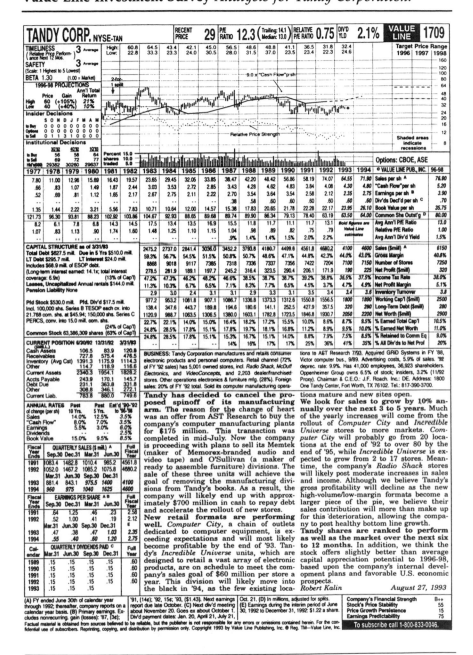

proprietary. The first is a "time lines" indicator, which ranges from 1 (highest) to 5. This value tries to quantify how quickly the particular stock will respond to market changes in the next 12 months. Stocks with ratings of 1 and 2 tend to favor strong earnings and price momentum. Conversely, stocks with ratings of 4 or 5 are characterized by poor earnings histories and tend to lag behind the market. The second indicator is a "safety" indicator, which also ranges from 1 (best) to 5. This takes into account the company's volatility and financial stability. Stocks with a rating of 1 are the least volatile and have the best financial stability. The third statistic is the stock's beta.

Graphs. In this section, two graphs are shown, with all data plotted on a monthly basis. The top graph includes three trends, as follows:

1. A high-low bar graph shows the stock price and its historical trend for the most recent 10-year period.

2. A relative price strength dotted line describes the stock's historical market price performance relative to the Value Line Composite Average of approximately 2,600 stocks (traded on the NYSE, on the AMEX, and over the counter). Known simply as the Value Line index (VLE),[8] this index is computed as a geometric average of all the composite stock prices that make up the index. The formula is:

$$VLE = \sqrt[n]{P_1 \cdot P_2 \cdot P_3 \cdot \ldots \cdot P_n} \qquad (1\text{--}4)$$

where:

n = Total number of stocks in the index

P_i = Current stock price (in dollars) for stock 1, 2 . . . to n

---

[8] The symbol VLE, used here for the Value Line Index, is the trading symbol used for its index options contracts that are traded on the **Philadelphia Stock Exchange (PHLX)**.

The *VLE* has a base level of 100 as of June 30, 1961. Because of the method of computation used, each stock has the same weight as every other stock in the index; in this, it is unlike a capitalization-weighted index (e.g., the *S&P's 500*). It is the opinion of many analysts that a geometric average-based index imparts a downward bias to the index so that it climbs slower and declines faster than an index based on an arithmetic average such as the 30-stock DJIA or the 20-stock Major Market Index.[9]

3. A value line (solid line), whose "value" equals the company's cash flow (reported earnings plus depreciation) times a number that is selected to correlate with the stock's 3- to 5-year projected target price, with the cash flow also projected out 3 to 5 years. The graph also indicates periods of recession (as shaded areas), stock splits, and the yearly high and low trading prices for each year.

The bottom graph is a vertical bar graph illustrating the monthly trading volume for the stock as a percentage of the total shares outstanding. If the stock has tradable options contracts, the exchanges on which they are traded are given. For example, Exhibit 1–14 indicates that options contracts on Tandy stock are traded on the **Chicago Board of Options Exchange (CBOE)** and the American Stock Exchange (ASE).

Like Standard & Poor's analysis, the remainder of the Value Line report is divided into several sections. These include an abridged form of balance sheet, with annual rates for cash flow, earnings, dividends, **book value,** quarterly sales figures, earnings per share, and dividends paid. There is a business summary of the corporation's primary product line and corporate operations. The summary typically includes the number of employees and shareholders, the major stockholders, the primary corporate officer, the state of incorporation, the corporate address, and the telephone number. Also included are a 400-word report on recent developments and prospects. The analyst's name and the report date appear at the end.

---

[9] A comprehensive description of most major financial market indexes can be found in *The Handbook of Financial Market Indexes, Averages, and Indicators,* by Howard M. Berlin (Homewood, IL: Business One Irwin, 1990).

Finally, a box at the bottom of the page gives Value Line's index for financial strength (a letter rating) and three proprietary numerical ratings for stock price stability, price growth persistence, and earnings predictability. All three have a maximum desirable value of 100.

Chapter Two

Corporate Bonds

INTRODUCTION

Unlike stocks, which are often referred to as **equity instruments, bonds,** regardless of their source of issue, are **fixed-income instruments.** Bonds are often referred to as **debt instruments,** because they are basically akin to loans or IOUs. These are pledges to repay **principal** at the end of a stated period, as well as to make periodic **interest** payments at a stated rate during the length of the loan. Bonds are issued by a wide spectrum of institutions. One key feature that sets bonds apart from other **fixed-income securities** is that bonds are considered long-term debt.

This chapter is concerned with bonds that are issued by corporations. Bonds and other fixed-rate securities issued by the US Treasury are discussed in Chapter 3, tax-free bonds issued by state and local governments are discussed in Chapter 4, and government agency bonds are discussed in Chapter 5.

CORPORATE BONDS

When a corporation issues bonds, the bondholders receive consideration of the payment of the periodic interest before the preferred and common stockholders are entitled to receive stock dividends. Consequently, any corporate debt must be serviced to lenders (bondholders) before owners (stockholders) are entitled to a portion of corporate profits (if there are any). As a result of their stature, corporate bonds are also known as **senior securities.** A bond issued by a corporation is a safer investment than its stock (common or preferred), because of the prior claim on assets to which it entitles its holder.

Corporations can issue several types of bonds, in two broad categories: secured and unsecured. *Secured corporate bonds* are issues that are backed by some form of corporate asset such as real property, equipment, cash, or investment instruments. *Unsecured corporate bonds,* also referred to as **debentures,** are backed only by the full faith and credit of the company—its ability to meet its debts. Two important criteria an investor should consider when deciding whether to purchase a given bond are the financial ability of the corporation to service its debt and whether or not the bond issue is secured. Bond **ratings,** which help in gauging the investment risk of corporate bonds, are discussed later in this chapter.

As pointed out previously, bonds are fixed-income securities; they pay a fixed rate of interest over the life of the bond. With the exception of certain bond derivatives, such as floating-rate bonds, income bonds, and **zero coupon bonds,** each bond has a stated fixed rate of interest that does not change. As long as the corporation is solvent, it must (1) pay this periodic interest and (2) repay the principal at maturity. As with stocks, however, the day-to-day value of bonds does vary, and it is possible for a given bond to be worth more or less than either its face value or its purchase price. Unlike Treasury bills, municipal bonds, or agency bonds, corporate bonds are generally issued in **face value** multiples of $1,000 (par value).

Reading Corporate Bond Quotations

Corporate bonds are traded on the NYSE, the AMEX, several of the regional exchanges, and over the counter. Not all the newspapers that publish stock listings also publish corporate (or any other) bond tables. With few exceptions, daily bond listings seem to be the sole province of specialized investment newspapers. *The Wall Street Journal, Barron's,* and *The New York Times* publish separate corporate bond tables for the NYSE issues and the AMEX issues that were traded on a given day. On the other hand, *Investor's Business Daily* consolidates NYSE and AMEX bonds into a single table. Of these publications, the corporate bond tables of *Investor's Business Daily* appear to be the most informative.

EXHIBIT 2–1
***NYSE and AMEX Corporate Bond Quotations from* Investor's Business Daily.**

S&P Rates	Bond	Ex	Coupon Rate	Mat-ures	Yld. Cur.	Yld.to Mat.	Vol.	Bond Close	Chg
A−	AldCorp	NY	ZrCpn	08/00	...	6.5	26	63¼	− ¾
A−	AldCorp	NY	ZrCpn	08/95	...	5.2	5	89⅝	+ ⅛
BBB−	Amax	NY	14.500	12/94	12.9	5.9	19	112	+ ¼
BBB	Amer&For	NY	5.000	03/30	8.0	8.3	10	62⅝	...
AAA	Amoco	NY	8.625	12/16	7.7	7.5	75	112¼	+ ¼
AAA	Amoco	NY	7.875	08/96	7.7	7.2	73	101⅞	+ ⅞
A	AmBrnd	NY	9.125	03/16	8.4	8.3	40	108	+ 1¼
CALL	AmBrnd	NY	8.500	10/03	7.5	6.6	3	114	+ 2
NR	AmFinOH	Pa	12.000	09/99	12.2	12.4	12	98½	+ 1
NR	AmFinOH	Pa	10.000	10/99	10.6	11.3	4	94¼	+ ¼
NR	AmFinOH	Pa	10.000	10/99	10.7	11.4	66	93⅞	− ⅛
B	Armco	NY	8.500	09/01	8.9	9.2	25	96	+ ⅜
B	Armco	NY	13.500	06/94	12.7	7.1	10	106⅛	+ ⅛
A+	AtlRichfd	NY	7.700	12/00	7.5	7.3	15	102	...
A+	AtlRichfd	NY	8.625	04/00	8.4	8.0	10	103¼	− ½
B+	Aubrn−C	NY	16.875	05/20	11.8	11.7	173	142½	+ 2½
BBB	AMR Cp	NY	9.000	09/16	8.5	8.5	988	105½	+ ¾
AA	AT&T	NY	5.125	04/01	5.5	6.1	149	93¾	+ ⅛
AA	AT&T	NY	6.000	08/00	6.0	6.0	245	100	...
AA	AT&T	NY	7.125	01/02	6.8	6.3	193	105⅜	+ ⅝
AA	AT&T	NY	8.125	01/22	7.6	7.5	335	106¾	+ ⅝
AA	AT&T	NY	8.125	07/24	7.6	7.5	10	106⅞	+ ⅜
AA	AT&T	NY	4.750	06/98	4.9	5.6	5	96½	+ ½
NR	AT&T	NY	4.500	02/96	4.5	4.7	255	99½	+ ⅛
AA	AT&T	NY	4.375	05/99	4.7	5.7	17	93¼	+ ¼
NR	AT&T	NY	5.500	01/97	5.5	5.4	10	100¼	+ ⅛
BBB+	Barnett	NY	8.500	03/99	7.7	6.4	49	110⅛	...
BB+	Baroid	NY	8.000	04/03	8.0	8.0	5	100	...
AA	BellTelPa	NY	7.500	05/13	7.3	7.3	5	102⅛	+ ⅛
AA	BellTelPa	NY	7.125	01/12	7.1	7.1	44	100¾	+ ½
AAA	BelsthTel	NY	6.250	05/03	6.3	6.3	16	99½	+ ¼

Reprinted by permission of *Investor's Business Daily*, June 14, 1993, © INVESTOR'S BUSINESS DAILY, INC., 1993.

As illustrated by Exhibit 2–1, which appeared in *Investor's Business Daily*, corporate bond quotes are given in the following format:

❶	❷	❸	❹	❺	❻	❼	❽	❾	❿
S&P Rate	**Bond**	**Ex**	**Coupon Rate**	**Matures**	**Yield Cur.**	**Yield to Mat.**	**Vol.**	**Bond Close**	**Chg**

The columns used in the format are described below.

❶   S&P rate.   The bond rating assigned by Standard & Poor's. The bond rating is related to its investment risk: the higher the rating, the lower the risk. As a consequence, issues with higher bond ratings generally have lower coupon rates. For example, the Atlantic Richfield bond listed below has a Standard & Poor's rating of A+, which puts it in the "intermediate grade" category.

S&P Rate	Bond	Ex	Coupon Rate	Matures	Yield Cur.	Yield to Mat.	Vol.	Bond Close	Chg
A+	AtlRichfd	NY	7.700	12/00	7.5	7.3	15	102	. . .

❷   Bond.   The name of the company issuing the bond. The companies are listed in alphabetical order, and the company name is usually abbreviated, as illustrated below:

S&P Rate	Bond	Ex	Coupon Rate	Matures	Yield Cur.	Yield to Mat.	Vol.	Bond Close	Chg
A+	AtlRichfd	NY	7.700	12/00	7.5	7.3	15	102	. . .

The abbreviation for a particular company may not necessarily be exactly the same as the abbreviation used for the stock quotation. *Investor's Business Daily*, in its corporate bond tables, for example, uses the abbreviation CmwEd for Commonwealth Edison, while its stock tables use Comnwlth Ed.

❸   Exchange.   An abbreviation of the exchange on which the bond is traded. Even though *Investor's Business Daily's* table primarily lists bonds traded on the NYSE (NY) and the AMEX

(Am), several bonds traded on the Pacific Stock Exchange (Pa) may also be listed on occasion.

S&P Rate	Bond	Ex	Coupon Rate	Matures	Yield Cur.	Yield to Mat.	Vol.	Bond Close	Chg
A+	AtlRichfd	NY	7.700	12/00	7.5	7.3	15	102	. . .
NR	TrumpCstl	Am	11.350	11/99	. . .	FLAT	34	94	$- \frac{3}{4}$
D	TWA	Pa	15.000	07/94	. . .	. . .	130	$103\frac{1}{2}$	$+ \frac{1}{2}$

④ Coupon rate. The fixed annual coupon percentage rate, also called the **coupon yield.** With very few exceptions, interest is paid semiannually.

S&P Rate	Bond	Ex	Coupon Rate	Matures	Yield Cur.	Yield to Mat.	Vol.	Bond Close	Chg
AAA	BelsthTel	NY	7.875	08/32	7.5	7.5	59	$104\frac{1}{2}$	$+\frac{5}{8}$
B	Coleman	NY	ZrCpn	05/13	. . .	7.0	2	$25\frac{3}{8}$	. . .
B+	ChryslrFinl	NY	n.a.	04/97	. . .	. . .	10	$99\frac{1}{2}$	$+\frac{1}{4}$

Zero coupon bonds, which do not pay interest periodically, are identified by the abbreviation ZrCpn, while the abbreviation n.a. is used to identify any bond with a variable or adjustable rate.

⑤ Matures. The date on which the bond matures, expressed in a month/year format. The month and year are each represented as a two-digit number. The year is abbreviated to the last two digits of the year, and it is understood that the first two digits are either 19 or 20. For maturity dates beyond 1999, 00 represents the year 2000. In the entry below, 05/13 represents a maturity date of May 2013.

S&P Rate	Bond	Ex	Coupon Rate	Matures	Yield Cur.	Yield to Mat.	Vol.	Bond Close	Chg
B	Coleman	NY	ZrCpn	05/13	. . .	7.0	2	$25\frac{3}{8}$	. . .

⑥ Current yield.   The yield, as a percentage of a bond's current price, that is paid as interest. For bonds priced above **par** (100), the current yield is less than the coupon rate; for bonds priced below par, the current yield is greater than the coupon rate. Only when a bond is exactly at par will the current yield equal the coupon rate. In the entry below, the current yield of 7.5 percent is less than the coupon rate (7.70 percent), since the bond is priced above par, at 102.

S&P Rate	Bond	Ex	Coupon Rate	Matures	Yield Cur.	Yield to Mat.	Vol.	Bond Close	Chg
A+	AtlRichfd	NY	7.700	12/00	7.5	7.3	15	102	. . .

⑦ Yield to maturity.   The yield of the bond if held to maturity. It takes into account (1) the present value of all interest payments (and assumes that these interest payments are reinvested at the bond's coupon rate), and (2) the current price. It also assumes that, at maturity, all bonds are priced at par. If a bond was bought at a **premium** (priced above par value of 100), the premium paid is lost at maturity. For issues priced below par, the bond is bought at a **discount** and is worth less than face value. Of the three types of bond yields discussed, the **yield to maturity** (**YTM**) is the most complex, but it provides a common basis upon which bond yields can be compared. It is possible that a bond bought at a premium will have a high current yield; a **discount bond,** by comparison, will have a higher yield to maturity.

⑧ Bond volume.   How many thousands of dollars worth of a given bond were traded on a certain day. This is in contrast with stock tables, which give the number of shares traded. In the following quotation, the number 15 means that 15 bonds with a face value of $15,000 (i.e., 15 $1,000 bonds) were traded.

S&P Rate	Bond	Ex	Coupon Rate	Matures	Yield Cur.	Yield to Mat.	Vol.	Bond Close	Chg
A+	AtlRichfd	NY	7.700	12/00	7.5	7.3	15	102	. . .

⑨ **Bond close.** The closing price of the bond as a percentage of par. Corporate bond prices are quoted as a percentage of par (or face value), equal to 100, and are generally expressed in whole points and eighths (0.125 point). Each whole point represents 1 percent of the bond's face value. For each $1,000 of face value, a full point equals $10, while an eighth equals $1.25. Bond prices generally move in the opposite direction from changes in interest rates.

⑩ **Change.** The net change from the bond's closing price of the previous day.

Exhibit 2–2 shows a portion of the AMEX bond table from *The Wall Street Journal*. This illustrates a slightly different format from the one used by *Investor's Business Daily*. On this list, corporate bond quotes are given in the following format:

Bond	Cur Yield	Vol.	Close	Net Chg.

Most notably, *The Wall Street Journal* bond tables do not give the bond's yield to maturity. Otherwise, the only other major differences from *Investor's Business Daily* are (1) that the bond's coupon rate and maturity are given immediately following the company name and (2) that the maturity indicates only the year without the month.

Examples are:

Bond	Cur Yield	Vol.	Close	Net Chg.
Atari 5¼402	c.v.	10	49	+ 1
Greyhnd 10s01	9.5	137	105¼	+ ¼
TurnBd zr04	. . .	8	40¾	− ¼
Westbr 11.7s96	11.7	5	100¼	− ¼

The first example (Atari 5¼402) describes a bond issued by Atari Corporation that has a coupon rate of 5¼ percent and that matures

EXHIBIT 2–2
AMEX Corporate Bond Quotations from **The Wall Street Journal.**

AMEX BONDS

Volume $3,259,000

SALES SINCE JANUARY 1

1993	1992	1991
$390,983,000	$443,400,000	$458,140,000

	Fri.	Thu.	Wed.	Tue.
Issues traded	56	57	48	55
Advances	23	20	25	23
Declines	16	20	11	23
Unchanged	17	17	12	9
New highs	3	3	7	4
New lows	0	0	1	1

Bonds	Cur Yld	Vol	Close	Net Chg.
AirExp 6s03	cv	125	89½ −	1½
Allnet 9S03	9.1	50	99	...
Atari 5¼02	cv	40	50½ −	1
Aurora 7¾401	cv	57	90½ +	3½
CII Fn 7½01	cv	5	72	...
ChckFul 8s06	cv	49	107½ +	½
CollAG 11⅜97	11.3	9	100¾ +	¼
CollAG 11⅞01	11.6	52	102½	...
CollAG 7½05	8.1	4	92⅝	...
ContHlt 14⅛96f	...	25	53½ +	1½
DrPep11½02f	...	169	73⅜ +	⅛
Ducom 7¾411	9.7	24	80 −	¾
Eckerd 11⅛01	10.8	30	103	...
Eckerd 13s06	12.9	115	100½ −	½
FruitL 12⅜03	11.7	9	105½ +	½
FruitL 7s11	7.7	10	90¾ +	⅝

in 2002. The maturity date is abbreviated as the last two digits of the year, it being understood that the first two digits are either 19 or 20. The letters c.v. indicate that this bond is a convertible bond (convertible bonds are discussed later in this chapter). The second example (Greyhnd 10s01) is a bond issued by Greyhound Corporation that has a coupon rate of 10 percent and that matures in the year 2001. The letter s between the coupon rate and the two-digit abbreviation for the maturity year is used for clarity to eliminate any confusion between the numbers representing the interest rate and the year. This notation is used when the interest rate does not include a fraction. The third example (TurnBd zr04) is a zero coupon bond issued by Turner Broadcasting System that matures in 2004. The last example (Westbr 11.7s96) is a bond issued by Westbridge Capital that has a coupon rate of 11.7 percent and that matures in 1996. Here, the rate is nonstandard and is expressed as a decimal. Again, the letter s is inserted between the coupon rate and the two-digit abbreviation for the maturity year to eliminate any confusion between the interest rate and the year.

Since zero coupon bonds do not pay interest periodically, no current yield is given. Any additional notes (such as letter codes used to indicate bankruptcy or registered bonds) are given at the end of the bond quotations. However, these codes are not standard from one newspaper to another.

Almost all the newspapers that publish daily corporate bond tables used to include bond 52-week high and low prices, but most have discontinued this information to save space. Although both *The Wall Street Journal* (a daily) and *Barron's* (a weekly) are published by Dow Jones & Company, only *Barron's* provides the 52-week highs and lows as well as the high and low prices for the week (Exhibit 2–3). *S&P's Bond Guide*, like its companion, *S&P's Stock Guide*, is available from most brokerage firms and also lists bond 52-week highs and lows. As published in *Barron's*, the format is as follows:

52-Weeks		Name and	Cur	Sales	Weekly				Net
High	Low	Coupon	Yield	$1,000	High	Low	Last		Chg.
104^1/$_2$	99^3/$_8$	AMR 8.10s98	7.9	1203	103	103	103	–	1^1/$_2$

This example is a bond issued by AMR that has a coupon rate of 8.10 percent and matures in 1998. This example is unlike the daily corporate bond tables of *The Wall Street Journal, Investor's Business Daily,* and *The New York Times* in that the last column presents the net change from the previous Friday's close.

For the most part, bond tables are informative. However, there are bits of information that are not generally given. Unlike Treasury bond listings (Chapter 3), corporate bond tables (except for *Investor's Business Daily*) do not normally state the months in which interest is paid. This information is useful because, according to common practice, the seller is paid all interest accrued from the last semiannual interest payment up until the day before **settlement**

EXHIBIT 2–3
Corporate Bond Quotations from **Barron's.**

52-Weeks High	Low	Name and Coupon	Cur Yld	Sales $1,000	Weekly High	Low	Last	Net Chg.
NEW YORK EXCHANGE								
A-B-C								
63¼	56¼	AForP 5s30	8.1	25	63¼	61¾	61¾	− 1½
105¾	95¼	AMR 9s16	8.6	124	105	104¼	105	− ¼
46¾	42⅞	AMR zr06	...	46	46	45½	45½	− ⅜
106½	99	AMR 8.10s98	7.6	30	106⅛	105⅜	106⅛	+ ⅞
102	100¼	ANR 8⅝93	8.6	2	100¼	100¼	100¼	...
100	86	Advst 9s08	cv	25	96⅞	96	96⅞	+ 1⅜
103	83	AirbF 6¾01	cv	78	101⅝	100½	101⅝	+ ⅞
106	105	AlaP 10⅝17	10.0	15	106	106	106	...
87	75	AlskAr 6⅞14	cv	179	84	82	83¼	+ 1¼
38¼	33⅝	AlskAr zr06	...	318	37¼	36¼	36¾	− ⅞
90¾	77	Albnylnt 5s02	cv	11	90¾	89	90¾	+ 1½
75¼	61	AlldC zr98	...	158	75¼	74	75	+ 1½
89	78⅛	AlldC zr96	...	12	89	89	89	+ ¾
64⅞	52	AlldC zr2000	...	75	64⅞	63⅞	64⅞	+ ¾
81⅛	68⅞	AlldC zr97	...	75	81⅛	79⅝	80	+ 1
70¼	57½	AlldC zr99	...	45	69½	69⅜	69½	− ⅜
59	47½	AlldC zr01	...	50	59	58¾	59	+ 1
51	40½	AlldC zr03	...	50	50⅞	50⅞	50⅞	+ ¼
43	32¾	AlldC zr05	...	45	42¼	41¾	42¼	+ ¾
36½	27¼	AlldC zr07	...	155	36½	35½	36½	+ 1
30	22⅜	AlldC zr09	...	165	30	29⅝	30	+ ¼
98	85	Allwst 7¼14	cv	90	92½	92¼	92½	− 1¾
117	110½	AMAX 14½94	13.0	58	111½	111	111½	+ ⅜
114	104¾	AmBrnd 8½03	7.5	3	113⅞	113⅞	113⅞	+ ⅞
102	98½	AmBrnd 5¼95	5.2	20	101½	101½	101½	− ½
102	99⅛	ACyan 7⅜01	7.3	15	101	100¾	101	...
103¾	101⅜	ACyan 8⅜06	8.2	17	103½	102⅝	102⅝	− ⅞
121¾	100	AmStor 01	cv	133	119	117½	118¼	+ ⅝
97¾	90¼	ATT 4¾98	4.9	457	97¾	97⅛	97¾	+ ½
99¾	94⅛	ATT 4⅜96	4.4	135	99⅜	99	99	− ½
101½	95¾	ATT 5½97	5.5	451	100⅜	100⅛	100⅛	...
95	87¼	ATT 4⅜99	4.6	498	94⅝	94	94⅜	+ ⅛
100¾	92¼	ATT 6s00	6.0	1676	100½	100¼	100¼	...

(delivery). The **accrued interest** is determined by the following formula:

$$\text{Accrued interest} = \frac{I \cdot DH \cdot FV}{180} \qquad \textbf{(2–1)}$$

where:

DH = Days held from last semiannual interest payment to the day before settlement

FV = Bond face value (in dollars)

I = Annual coupon rate (as a decimal)

Interest for corporate bonds is computed on the basis of a 360-day year in which each month is assumed to have 30 days. Even though February actually has 28 days (29 in a leap year), and January, for example, has 31 days, these months are treated as if they had 30 days. If a bond with coupon interest payment dates of February 1 and August 1 is settled on March 12, the number of days of accrued interest will be:

February	30 days
March	11
	41 days

Example: Calculating Accrued Interest

Suppose that an A− rated bond issued by Pennzoil has an $8^{3/8}$ percent coupon and pays semiannual interest on March 1 and September 1. If 10 bonds, each with a face value of $1,000, are sold such that the settlement date is April 4, there are 33 days of accrued interest. Using Equation 2–1,

$$\text{Accrued interest} = \frac{(0.08375) \cdot (33) \cdot (\$10,000)}{360}$$

$$= \$76.77$$

of accrued interest that is due the seller. On the next interest payment date, the buyer will receive the entire interest for the 6-month

---

period ($418.75). Since the buyer has already paid $76.77 in accrued interest to the seller, the buyer will now have a net of $418.75 − $76.77, or $341.98 of interest paid for the semiannual interest period.

Another item that is missing from daily or weekly bond tables is an indication of whether or not there is a **call** date. Many bonds, as part of their issue, have one or more provisions that allow the issuer to redeem or "call in" a part or all of the issue earlier than its maturity date. This call provision can range from as little as several years after issue (very doubtful) to as close as one interest payment period (i.e., 6 months) before maturity. In return for calling the bond before maturity, the issuer will often pay a premium of several points. For example, if a $1,000 corporate bond is called at 102, the issuer will pay $1,020 to the bondholder, plus the interest due on that date. Beyond the call date, no further interest is paid.

Finally, for convertible bonds, which are discussed later in this chapter, the conversion rate is not published. Most of these missing data are shown in *S&P's Bond Guide*. Exhibit 2–4 illustrates a portion of *S&P's Bond Guide*, showing the interest payment dates. For the Pennzoil issue mentioned in the previous example, the interest payment dates are given as Ms (March-September), where the capital letter denotes the maturity month (i.e., March). When no number is given, interest is assumed to be paid on the first of the month. Another example is jD15, which means that interest is paid on June 15 and December 15 and that the bond matures on December 15.

Calculating Bond Dollar Prices

Corporate bond prices are quoted as a percentage of par, equal to 100 percent of face value, and are generally expressed in whole points and eighths (0.125 point), although some bond values can be expressed by fractions as low as thirty-seconds. Each whole point represents 1 percent of the issue's face value. For each $100 of face value, a full point is equal to $1, while an eighth equals

EXHIBIT 2–4
S&P's Bond Guide.

Exchange / Individual Issue Statistics (Title-Industry Code & Co. Finances (In Italics))	Interest Dates (Ind)	S&P Debt Rating	Date of Last Rating Change (Fixed Charge Coverage 1986)	Prior Rating (1987)	Eligible (1988)	Bond Form (Year End)	Regular Price (Cash & Equiv.)	Regular (Begins) Thru (Curr. Assets)	Sinking Fund Price (Curr. Liab.)	Sinking Fund (Begins) Thru (Balance Sheet Date)	Refund/Other Restriction Price (L. Term Debt (Mil $))	Refund/Other Restriction (Begins) Thru	Outst'g (Mil $) (Capitalization (Mil $))	Underwriting Firm (Total Debt % Capital)	Underwriting Year	Price Range 1989 High	Price Range 1989 Low	Mo. End Price Sale(s) or Bid	Curr. Yield	Yield to Mat.
Pennsylvania Pwr & Light (Cont.)																				
1st 10⅞s 2016	Jj	A–	7/86	BBB+	X	R	109.06	12-31-89	Z100	....	®107.99	12-31-90	125	F2	'86	107	103¾	104⅝	10.39	10.36
1st 9s 2016	Ao	A–	7/86	BBB+	X	R	107.40	3-31-90	Z100	....	®106.70	3-31-91	125	H7	'86	91⅜	87	88⅛	10.21	10.31
1st 9½s 2016	aO	A–			X	R	108.10	9-30-89	Z100	....	®106.75	9-30-91	125	F2	'86	95¾	91⅛	92⅛	10.31	10.37
1st 10s 2019	Jj	A–			X	R	109.35	12-31-89	Z100	....	®107.01	12-31-93	125	F2	'89	99¼	94½	95⅜	10.48	10.51
Pennzoil Co.	*49d*		*2.17*	*1.29*	*2.12*	*Dc*	*2128*	*2856*	*365.0*	*12-31-88*	*1415*		*2978*	*48.0*						
• SF Deb 8⅜s '96	Ms	A–	4/88	BBB+	X	R	100.87	2-28-90	100.03	2-28-90	....	....	8.30	W6	'71	93½	93	91¼	9.18	10.16
• SF Deb 8⅝s '96	Ms	A–	4/88	BBB+	X	R	100.87	2-28-90	*100.03	2-28-90	....	....	31.2	Exch.	'86	97¼	95	93⅛	9.26	10.02
• SF Deb 8¾s 2001	jD31	A–	4/88	BBB+	X	R	103.50	12-31-89	100	....	....	....	2.76	W6	'77	95½	90	88½	9.89	10.39
• SF Deb 9s 2001	jD31	A–	4/88	BBB+	X	R	103.50	12-31-89	*100	....	....	....	67.6	Exch.	'86	96⅛	95⅛	92⅞	9.69	10.00
• SF Deb 12⅛s 2007	jD	A–	4/88	BBB+	X	R	107.82	11-30-89	100	(12-1-93)	®105.59	11-30-92	5.14	M3	'82	No Sale		104⅝	11.59	11.51
• SF Deb 12¼s 2007	jD	A–	4/88	BBB+	X	R	107.82	11-30-89	100	(12-1-93)	®105.59	11-30-92	94.9	Exch.	'86	No Sale		107⅜	11.41	11.29
SF Deb 10s 2011	Ms	A–	4/88	BBB+	X	R	106.96	2-28-90	100	(3-1-97)	®104.09	2-2-96	200	M3	'86	99⅜	94¾	95⅞	10.43	10.48
SF Deb 10⅛s 2011	fA	A–	4/88	BBB+	X	R	108.10	7-31-89	100	(8-1-97)	®104.50	7-31-96	150	M3	'86	99½	95	96	10.55	10.59
SF Deb 9s 2017	Ao	A–	4/88	BBB+	X	R	108.10	3-31-90	100	(4-1-98)	®104.50	3-31-97	100	M3	'87	89¾	85⅛	86⅛	10.45	10.55
SF Deb 10⅝s 2018	Ao	A–			X	R	109.87	3-31-90	100	(4-1-99)	®107.79	3-31-98	250	M3	'88	103⅜	97⅜	98⅜	10.80	10.81
• Deb 15s '92	Mn	A–	4/88	BBB+	X	R	100	....	....	....	....	....	18.6	M3	'82	104	101	99¾	15.04	15.09
• Deb 15½s '92	Mn	A–	4/88	BBB+	X	R	100	....	....	....	....	....	131	Exch.	'86	103	100½	s101	15.35	15.08
Nts 8¼s '91	fA	A–	4/88	BBB+	X	R	NC	....	....	....	....	....	150	M3	'86	97⅛	95⅜	95½	8.64	10.46
Nts 9⅛s '96	Ms	A–	4/88	BBB+	X	R	100	(3-1-93)	....	....	....	....	100	M3	'86	98⅛	95⅛	95¾	9.53	9.99
Penril Corp	*24*		*0.64*	*0.27*	*4.78*	*Jl*	*1.98*	*21.00*	*6.18*	*10-31-88*	*15.90*		*20.70*	*77.8*						
◆Sr Sub Nts[1] 10⅞s '93	§Fa	NR	5/87	D	Z	R			Default 2-1-87 int				[2]0.94	D9	'83	No Sale		54⅛	....	Flat
People Express Airlines[3]	*4*		*1.44*	*d0.29*	....	*Dc*	*0.15*	*20.80*	*96.10*	*9-30-88*	*438.0*		*621.0*	*72.1*						
Sec Eq Ctfs 14⅜s '96	Ao15	NR				R	102	(4-5-93)	100	....	....	....	115	M6	'86	92	87	91¾	15.67	16.39
[4]Nts([5]'88) 16½s '91	jj15	NR				R	NC	....	....	....	....	....	40.0	M6	'84	99⅞	97	97	17.01	18.11
Peoples Gas Light&Coke[6]	*73b*		*4.56*	*3.37*	*3.76*	*Sp*	*65.90*	*351.0*	*229.0*	*12-31-88*	*420.0*		*857.0*	*49.2*						
1st&Ref L 6¼s '92	fA15	AA–	1/85	A+	X	R	100.91	8-14-89	100.28	8-14-89	....	....	32.0	H1	'67	92	88⅛	88¼	7.08	10.47
1st&Ref M 8⅞s '95	mS15	AA–	1/85	A+	X	R	102.41	9-14-89	100.39	9-14-89	....	....	17.5	F2	'70	97	91	91⅜	9.71	10.76
1st&Ref N 7⅝s '97	Ao15	AA–	1/85	A+	X	R	102.31	4-14-90	100.15	4-14-90	....	....	29.6	G8	'72	89	85⅝	86⅜	8.83	10.14
1st&Ref O 8¼s '98	jJ15	AA–	1/85	A+	X	R	103.10	7-14-89	100	....	....	....	22.6	F2	'73	91⅝	87	87¾	9.40	10.33
PepsiCo Inc	*11e*		*3.44*	*4.24*	....	*Dc*	*1664*	*3363*	*3449*	*9-03-88*	*2803*		*6903*	*57.1*						
Nts 8¼s '89	mN	A+	1/89	AA–	X	R	NC	....	....	....	....	....	150	M6	'87	99⅛	98⅜	98½	8.38	10.95
Nts 9⅜s '93	mS	A+	1/89	AA–	X	R	100	(9-1-91)	....	....	....	....	150	F2	'88	99½	97	97¼	9.64	10.16
• Nts 7⅝s '98	jD18	A+	1/89	AA–	X	R	NC	....	....	....	....	....	165	M6	'86	88	83⅜	85⅛	8.96	10.06
Petro-Lewis Corp	*49b*		*3.79*	*n/a*	*n/a*	*Je*														
Sub Nts Zero Cpn '89	[7]	NR	3/87	C		R	100	....	....	....	....	....	[2]14.9	D9	'81	82	79¾	79¾	....	Flat
Pfizer, Inc	*21a*		*16.76*	*16.18*	*13.71*	*Dc*	*808.0*	*4095*	*2344*	*12-31-88*	*227.0*		*5521*	*21.6*						
• SF Deb 8½s '99	Ao15	AAA	5/86	AA	X	R	101.94	4-14-90	100	....	....	....	50.1	L3	'74	96	92	s93¼	9.12	9.56
Phelps Dodge Corp.	*44b*		*2.29*	*5.26*	....	*Dc*	*98.80*	*665.0*	*353.0*	*9-30-88*	*455.0*		*2031*	*22.4*						
• SF Deb 8.10s '96	Jd15	BBB	6/88	BB+	X	R	101.215	6-14-89	100	....	....	....	59.1	M6	'71	97⅛	95	89⅞	9.01	10.11
Philadelphia Electric	*75*		*2.22*	*2.14*	....	*Dc*	*212.0*	*917.0*	*1025*	*9-30-88*	*5338*		*10295*	*55.7*						
• 1st & Ref 5s '89	aO	BBB–	9/82	BBB	X	CR	100	....	....	....	....	....	50.0	M6	'59	96¾	96⅝	97¼	5.14	10.80
• 1st & Ref 6½s '93	Ms	BBB–	9/82	BBB	X	R	100.90	2-28-90	....	....	....	....	60.0	H1	'68	88¾	86⅝	87½	7.43	10.47
• 1st & Ref 4½s '94	Mn	BBB–	9/82	BBB	X	R	100.90	4-30-90	....	....	....	....	50.0	H1	'64	77½	75⅜	76½	5.88	10.60

Uniform Footnote Explanations-See Page 1. Other: [1] Plan int arrears payment. [2] Incl disc. [3] Subsid of People Express Inc(Texas Air). [4] (HRO)On 7-19-88 at 100. [5] Plan seek indent chge to 10 ½% 2006. [6] Subsid of Peoples Energy. [7] Due Aug 15.

12.5 cents. Issues priced above par value of 100 (a premium) are worth more than face value. Bonds priced below par (a discount) are worth less than face value. As an aid, the decimal equivalents of thirty-seconds are given in Appendix A.

Two Examples: Calculating Bond Dollar Prices

Determine the dollar price of a $1,000 corporate bond quoted at a premium of 105³/₈ and for a $1,000 bond quoted at a discount of 97¹/₂.

1. A quote of 105³/₈ is equivalent to 105.375 points. The dollar price is:

$$\text{Price} = \frac{105.375}{100} \cdot \$1,000$$

$$= \$1,053.75$$

2. A quote of 97¹/₂ is equivalent to 97.50 points. The equivalent dollar price is:

$$\text{Price} = \frac{97.50}{100} \cdot \$1,000$$

$$= \$975.00$$

Calculating Bond Yields

Current yield. A bond's **current yield** is the percentage rate of its current price that will be paid in annual interest. It is calculated from:

$$\text{Current yield} = \frac{I \cdot FV}{PV} \cdot 100 \qquad\qquad \text{(2–2)}$$

where:

FV = Bond face value (in dollars)

I = Annual coupon rate (as a decimal)

PV = Current value (in dollars)

The quantity $I \cdot FV$ represents the amount of annual interest in dollars received, which is compared to a percentage of the issue's present value. For bonds priced above par, the current yield is less than the coupon rate; for bonds priced below par, the current yield is greater than the coupon rate. Only when the bond is exactly at par will the current yield equal the coupon rate.

Two Examples: Calculating a Bond's Current Yield

From Exhibit 2–1, the 9.125 percent bond of American Brands that matures in March 2016 (03/16) is priced at 108. For a $1,000 bond, the current yield is (Equation 2–2):

$$\text{Current yield} = \frac{(0.09125) \cdot (\$1,000)}{\$1,080} \cdot 100$$

$$= 8.449\%$$

which agrees with the published rate of 8.4 percent when rounded off to one decimal place. Note that since the bond is selling above par, the current yield is less than the coupon rate. The bondholder receives $91.25 in interest each year for each $1,000 bond. If the interest payments are made semiannually, one payment is $45.62 while the other payment is $45.63.

On the other hand, the 8.5 percent bond of Armco that matures in September 2001 (09/01) is priced at 96. The current yield of a $1,000 bond is:

$$\text{Current yield} = \frac{(0.085) \cdot (\$1,000)}{\$960} \cdot 100$$

$$= 8.854\%$$

which agrees with the published rate of 8.9 percent when rounded off to one decimal place. Note that this bond is selling below par and the current yield is greater than its coupon rate. The bondholder receives $85.00 in interest each year for each $1,000 bond.

Yield to maturity.   Unlike the current yield, which is a very simple calculation, a bond's yield to maturity considers how much time is left before the bond matures at par value (100) in addition to its coupon rate and purchase price. The standard formula for calculating the yield to maturity is based on the bond's current price, or present value (PV), as follows:

$$PV = \sum_{t=1}^{n} \frac{0.5\,I}{\left[1 + \dfrac{YTM}{2}\right]^n} + \frac{100}{\left[1 + \dfrac{YTM}{2}\right]^n} \tag{2–3}$$

where:

I = Annual coupon rate (as a percentage)

n = Number of full remaining semiannual interest payments

This formula is both very awkward and difficult for the average person to use in solving for *YTM*. However, there are a number of business-type calculators as well as computer programs for personal computers that simplify the process and permit accurate calculation of a bond's yield to maturity. If such aids are not available, a very good approximation for determining a bond's *YTM* is:

$$YTM = \frac{2 \cdot (I \pm AYD)}{(100 + CP)} \cdot 100 \qquad (2\text{-}4)$$

where:

AYD = Annual yearly discount (as a percentage)

CP = Current price (in points as a fraction of par)

I = Annual coupon rate (as a percentage)

The annual yearly discount (AYD) is the difference between par (100) and the bond's current price averaged over the number of years left until maturity. For bonds bought at a discount, the AYD is added to the annual coupon rate. For bonds bought at a premium, it is subtracted.

Two Examples: Calculating a Bond's Yield to Maturity

In Exhibit 2–1, two bonds are quoted on June 11, 1993, as follows:

S&P Rate	Bond	Ex	Coupon Rate	Mat- ures	Yield Cur.	Yield to Mat.	Vol.	Bond Close	Chg
A+	AtlRichfd	NY	7.700	12/00	7.5	7.3	15	102	. . .
B	StoneC	NY	11.500	09/99	13.5	15.3	1243	85^1/$_8$	+ 1^1/$_8$

The first quote is for an Atlantic Richfield bond having a 7.70 percent coupon, which matures in December 2000. On the day of its quotation, the bond had approximately $7\frac{1}{2}$ years until maturity and was priced at 102 (a premium). The annual yearly discount is:

$$AYD = \frac{100 - 102}{7.5 \text{ years}}$$

$$= -0.27\%$$

Note that the *AYD* is negative for a bond bought at a premium, and must be subtracted from the coupon rate. The *YTM* (Equation 2–4) is:

$$YTM = \frac{2 \cdot (7.70 - 0.27)}{(100 + 102)} \cdot 100$$

$$= 7.36\%$$

which is only 6 **basis points** (0.06 percent) from the published yield of 7.3 percent.

The second quote is for a Stone Container bond with an 11.5 percent coupon, which matures in September 1999. On the day of its quotation, the bond had approximately 6 years until maturity and was priced at $85\frac{1}{8}$ (a discount). The annual yearly discount is:

$$AYD = \frac{100 - 85.125}{6 \text{ years}}$$

$$= 2.48\%$$

Here, the *AYD* is positive for a bond bought at a discount, which must be added to the coupon rate. The yield to maturity (Equation 2–4) is:

$$YTM = \frac{2 \cdot (11.5 + 2.48)}{(100 + 85.125)} \cdot 100\%$$

$$= 15.10\%$$

which is only 20 basis points (0.20 percent) from the published yield of 15.3 percent.

These two examples point out that no rule-of-thumb formula (such as Equation 2–4) is 100 percent correct all the time. Equation 2–4 becomes less accurate as the time to maturity increases and as the discount (or premium) increases. Its use is not appropriate for zero coupon bonds (with a **deep discount**) or for straight bonds with maturities greater than 25 years.

Bond Ratings

The system of rating debt securities was originated by John Moody. Its purpose is to assess the issuer's ability to (1) pay the interest and (2) repay the principal of a specific debt issue when due. Although there are many different types of debt that may be serviced, the types that receive the primary focus of commercial rating companies, such as Moody's Investor Service, Standard & Poor's Corporation, Duff & Phelps, and Fitch Investor Service, are corporate and municipal bond issues. Of these four rating companies, Moody's and Standard & Poor's are perhaps the best known, and their ratings are the most widely used.

A rating assigned by a given bond rating firm is simply the firm's best assessment of the creditworthiness of the particular issue, based on the facts at hand. If the underlying considerations change, the bond rating may change, up or down. Furthermore, bonds of different issuers that carry the same rating are not necessarily of equal quality.

The rating scale used by the four major bond rating firms is summarized in Exhibit 2–5. The rating scales used by the rating companies can be divided into the following two broad categories: investment grade (high and medium grade) and noninvestment grade (speculative and default). Since the mid-1980s, speculative, high-yield bonds have been called *junk bonds*, because of the high probability that the periodic interest payments and/or repayment of principal at maturity will not occur as promised.

Standard & Poor's Corporation sometimes uses plus (+) and minus (−) modifiers along with ratings from AA to CCC (e.g., A+ or BB−) to show relative standing within a major rating category. Moody's applies the numerical modifier 1, 2, or 3 to each major rating category from Aa to B for corporate bonds. The modifier 1 (e.g., Aa1) indicates that the issue ranks at the highest

EXHIBIT 2-5
Bond Rating Scales.

Category	Moody's	Standard & Poor's	Duff & Phelps	Fitch	Criteria
High grade	Aaa	AAA	1	AAA	Issues judged to be of the best quality. These issues carry the lowest degree of investment risk and are frequently referred to as *gilt-edged*. The capacity to pay principal and interest is extremely strong.
	Aa	AA	2–4	AA	Issues judged to be of high quality by all standards. The issuers have a strong capacity to pay principal and interest. These issues are rated lower because their margins of protection are not as strong as those of issues with higher ratings.
Medium grade	A	A	5–7	A	Issues judged to have many favorable investment attributes, issued by firms with a strong capacity to pay interest and principal. These issues are somewhat more susceptible to changes in economic conditions than are issues with higher ratings.
	Baa	BBB	8–10	BBB	Bonds whose issuers are judged to have adequate capacity to pay interest and principal. Although these issues exhibit adequate protection, changes in economic conditions or other circumstances are more likely to weaken the capacity of the firm to pay interest and repay principal for debt in this category than for debt in higher-rated categories.

EXHIBIT 2–5 *(concluded)*

Category	Moody's	Standard & Poor's	Duff & Phelps	Fitch	Criteria
Speculative grade	Ba	BB	11–13	BB	Issues judged as having speculative elements. The future of these issues cannot be considered well assured. Bonds in this category are frequently referred to as *junk bonds*.
	B	B	14	B	Issues that generally lack the characteristics of a desirable investment; also referred to as *junk bonds*. Assurance of interest and principal payments over a long period of time may be small.
Default	Caa	CCC	15	CCC	Issues of poor quality that may be in default or in danger of default with respect to payments of interest or principal.
	Ca	CC	16	CC	Issues judged to be highly speculative, which are either in default or have other market shortcomings.
	C		17		The lowest class of rated bonds, regarded as having extremely poor prospects of ever attaining any real investment standing.
		C		C	Issues on which no interest is being paid.
		D		DDD, DD, D	Issues in default, with principal and interest payments in arrears.

Sources: *Moody's Bond Record, S&P's Bond Guide,* and Fitch Investor Service's *Rating Register.*

end of its rating category, the modifier 2 indicates a mid-range ranking, and the modifier 3 indicates that the issue ranks last in its category. For municipal bonds (Chapter 4), Moody's uses the modifier 1 only for bonds in the Aa, A, Baa, Ba, and B groups, to indicate the strongest investment attributes.

When no rating is assigned, or when a rating has been suspended or withdrawn, the reasons may be unrelated to the quality of the issue. Such may be the case if (1) a bond issue was not submitted to be rated, (2) the issue belongs to a group of securities that are not rated as a matter of policy, (3) there are insufficient data on which to base a rating, or (4) the bonds are privately placed.

ZERO COUPON BONDS

In April 1981, J.C. Penney Company publicly issued approximately $200 million worth of 8-year **notes.** This issue was different from other issues in that these securities did not carry either interest coupons or a schedule of interest payments. In the traditional sense, because there are no interest payments, there are no coupons to clip—hence the term *zero coupon bond*. All that remained was the principal certificate, or corpus. Unlike most bonds, which are worth face value at their original date of issue, zero coupon bonds (also called *zeros*) are issued at a price below face value (i.e., at a discount). How much of a discount depends on the time to maturity as well as on the interest rates for other fixed-rate instruments of similar maturity. Because they are discounted at their original issue, zero coupon bonds are classified (by the IRS) as **original issue discount (OID)** securities.

Corporate zero coupon bonds have their pros and cons. Buying a zero is similar to buying a **certificate of deposit (CD)** at a given interest rate. The compounding of interest over the CD's life increases the amount the owner receives at maturity; that is, the owner receives the original amount invested plus the compounded interest. With a zero coupon bond, as with a CD, the rate of compounding interest is fixed over the bond's life. Zeros are unlike CDs, however, in that the daily **market value** of zero coupon bonds does change in response to major market interest rate fluctuations (e.g., the prime rate), as well as according to the time left before maturity or call. Zeros can be an attractive alternative to standard corporate bonds, as the potential for appreciation of the bonds' price is greater than for bonds priced at par or at a premium.

Zero coupon bonds are quoted in the same manner as ordinary corporate bonds except that a coupon rate and current yield are not listed, since zero coupon bonds do not pay periodic interest. For example, Exhibit 2–1, from *Investor's Business Daily*, uses the following format for a zero coupon bond issued by Coleman:

S&P Rate	Bond	Ex	Coupon Rate	Matures	Yield Cur.	Yield to Mat.	Vol.	Bond Close	Chg
B	Coleman	NY	ZrCpn	05/13	. . .	7.0	2	25³⁄₈	. . .

Although the current yield is not calculated, it is still possible to determine the yield to maturity. This is done the same as when the compound interest formula is used, except that the equation is solved for the interest rate, as follows:

$$YTM = n\left[\left(\frac{MV}{PV}\right)^{1/nY} - 1\right] \cdot 100\% \qquad (2\text{–}5)$$

where:

MV = Matured value (100 points)

n = Number of compounding periods remaining until maturity

PV = Present value or price (in points as a fraction of par)

Y = Number of years to maturity

The quantity nY equals the number of compound interest periods. Any difference between the calculated and the published yield to maturity can usually be attributed to the fact that the quoted prices do not occur exactly on the dates for interest compounding.

Example: Computing the Yield to Maturity for a Zero Coupon Bond

For the Coleman zero coupon bond maturing in May 2013, the price was quoted on June 2, 1993, at 25³/₈. Since the maturity is 39 semiannual ($n = 2$) interest periods away, the *YTM* (Equation 2–5) is:

$$YTM = (2)\left[\left(\frac{100}{25.375}\right)^{1/39} - 1\right] \cdot 100\%$$

$$= (2) \cdot (1.0358 - 1) \cdot (100\%)$$

$$= \mathbf{7.16\%}$$

which compares with the published yield of 7.0 percent. The difference of 16 basis points (0.16 percent) can be attributed to the fact that this date (June 2, 1993) falls between the interest payment dates of May 1 and November 1. There is about 1 month of interest that will affect the yield calculation. If this extra month is taken into account, there are 39.83 compounding periods left. The yield to maturity is 7.01 percent; when rounded off, it is 7.0 percent, which agrees with the published yield.

CONVERTIBLE BONDS

Convertible bonds are a hybrid, allowing investors to own both stock and bonds in the same company. The name of these bonds comes from the fact that this type of bond can be exchanged or converted into another type of security (i.e., common shares of the company). Companies usually issue convertible bonds as a way of cheaply increasing their capital without immediately diluting the common stock. Eventually, many of these bonds will be converted into stock, but the conversions will take place at a later time, reducing the impact.

Because convertible bonds are generally issued with no collateral backing other than the full faith and credit of the issuing company, this type of security is issued as a *debenture*. Convertibles are rated similarly to corporate **straight bonds** (nonconvertible bonds). The company in its **indenture** agreement states the terms under which the bond is issued. These terms include facts about the conversion privilege, such as:

- How many shares will be received for each $1,000 bond (the conversion ratio)
- How long the conversion privilege lasts
- Whether there are any changes in the conversion privilege

Convertible bonds have the following three important characteristics:

- *Convertible bonds pay interest.* As a general rule, convertibles yield more interest than the dividends received on the firm's common stock. However, the interest is generally less than on straight bonds of equivalent maturity and quality.
- *Convertible bonds offer greater possibility of appreciation.* A bond's price is usually linked to the earnings and growth performance of the issuing corporation. The prices of stock and bonds generally move in the same direction but not necessarily at the same rate. As the bond's price increases, they act more like stocks than bonds. There is an increase in risk and a decrease in yield.
- *Convertible bonds have some measure of safety and stability.* There is also some stability and safety associated with straight bonds and preferred stock. The price of convertible bonds, like that of straight bonds, will move in the opposite direction from interest rate changes. The issuing firm is obligated to pay interest on convertibles before it pays dividends on preferred and common stock, but only after the firm's senior debt is paid.

EXHIBIT 2–6
Convertible Bond Tables from **Investor's Business Daily.**

Super Convertible Bond Tables

S&P Rates	Convertible Bond	Exch	Coupon Rate	Mat-ures	Cur. Yld.	Yld.to Mat.	Vol.	Bond Close	Chg	Conv. Price	Stk. Close	%Prem (Disc)
NR	ConvxCm	O	6.000	03/12	9.0	9.9	100	67	...	21.75	5¾	153.4
CCC+	CooperCo	NY	10.625	03/05	16.6	18.1	3	64	+3¾	27.45	.19	....
BBB−	CrayRes	NY	6.125	02/11	7.4	7.9	19	83	...	78.00	27½	135.4
BBB+	CCBFincl	O	8.750	06/10	6.6	5.8	30	132	...	26.67	36⅛	−2.6
A	CIGNA	NY	8.200	07/10	7.9	7.8	80	104	...	68.25	58¾	21.6
NR	CII Finacl	Am	7.500	09/01	10.8	13.9	9	69⅛	...	21.87	5¾	181.2
NR	Daka	O	7.000	03/03	6.7	6.3	1900	105	+1	12.00	10	26.0
BBB	DanaCp	NY	5.875	06/06	5.5	5.1	11	107	+1½	50.43	53¾	94.7
CCC	Datpoint	NY	8.875	06/06	11.3	12.2	32	78¾	+ ⅛	18.11	5	185.2
B−	DatGenerl	NY	7.750	06/01	8.0	8.3	26	97	+ ¼	19.20	9⅞	88.6
BB−	DixieYrn	O	7.000	05/12	8.0	8.3	5	88	...	32.20	12¾	122.2
A−	DowChm	O	5.750	04/01	5.3	4.4	10	109	...	37.50	34¼	19.3
NR	DrugEmpo	O	7.750	10/14	10.1	10.5	100	76½	...	15.35	7	67.8
BB+	ElanIntl	Am	ZrCpn	10/12	...	FLAT	25	41½	...	.....	.....	....
B−	EmplBnPl	NY	6.750	07/06	10.4	12.2	10	64¾	− ⅝	44.00	7⅞	261.8
B+	Enclean	O	7.500	08/01	10.7	13.7	100	70	...	18.00	4⅛	205.5
BBB+	EKodak	NY	ZrCpn	10/11	...	6.4	58	31¼	...	47.15	51⅛	8.7
B−	Fieldcrst	NY	6.000	03/12	7.5	8.1	103	80	−1	44.25	27⅞	27.0
BB+	FirtUnRE	NY	10.250	07/09	9.6	9.4	16	107	...	21.33	10¼	122.7
BB−	FrptMcM	NY	6.550	01/01	6.9	7.6	1	94¼	− ½	23.74	19½	44.3
BB−	FrptMcM	NY	ZrCpn	08/06	...	8.9	35	31⅝	+ ⅛	20.63	19½	25.3
NR	FstRepblc	NY	7.250	12/02	6.6	5.9	11	110	...	14.08	12¾	21.5
CCC	GenRad	NY	7.250	05/11	10.1	10.9	56	71½	−3	14.38	3⅛	229.0
B−	Grancare	O	6.500	01/03	6.6	6.8	5	98	...	27.15	18	47.8
CALL	GrowGrp	NY	8.500	02/06	6.3	4.7	141	136	+4	12.61	17¾	−3.4
BBB−	Grummn	NY	9.250	08/09	8.2	7.9	296	112½	...	34.75	39⅛	−0.1
BBB−	Guilford	NY	6.000	09/12	6.0	6.0	60	99⅝	− ⅜	29.50	22¼	32.1
A+	Halburtn	NY	ZrCpn	03/06	...	6.0	10	46⅞	− ⅛	60.37	37⅝	82.6
NR	HealthCh	Am	10.375	04/99	10.8	11.4	10	95¾	...	20.00	3¾	410.7
B−	HeclaMng	NY	ZrCpn	06/04	...	8.1	1	41¾	...	14.81	12⅞	55.7
B	Hexcel	O	7.000	08/11	8.8	9.3	10	80	...	31.87	9⅞	158.2
B−	Hillhvn	Am	7.750	11/02	6.4	5.0	26	120½	−1⅝	3.36	3.10	22.2
D	HillDept	NY	11.000	07/02	...	FLAT	25	4	...	14.00	¼	138.9
A−	HmeDepot	NY	4.500	02/97	3.4	n.a.	18	131	+3	38.75	43½	16.7
BBB+	HoraceM	NY	4.000	12/99	4.0	4.1	2	99½	+1	35.00	24¼	43.6
NR	HudsnGenl	Am	7.000	07/11	9.7	10.4	22	72½	+1	32.75	12½	90.0
BB+	IndpBcp	O	7.000	06/11	7.4	7.5	5	95	...	36.25	24¾	39.1
B+	InspirRs	NY	8.500	06/12	8.5	8.5	142	100	+1½	8.08	3⅞	108.6
B+	Interface	O	8.000	09/13	8.2	8.2	10	98	...	16.91	11½	44.1
NR	IntersJohn	NY	7.750	03/11	8.7	9.0	11	89	...	17.75	8	97.5

S&P Rates	Convertible Bond	Exch	Coupon Rate	Mat-ures	Cur. Yld.	Yld.to Mat.	Vol.	Bond Close	Chg	Conv. Price	Stk. Close	%Prem (Disc)
NR	IntgHlth	O	6.000	01/03	6.0	5.9	500	100½	...	32.13	23¼	38.9
NR	IntlFood	O	9.000	12/07	9.0	9.0	10	100	...	.....	.....	....
B	IMC Ftlzer	NY	6.250	12/01	7.7	9.5	20	81½	...	63.50	28⅞	79.2
NR	Jacobson	O	6.750	12/11	8.3	8.9	68	81	...	32.67	13	103.6
NR	Jameswy	NY	8.000	05/05	14.3	16.6	32	56	...	13.80	2¼	243.5
NR	JBaker	O	7.000	06/02	4.7	1.2	100	149½	...	16.12	21⅝	12.7
BBB−	Kaman	O	6.000	03/12	6.9	7.3	90	86½	...	23.36	10⅞	85.8
BBB+	KerrMc	NY	7.250	06/12	6.3	5.9	23	115	−3	45.30	50¾	2.7
B−	KllyO&G	Am	8.500	04/00	7.8	6.9	22	108½	+ ½	23.50	21¾	17.2
NR	Kollmorg	NY	8.750	05/09	9.6	9.9	20	91	−1	34.35	5⅝	455.7
NR	LaPetiteA	O	6.500	06/11	10.0	11.0	10	65	...	19.50	9¼	37.0
BBB−	Leucadia	NY	5.500	02/03	5.8	6.1	25	95½	−1	28.75	37½	....
A+	Loews	NY	ZrCpn	10/04	...	6.0	11	51⅛	...	150.08	93⅝	99.5
NR	LynchC	Am	8.000	07/06	7.8	7.7	5	102¼	+1⅛	31.00	24¾	28.1
D	LTV Intl	NY	10.250	11/95	...	n.a.	192	27½	+ ½	10.75	⅛	....
B	MascoInd	O	6.000	12/11	5.2	4.7	1000	115½	−1½	18.00	20⅝	2.0
BBB	MascCorp	NY	5.250	02/12	5.4	5.5	25	97½	− ¼	42.28	29¼	40.9
B−	Maxxim	Am	6.750	03/03	6.0	5.0	5	113	+3	18.00	17⅛	18.8
BBB	Mead	NY	6.750	09/12	6.4	6.3	6	105¼	+ ¼	52.85	45	23.6
CALL	MedcoCn	O	6.000	09/01	6.0	3.3	2000	119	+1	8.00	29	....
BBB+	Mellon	NY	7.250	09/99	6.4	4.8	35	113	−3	50.51	53¾	6.2
CCC+	Midlantic	O	8.250	07/10	8.5	8.5	200	97½	...	48.00	19¾	137.0
NR	MobilTel	O	6.750	05/02	3.0	n.a.	22	222	−2	10.00	22¼	−0.2
NR	Moog Inc	Am	9.875	01/06	9.6	9.5	10	103	...	22.88	6¾	249.1
NR	MoranE	NY	8.750	01/08	11.5	12.3	15	76	...	17.54	3	344.3
A+	Motorola	NY	ZrCpn	09/09	...	1.7	5	76	+1	33.57	84½	−1.5
B−	MEDIQ	Am	7.250	06/06	8.5	9.2	5	85½	− ¼	10.55	4⅝	95.0
BB−	Novacare	NY	5.500	01/00	5.9	6.8	91	93	− ½	26.65	15⅛	63.9
A+	NBD Bc	NY	7.250	03/06	6.2	5.4	50	116½	+1	30.40	31½	12.4
D	NVR LP	Am	10.000	06/02	...	FLAT	10	32	+2⅛	11.83	.14	765.3
NR	Obrien	Am	11.000	03/11	9.7	9.4	55	113½	+1⅛	5.46	4¾	30.5
A+	OldRepblc	NY	n.a.	08/02	...	n.a.	2	110	−2	25.63	22⅛	27.4
CALL	Olsten	Am	4.875	05/03	5.0	5.3	4	97	...	17.53	23	....
CCC+	OrbiSci	O	6.750	03/03	6.2	5.6	100	108½	...	14.37	12	29.9
BB+	OryxEn	NY	7.500	05/14	7.7	7.7	8	98	...	39.13	21¼	80.4
B+	OutbrdM	NY	7.000	07/02	6.5	5.9	15	107½	+1	22.25	18⅝	28.4
B	OHM Crp	O	8.000	10/06	9.4	10.1	16	85	...	24.00	7¾	163.2
NR	PacifSci	NY	7.750	06/03	8.1	8.3	15	96	− ½	38.00	14¾	147.3
CCC−	Patten	NY	8.250	05/12	10.3	10.7	20	80	+2	9.83	3⅜	133.0
NR	Pennzoil	NY	6.500	01/03	5.3	3.7	18	122	−2½	84.13	87⅝	17.1

Reprinted by permission of *Investor's Business Daily*, June 14, 1993, © INVESTOR'S BUSINESS DAILY, INC., 1993.

As illustrated by Exhibit 2–6, which appeared in *Investor's Business Daily*, convertible bond quotes are typically expressed in the following format:

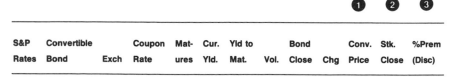

										❶	❷	❸
S&P Rates	**Convertible Bond**	**Exch**	**Coupon Rate**	**Mat-ures**	**Cur. Yld.**	**Yld to Mat.**	**Vol.**	**Bond Close**	**Chg**	**Conv. Price**	**Stk. Close**	**%Prem (Disc)**

In comparison with *Investor's Business Daily*'s straight bond tables, such as the one shown in Exhibit 2–1, the first ten columns are the same. The bonds' current yield and yield to maturity may be determined by Equations 2–2 and 2–4, respectively. The last three columns used in the format are described in the following.

❶ Conversion price. The stock price at which a bond is convertible into common shares. The conversion price (*CP*) is inversely related to the bond's **conversion ratio (*CR*),** which is the number of shares of the issuing firm's common stock that can be obtained by surrendering the convertible bond.

The conversion ratio (*CR*) is calculated by the following equation:

$$CR = \frac{\$1000}{CP} \qquad (2\text{-}6)$$

For the following entry, the **conversion price** of the convertible bond issued by JBaker is $16.12.

S&P Rates	Convertible Bond	Exch	Coupon Rates	Mat-ures	Cur. Yld.	Yld to Mat.	Vol.	Bond Close	Chg	Conv. Price	Stk. Close	%Prem (Disc)
NR	JBaker	0	7.000	06/02	4.7	1.2	100	149$^{1}/_{2}$	. . .	16.12	21$^{3}/_{8}$	12.7

The conversion ratio is $1,000/$16.12 per share, and thus 62.03 common shares will be received for each $1,000 bond converted. As would be specified in the firm's indenture agreement, the conversion price (or conversion ratio) may change over time. Conversion prices are also adjusted for stock splits such that if a stock were to have a 3-for-1 split, the conversion price would be reduced by a third.

❷ Stock closing price. The closing price of the common shares of the bond's issuer. The bondholder will want to convert to common shares when the stock price is higher than the conversion price.

❸   Percent premium or discount.   The bond's *conversion premium* (or discount), expressed as a percentage of the bond price relative to its conversion value. The terms **premium** and *discount* have two meanings with respect to straight and convertible bonds. In one sense, as discussed previously, these terms describe the relationship between a straight bond's current market price and *par*. With regard to convertible bonds, however, the terms *premium* and *discount* relate the bond's market price to its conversion value (i.e., parity). To distinguish straight bonds from convertibles, the terms *conversion premium* and *conversion discount* are used for convertible bonds only.

The conversion premium (or discount) is often used to measure a bond's worth in terms of the three characteristics discussed previously (interest payment, appreciation, and safety or stability). When the percent conversion premium is low, the convertible bond will respond more readily to price movements of the firm's common stock.

The conversion premium (or discount) is calculated by first computing the bond's **conversion value (CV),** which is the current value of the total shares into which a bond can be converted, as follows:

$$CV = CR \cdot SP \qquad\qquad (2\text{--}7)$$

where:

SP = Stock price (in dollars)

The conversion value, also called *conversion parity,* is the theoretical value of a convertible bond, which may or may not be equal to the bond's current market value. The bond is said to be selling at **parity** (i.e., par) when the market price equals the conversion value. As with straight bonds, the terms *premium* and *discount* have the same basic meanings when comparing the bond's market price with its conversion value.

Using both the bond's conversion value and its current market price, the conversion premium is calculated as:

$$\text{Conversion premium (discount)} = \frac{MP - CV}{CV} \cdot 100 \quad (2\text{-}8)$$

where:

CV = Bond conversion value (in dollars)

MP = Bond market value (in dollars)

Example: Calculating the Percent Conversion Premium, Current Yield, and Yield to Maturity of a Convertible Bond

The quotation for a convertible bond issued by NBD Bancorp for June 2, 1993, is as follows:

S&P Rates	Con-vertible Bond	Exch	Coupon Rate	Mat-ures	Cur. Yld.	Yld to Mat.	Vol.	Bond Close	Chg	Conv. Price	Stk. Close	%Prem (Disc)
A+	NBD Bc	0	7.250	03/06	6.2	5.4	50	$116^{1}/_{2}$	+1	30.40	$31^{1}/_{2}$	12.4

For a conversion price of $30.40, the conversion ratio (Equation 2–6) is:

$$CR = \frac{\$1,000}{\$30.40}$$

$$= \mathbf{32.89}$$

such that each $1,000 bond will be converted to 32.89 shares of NBD Bancorp common stock. The bond's conversion value of 32.89 shares at a stock price of $31.50 per share is (Equation 2–7):

$$CV = (32.89) \cdot (\$31.50)$$

$$= \mathbf{\$1,036.04}$$

For a closing price of $116\frac{1}{2}$, the dollar value of the $1,000 bond is then $1,165 and the conversion premium is (Equation 2–8):

$$\text{Conversion premium} = \frac{1165 - 1036.04}{1036.04} \cdot 100$$

$$= \mathbf{12.4\%}$$

which agrees with the published value when rounded off to the nearest tenth of a percent.

The current yield (Equation 2–2) is:

$$\text{Current yield} = \frac{(0.0725) \cdot (\$1,000)}{\$1165} \cdot 100$$

$$= \mathbf{6.22\%}$$

which agrees with the published value when rounded off to the nearest tenth.

On the day of its quotation, the bond had approximately $12\frac{3}{4}$ years until its maturity and was priced at $116\frac{1}{2}$ (a premium). The annual yearly discount is:

$$AYD = \frac{100 - 116.5}{12.75 \text{ years}}$$

$$= \mathbf{-1.29\%}$$

The yield to maturity (Equation 2–4) is:

$$YTM = \frac{2 \cdot (7.75 - 1.29)}{(100 + 116.5)} \cdot 100$$

$$= 5.5\%$$

which is 10 basis points higher than the published yield. Remember, this is an approximate formula and is more accurate for short terms than for long terms.

Chapter Three

Treasury Bills, Notes, and Bonds

INTRODUCTION

The US Government offers two broad classes of marketable fixed-rate securities: discount and coupon. These issues differ only in how the interest is paid. The discounted securities are represented by short-term Treasury bills with maturities of 1 year or less, while the longer-term coupon securities are issued in the forms of notes and bonds. Debt instruments of the US Treasury span maturities from as little as 13 weeks to as much as 30 years.

The Treasury raises most of its funds, aside from the taxes it collects through the IRS, by selling marketable securities. These are debt obligations of the United States, and, as such, they represent the largest aggregate debt burden the world has known. This huge debt burden, coupled with the approximately $20 billion minimum in securities that the Treasury auctions off every week, makes the market in Treasury securities perhaps the most active and liquid in the world. For detailed in-depth information about Treasury securities, the reader is recommended to read *The Dow Jones–Irwin Guide to Buying and Selling Treasury Securities*[1] or *The Handbook of Treasury Securities*.[2]

---

[1] Howard M. Berlin, *The Dow Jones–Irwin Guide to Buying and Selling Treasury Securities* (2d edition, Homewood, IL: Business One Irwin, 1988).

[2] Frank J. Fabozzi (Ed.), *The Handbook of Treasury Securities* (Chicago, IL: Probus Publishing Co., 1987).

TREASURY BILLS

Treasury bills, or **T-bills** as they are most commonly called, are the US government's short-term obligations. These have maturities of either 13 weeks (91 days or 3 months), 26 weeks (182 days or 6 months), or 52 weeks (364 days or 1 year). T-bills are issued in minimum amounts of $10,000, with increments of $5,000.

Reading T-Bill Quotations

Major dealers in Treasury securities make available every afternoon a list of OTC trading prices of all marketable (i.e., secondary market) issues. This list is published daily in major newspapers. Quotations for all T-bill issues that are traded on the **secondary market** are arranged in chronological order, from the issue that matures earliest to the one that has the longest maturity.

As illustrated by Exhibit 3–1, which appeared in *The Wall Street Journal,* T-bill quotes are typically given in the following format:

①	②	③	④	⑤	⑥
	Days				
	to				**Ask**
Maturity	**Maturity**	**Bid**	**Asked**	**Change**	**Yield**

The columns used in the format are now described.

① Maturity. The date on which the T-bill matures. The year is abbreviated to the last two digits.

② Days to maturity. The number of calendar days from the day following the quote date to the maturity date. Not all newspapers include this information.

③ Bid. The annualized percentage return for which a dealer (i.e., the buyer) has offered to buy this T-bill. In the quota-

EXHIBIT 3–1
T-Bill Quotations from **The Wall Street Journal.**

Maturity	Days to Mat.	Bid	Asked	Chg.	Ask Yld.
TREASURY BILLS					
Aug 13 '92	0	3.14	3.04	....	0.00
Aug 20 '92	7	3.11	3.01	+ 0.02	3.06
Aug 27 '92	14	3.09	2.99	+ 0.02	3.04
Sep 03 '92	21	3.08	2.98	+ 0.02	3.03
Sep 10 '92	28	3.08	2.98	+ 0.02	3.03
Sep 17 '92	35	3.08	3.04	+ 0.01	3.09
Sep 24 '92	42	3.09	3.05	+ 0.01	3.11
Oct 01 '92	49	3.08	3.04	+ 0.01	3.10
Oct 08 '92	56	3.11	3.07	+ 0.02	3.13
Oct 15 '92	63	3.11	3.09	....	3.15
Oct 22 '92	70	3.11	3.09	– 0.01	3.16
Oct 29 '92	77	3.12	3.10	....	3.16
Nov 05 '92	84	3.12	3.10	– 0.01	3.17
Nov 12 '92	**91**	**3.13**	**3.11**	**....**	**3.18**
Nov 19 '92	98	3.13	3.11	– 0.01	3.19
Nov 27 '92	106	3.13	3.11	– 0.01	3.18
Dec 03 '92	112	3.14	3.12	....	3.19
Dec 10 '92	119	3.14	3.12	....	3.20
Dec 17 '92	126	3.14	3.12	– 0.01	3.21
Dec 24 '92	133	3.16	3.14	+ 0.01	3.22
Dec 31 '92	140	3.12	3.10	– 0.01	3.18
Jan 07 '93	147	3.15	3.13	+ 0.01	3.21
Jan 14 '93	154	3.18	3.16	+ 0.01	3.26
Jan 21 '93	161	3.19	3.17	+ 0.02	3.26
Jan 28 '93	168	3.19	3.17	+ 0.01	3.26
Feb 04 '93	175	3.20	3.18	+ 0.01	3.27
Feb 11 '93	**182**	**3.20**	**3.18**	**....**	**3.29**
Mar 11 '93	210	3.21	3.19	+ 0.02	3.29
Apr 08 '93	238	3.22	3.20	....	3.30
May 06 '93	266	3.23	3.21	+ 0.01	3.32
Jun 03 '93	294	3.24	3.22	+ 0.02	3.33
Jul 01 '93	322	3.27	3.25	+ 0.01	3.37
Jul 29 '93	350	3.29	3.27	+ 0.01	3.40

tion below, the bid quote of 3.08 means that a buyer has offered to purchase this T-bill at an annualized rate of 3.08 percent.

Maturity	Days to Maturity	Bid	Asked	Change	Ask Yield
Sep 10 '92	28	3.08	2.98	+0.02	3.03

❹ **Asked.** The annualized percentage return that the seller would like the buyer to accept. In the quotation above, the seller would like the buyer to accept an annualized return of 2.98 percent.

Bid and asked quotes for T-bills are different from quotes for bonds. Unlike notes and bonds, T-bills are quoted on the basis of percentage rates rather than buying and selling prices. On a yield basis, the bid quote for T-bills is always higher than the asked quote. This causes the asked price to be higher than the bid price and corresponds to the commonsense practice whereby you (as the buyer) pay a higher price for a T-bill than you would receive if you (now acting as the seller) immediately tried to sell the same T-bill.

Since Treasury issues are traded over the counter, it is not possible to determine the exact price of the last trade. The quoted bid price represents the highest price being bid by buyers, while the quoted asked price is the lowest price being asked by sellers. Furthermore, bid and asked quotes are usually based on T-bills with a face value of $1 million. For T-bills with a smaller face value, the bid quote will be progressively lower, while the asked quote will be higher than the price quoted in the newspapers.

⑤ Change. The change in the bid quote from the quote for the previous trading day. In the example below, the quoted bid is 0.02 percent higher than the previous day's bid of 3.06 percent.

Maturity	Days to Maturity	Bid	Asked	Change	Ask Yield
Sep 10 '92	28	3.08	2.98	+0.02	3.03

⑥ Asked yield. The T-bill's annualized rate of return if it is held to maturity and calculated on the amount invested, not on the face value of the T-bill. The yield quote is based on the asked quote.

The asked yield is also known as the **equivalent coupon rate,** the *effective yield,* the *investment yield,* the *bond equivalent yield,* or the *annual percentage rate (APR).* The APR can be directly compared to the stated annual interest rates of other fixed-rate investments, such as CDs, which are not quoted at a discount.

Calculating T-Bill Dollar Prices

From published quotations, the actual buying and selling prices for 13-, 26-, and 52-week T-bills may be calculated from either the discounted asked (or bid) quote plus the exact number of days to maturity from (but not including) the quote date. The equivalent dollar price of either bid or asked quotes is found from:

$$\text{Price} = FV - \frac{(FV \cdot R \cdot DM)}{360} \qquad (3\text{--}1)$$

where:

DM = Number of days to maturity (not including the quote date)

FV = T-bill face value (in dollars)

R = Discounted asked or bid quote (as a decimal)

Example: Calculating T-Bill Dollar Prices

The fifth entry in Exhibit 3–1 is for a T-bill that matures on September 10, 1992. On August 11, 1992, this T-bill was quoted as follows:

Maturity	Days to Maturity	Bid	Asked	Change	Ask Yield
Sep 10 '92	28	3.08	2.98	+0.02	3.03

Since this quotation was made on August 11 with 28 days to maturity, the seller of a $10,000 T-bill would receive $9,976.04 (Equation 3–1), as follows:

$$\text{Bid price} = \$10,000 - \frac{(\$10,000 \cdot 0.0308 \cdot 28)}{360}$$

$$= \$10,000 - \$23.96$$

$$= \mathbf{\$9,976.04}$$

On the other hand, the asked quote of 2.98 percent is the annualized percentage return that the buyer would pay. For the same $10,000 T-bill, the buyer would then pay $9,976.82 (Equation 3–1), as follows:

$$AP = \$10,000 - \frac{(\$10,000 \cdot 0.0298 \cdot 28)}{360}$$

$$= \$10,000 - \$23.18$$

$$= \mathbf{\$9,976.82}$$

where:

AP = Asked price

Notice that the asked price is higher than the bid price. Here, the spread of $0.78 between the asked and bid prices may seem small, but remember, this example is a $10,000 T-bill. For a $1 million T-bill, the spread would be $78.

Calculating T-Bill Yields

Yields are calculated from the asked price and the exact number of days to maturity from the quote date, and are different for 13- to 26-week T-bills and 52-week T-bills.

13-week and 26-week T-bills. The annualized yield is determined from the asked price (in dollars), as follows:

$$\text{Yield} = \frac{(FV - AP) \cdot 365}{DM \cdot AP} \cdot 100 \qquad\qquad \textbf{(3--2)}$$

where:

AP = Asked price (in dollars)

DM = Number of days to maturity (not including the quote date)

FV = T-bill face value (in dollars)

Example: Calculating the Yield of a 13-Week T-Bill

Using the same quotation as in the previous example, on August 11, 1992, the annualized yield for the $10,000 T-bill maturing on September 10, 1992, with an asked quote of 2.98 percent ($9,976.82) is (from Equation 3–2):

$$\text{Yield} = \frac{(\$10{,}000 - \$9{,}976.82) \cdot 365}{28 \cdot \$9{,}976.82} \cdot 100$$

$$= \frac{8{,}460.70}{279{,}350.96} \cdot 100$$

$$= \textbf{3.03\%}$$

which agrees with the quoted yield.

52-week T-bills. The determination of the annualized yield for 52-week (364-day) T-bills is done differently from that for 13- and 26-week T-bills, as follows:

$$\text{Yield} = \frac{\sqrt{B^2 - 4AC} - B}{2A} \qquad (3\text{–}3)$$

where:

$$A = \frac{DM}{2Y} - 0.25$$

$$B = \frac{DM}{Y}$$

$$C = \frac{AP - FV}{AP}$$

AP = Asked price (in dollars)

DM = Number of days to maturity (not including the quote date)

FV = T-bill face value (in dollars)

Y = Number of days in the year following the issue date (365 or 366)

The last T-bill in Exhibit 3–1 is quoted on August 11, 1992, as:

Maturity	Days to Maturity	Bid	Asked	Change	Ask Yield
Jul 29 '93	350	3.29	3.27	+0.01	3.40

Since this maturity date is 350 days away from the August 11, 1992, quote date, this was a 52-week T-bill when originally issued. Using the asked quote of 3.27 percent for a $10,000 T-bill, the seller would receive $9,682.08 (Equation 3–1), as follows:

$$AP = \$10,000 - \frac{(\$10,000 \cdot 0.0327 \cdot 350)}{360}$$

$$= \$10,000 - \$317.92$$

$$= \mathbf{\$9,682.08}$$

The annualized yield is then determined as:

$$A = \frac{350}{2 \cdot 365} - 0.25$$

$$= \mathbf{0.2295}$$

$$B = \frac{350}{365}$$

$$= \mathbf{0.9589}$$

$$C = \frac{\$9,682.08 - \$10,000}{\$9,682.08}$$

$$= \mathbf{-0.0328}$$

Substituting these intermediate values in Equation 3–3, we get:

$$\text{Yield} = \frac{\sqrt{(0.9589)^2 - (4)(0.2295)(-0.0328)} - 0.9589}{(2)(0.2295)}$$

$$= 3.40\%$$

which agrees with the quoted yield.

T-Bill Auction Results

The US government sells its newly issued T-bills by auction. Both 13- and 26-week T-bills are auctioned every week, on Mondays (or on Tuesdays when federal holidays fall on Mondays), while 52-week T-bills are auctioned every 4 weeks, on Thursdays. Exhibit 3–2 illustrates the results appearing in *The Wall Street Journal* for an auction of 13- and 26-week T-bills on June 21, 1993. The auction results generally contain the following information:

Amount sold
Average annual discount rate
Total bids (tenders) submitted
Range of yields and discounted prices of accepted bids
Amount of noncompetitive tenders
Average price
Coupon equivalent rate
Maturity date
Historical comparisons
CUSIP number

T-bills are sold at a discount such that the buyer pays less than their face value. The difference between the T-bill's face value at maturity and the amount paid is termed the **discount** and is determined as follows:

Discount = Face value − Purchase price

EXHIBIT 3–2
Published T-Bill Auction Results from **The Wall Street Journal.**

The five-year note was quoted at a yield of 5.19%, down from 5.22% late Friday.

Meanwhile yesterday, the Treasury sold $24.29 billion of three-month and six-month bills at its regular weekly auction. The three-month bill was sold at an average discount rate of 3.10% for a coupon-equivalent yield of 3.17% The six-month bill was sold at an average discount rate of 3.19% for a coupon-equivalent yield of 3.29%.

Rates are determined by the difference between the purchase price and face value. Thus, higher bidding narrows the investor's return while lower bidding widens it. The percentage rates are calculated on a 360-day year, while the coupon-equivalent yield is based on a 365-day year.

	13-Week	26-Week
Applications	$44,226,758,000	$51,421,458,000
Accepted bids	$12,110,883,000	$12,176,749,000
Accepted at low price	7%	11%
Accepted noncompet'ly	$1,233,366,000	$816,623,000
Average price (Rate)	99.216(3.10%)	98.387 (3.19%)
High price (Rate)	99.221 (3.08%)	98.392 (3.18%)
Low price (Rate)	99.214 (3.11%)	98.382 (3.20%)
Coupon equivalent	3.17%	3.29%
CUSIP number	912794E34	912794G99

Both issues are dated June 24. The 13-week bills mature Sept. 23, 1993, and the 26-week bills mature Dec. 23, 1993.

The dollar value of the discount is determined from:

$$\text{Discount} = \frac{FV \cdot DR \cdot DM}{360} \tag{3-4}$$

where:

DM = Number of days to maturity (not including the quote date)—91, 182, or 364, as appropriate

DR = Discount rate (as a decimal)

FV = T-bill face value (in dollars)

The discount is then equal to the interest that would be earned on the T-bill over the 91-, 182-, or 364-day period if the purchase price were at par. It should be noted that the discount is based on a 360-day year. On the other hand, the *coupon equivalent rate* (the *APR*) is based on a 365-day year, as follows:

$$APR = \frac{D \cdot 365}{(FV - D) \cdot DM} \qquad (3\text{--}5)$$

where:

D = Discount (in dollars)

DM = Number of days to maturity (not including the quote date)—91, 182, or 364, as appropriate

FV = T-bill face value (in dollars)

For the Treasury auction results, the quoted *APR* is based on the average price (rate).

In contrast to the discount rate, the annual percentage rate is based on the actual purchase price of the T-bill and therefore equals the actual yield of the investment. The *APR* is always higher than the discount rate, because the *APR* is computed on the basis of the purchase price, while the discount rate is based on the T-bill's value at maturity.

In determining the annualized yield from weekly T-bill auction results, the *discounted purchase price*, which is conventionally based on a par value of 100, becomes the asked price. The number of days to maturity is usually either 91 (for 13-week T-bills) or 182 (for 26-week T-bills), but in rare instances, 90 and 180 days are used. In determining the annualized yield from 52-week T-bill auction results, there are 364 days to maturity.

The Treasury always receives bids for T-bills totaling more than is scheduled to be auctioned. The ratio of the amount bid to the amount accepted is referred to as the **bid cover** and is calculated as follows:

$$\text{Bid cover} = \frac{\text{Amount bid}}{\text{Amount accepted}} \qquad (3\text{--}6)$$

A high bid cover (usually thought to be greater than 2.0) is indicative of strong interest in the auction.

Following the deadline for bids, the Treasury arranges the **competitive bids** in order from the lowest yield (i.e., the highest bid price) to the highest yield (i.e., the lowest bid price). Then, starting with the lowest bid and the total amount of noncompetitive bids, the face amounts of all competitive bids are totaled up until the entire issue is fully sold (subscribed). The last accepted bid, representing the highest discounted yield (i.e., the lowest discounted price) is termed the *stop-out rate,* or the **stop-out price.**

Example: Examining T-Bill Auction Results

Exhibit 3–2, from *The Wall Street Journal,* gives the results of the weekly auction of 13- and 26-week T-bills on June 21, 1993. Of the $44.27 billion it received in bids for the 13-week bills, the Treasury sold only $12.11 billion in face value via competitive and **noncompetitive bids.** Since $1.23 billion in T-bills was sold via noncompetitive bids, it follows that approximately $10.88 billion in T-bills was sold via competitive bids, with yields ranging from 3.08 percent to the stop-out rate of 3.11 percent, as follows:

Total sold	$12.11 billion
Sold noncompetitively	−1.23 billion
Sold competitively	$10.88 billion

The bid cover is:

$$\text{Bid cover} = \frac{\$44.23 \text{ billion}}{\$12.11 \text{ billion}}$$

$$= 3.65$$

which means that there was a strong interest in the sale.

At the average discount rate of 3.10 percent, the buyer at auction pays for a $10,000 T-bill maturing in 91 days (Equation 3–1), as follows:

$$\text{Purchase price} = \$10,000 - \frac{(\$10,000 \cdot 0.0310 \cdot 91)}{360}$$

$$= \$10,000 - \$78.36$$

$$= \mathbf{\$9,921.64}$$

On a par basis of 100, the $9,921.64 purchase price equals 99.216. This represents $99.216 for each $100 of face value. If a $25,000 T-bill, for example, was purchased at the average price, it would cost:

$$\text{Purchase price} = \$99.216 \cdot \frac{\$25,000}{\$100}$$

$$= \mathbf{\$24,804.00}$$

Based upon par value of 100 and the quoted average price of 99.216, the discount would then be 100 − 99.216, or 0.784. The APR or coupon equivalent rate is (Equation 3–5):

$$\text{Yield} = \frac{0.784 \cdot 365}{91 \cdot 99.216} \cdot 100$$

$$= \mathbf{3.169\%}$$

When rounded off to the second decimal place, this agrees with the quoted coupon equivalent of 3.17 percent shown in Exhibit 3–2.

TREASURY NOTES AND BONDS

Treasury notes (T-notes) and **Treasury bonds (T-bonds)** have longer maturities than T-bills. By regulation, T-notes have fixed maturities greater than 1 year but not greater than 10 years from their date of issue. The 2- and 3-year issues are available in denominations of $5,000, $10,000, $100,000, $1 million, $100 million, and $500 million. T-notes with original maturities of 4, 5, 7, and 10 years[3] are available in denominations of $1,000, $5,000, $100,000, and $1 million. Unlike T-bills, T-notes bear a specific fixed rate of interest, which is paid to the owner every 6 months.

On the other hand, T-bonds (which should not be confused with US savings bonds) are the Treasury's long-term obligations. Prior to 1986, newly issued T-bonds were available with 15-, 20-, and 30-year maturities. Prior to 1985, 30-year T-bonds were issued with a 25-year call option. Currently, T-bonds are issued only with 30-year maturities and are not callable. The original 20- or 30-year (with the call option) T-bonds can still be bought on the secondary market. T-bonds are available in denominations of $5,000, $10,000, $100,000, $1 million, $100 million, and $500 million (Exhibit 3–3). T-notes and T-bonds are treated essentially the same way, differing only in their lengths of maturity.

Reading T-Note and T-Bond Quotations

Just as for T-bills, major dealers in Treasury securities make available every afternoon a list of OTC trading prices of all tradable T-note and T-bond issues. Quotations for T-note and T-bond issues that are traded on the secondary market are arranged in chronological order, from the issue that matures earliest to the one that has the longest maturity (i.e., the "long bond"). Very often these quotations are not closing market prices but mid-afternoon prices.

---

[3] The Treasury stopped auctioning 7-year T-notes in 1993 to shorten the average maturity of its debt.

EXHIBIT 3–3
$500 Million T-Bond.

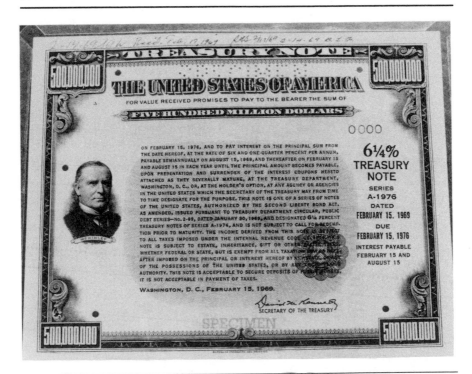

Photograph copyright 1987, Howard M. Berlin, Ltd.

As illustrated by Exhibit 3–4, which appeared in *The Wall Street Journal*, T-note and T-bond quotes are typically expressed in the following format:

Rate	Maturity	Bid	Asked	Change	Asked Yield

EXHIBIT 3–4
T-Bond Quotations from **The Wall Street Journal.**

GOVT. BONDS & NOTES

Rate	Maturity Mo/Yr	Bid	Asked	Chg.	Ask Yld.	Rate	Maturity Mo/Yr	Bid	Asked	Chg.	Ask Yld.
$4\frac{1}{4}$	Aug 87-92	99:28	100:12	....	0.00	$7\frac{7}{8}$	Jan 98n	110:01	110:03	+ 3	5.69
$7\frac{1}{4}$	Aug 92	100:00	100:02	− 1	0.00	$8\frac{1}{8}$	Feb 98n	111:05	111:07	+ 3	5.72
$7\frac{7}{8}$	Aug 92n	100:00	100:02	− 1	0.00	$7\frac{7}{8}$	Apr 98n	109:31	110:01	+ 2	5.78
$8\frac{1}{4}$	Aug 92n	100:00	100:02	− 1	0.00	7	May 93-98	101:20	101:28	− 3	4.45
$8\frac{1}{8}$	Aug 92n	100:08	100:10	....	1.67	9	May 98n	115:15	115:17	+ 3	5.79
$8\frac{1}{8}$	Sep 92n	100:22	100:24	....	2.32	$8\frac{1}{4}$	Jul 98n	111:29	111:31	+ 5	5.83
$8\frac{3}{4}$	Sep 92n	100:22	100:24	....	2.92	$9\frac{1}{4}$	Aug 98n	116:29	116:31	+ 4	5.86
$9\frac{3}{4}$	Oct 92n	101:04	101:06	....	2.73	$7\frac{1}{8}$	Oct 98n	106:07	106:09	+ 5	5.90
$7\frac{3}{4}$	Oct 92n	100:30	101:00	....	3.00	$3\frac{1}{2}$	Nov 98	102:11	103:11	+ 7	2.91
$7\frac{3}{4}$	Nov 92n	101:04	101:06	....	3.01	$8\frac{7}{8}$	Nov 98n	115:03	115:05	+ 5	5.94
$8\frac{3}{8}$	Nov 92n	101:09	101:11	....	3.01	$6\frac{3}{8}$	Jan 99n	102:06	102:08	+ 5	5.95
$10\frac{1}{2}$	Nov 92n	101:26	101:28	− 1	3.03	$8\frac{7}{8}$	Feb 99n	115:08	115:10	+ 4	6.00
$7\frac{7}{8}$	Nov 92n	101:07	101:09	....	2.99	7	Apr 99n	105:14	105:16	+ 5	5.99
$7\frac{1}{4}$	Dec 92n	101:16	101:18	− 1	3.07	$8\frac{1}{2}$	May 94-99	107:07	107:15	− 4	4.05
$9\frac{1}{8}$	Dec 92n	102:06	102:08	− 1	3.11	$9\frac{1}{8}$	May 99n	116:26	116:28	+ 4	6.05
$8\frac{3}{4}$	Jan 93n	102:09	102:11	....	3.09	$6\frac{3}{8}$	Jul 99n	102:07	102:09	+ 3	5.97
7	Jan 93n	101:22	101:24	....	3.17	8	Aug 99n	110:26	110:28	+ 6	6.07
4	Feb 88-93	98:27	99:11	− 2	5.33	$7\frac{7}{8}$	Nov 99n	110:02	110:04	+ 5	6.13
$6\frac{3}{4}$	Feb 93	101:25	101:29	+ 2	2.92	$7\frac{7}{8}$	Feb 95-00	107:10	107:14	+ 5	4.69
$7\frac{7}{8}$	Feb 93	102:08	102:12	....	3.10	$8\frac{1}{2}$	Feb 00n	113:21	113:23	+ 5	6.19
$8\frac{1}{4}$	Feb 93n	102:14	102:16	− 1	3.22	$8\frac{7}{8}$	May 00n	115:31	116:01	+ 6	6.24
$8\frac{3}{8}$	Feb 93n	102:16	102:18	− 1	3.22	$8\frac{3}{8}$	Aug 95-00	109:16	109:20	+ 4	4.89
$10\frac{7}{8}$	Feb 93n	103:25	103:27	....	3.15	$8\frac{3}{4}$	Aug 00n	115:07	115:09	+ 6	6.29
$6\frac{3}{4}$	Feb 93n	101:27	101:29	....	3.22	$8\frac{1}{2}$	Nov 00n	113:22	113:24	+ 6	6.34
$7\frac{1}{8}$	Mar 93n	102:10	102:12	− 1	3.30	$7\frac{3}{4}$	Feb 01n	108:29	108:31	+ 5	6.37
$9\frac{5}{8}$	Mar 93n	103:29	103:31	....	3.23	$11\frac{3}{4}$	Feb 01	134:28	135:00	+ 6	6.36
$7\frac{3}{8}$	Apr 93n	102:20	102:22	− 1	3.30	8	May 01n	110:18	110:20	+ 6	6.40
7	Apr 93n	102:16	102:18	....	3.35	$13\frac{1}{8}$	May 01	144:24	144:28	+ 5	6.36
$7\frac{5}{8}$	May 93n	103:02	103:04	− 1	3.41	$7\frac{7}{8}$	Aug 01n	109:21	109:23	+ 6	6.44
$8\frac{5}{8}$	May 93n	103:26	103:28	− 1	3.39	8	Aug 96-01	107:24	107:28	− 5	5.77
$10\frac{1}{8}$	May 93n	104:30	105:00	− 1	3.38	$13\frac{3}{8}$	Aug 01	147:06	147:10	+ 8	6.39
$6\frac{3}{4}$	May 93n	102:18	102:20	− 1	3.39	$7\frac{1}{2}$	Nov 01n	106:30	107:00	+ 6	6.48
7	Jun 93n	103:01	103:03	− 1	3.41	$15\frac{3}{4}$	Nov 01	164:17	164:21	+ 6	6.39
$8\frac{1}{8}$	Jun 93n	104:01	104:03	....	3.37	$14\frac{1}{4}$	Feb 02	154:31	155:03	+ 7	6.42
$7\frac{1}{4}$	Jul 92n	103:13	103:15		3.40	$7\frac{1}{2}$	May 02n	107:08	107:10		

The columns used in the format are described below.

❶ **Rate.** The stated annual percentage rate of interest.

❷ **Maturity.** The date on which the T-note or T-bond matures, expressed in a month-year format. T-notes and T-bonds usually mature on the 15th of the month. Although the Treasury typically used to issue its 30-year bond every quarter on a February, May, August, and November cycle, in 1993 it cut this schedule in half, auctioning T-bonds only semiannually, on a February and August cycle.

When two years are listed, the first is the T-bond's **call date,** the second is the **maturity date,** and the two are 5 years apart. In the following quotations, May 93-98 represents a T-bond that matures on May 15, 1998, but can be called 5 years earlier, on May 15, 1993.

Rate	Maturity	Bid	Asked	Change	Asked Yield
7	May 93-98	101:20	101:28	−3	4.45
7¼	May 16	99:01	99:31	+13	7.34

For call and maturity dates beyond 1999, 00 represents the year 2000. In the second entry, May 16 represents a maturity date of May 15, 2016.

An n after the maturity year indicates that the issue is a T-note. In the entry below, Nov 94n represents a T-note that matures on November 15, 1994.

Rate	Maturity	Bid	Asked	Change	Asked Yield
8¼	Nov 94n	108:14	108:16	−1	4.26

❸ **Bid.** The price in **points** at which a dealer has offered to buy the issue. The price, a percentage of par (100), is expressed in whole points and thirty-seconds (0.03125 point). Each whole point represents 1 percent of the issue's face value.

Whole points and thirty-seconds can be separated either by a colon (as done in *The Wall Street Journal*), a hyphen (as done in *The New York Times*) or a period (as done in *Investor's Business Daily*). When a colon or a hyphen is used, the thirty-seconds are written as two-digit numbers from 00 to 32. When a period is used, fractional thirty-seconds less than $10/32$ are written without leading zeros for 0 to 9. The following forms are equivalent:

$98^{8}/_{32}$ 98:08   98-08   98.8

④ Asked. The asked quote is the price that the seller would like the buyer to accept. Treasury securities are quoted on a bid-asked price basis instead of in the high-low-close price format used for corporate bonds. This is contrasted with T-bills, for which bid-asked quotations are percentage rates. For T-notes and T-bonds, the asked price is always higher than the bid quote, which corresponds to the commonsense practice according to which you (the buyer) pay a higher price for the security than the price you would receive if you (now acting as the seller) immediately tried to sell the same note or bond. As an example:

Rate	Maturity	Bid	Asked	Change	Yield
7¼	May 16	99:01	99:06	+ 13	7.34

The asked price of 99:06 is higher than the bid (99:01).

Since Treasury issues are traded over the counter, it is not possible to determine the exact price of the last trade. The quoted bid price represents the highest price being bid by the buyers, while the quoted asked price is the lowest price being asked by the sellers. Furthermore, bid and asked quotes are usually based on T-notes and T-bonds with a face value of $1 million. For issues with smaller face values, the bid quote will be progressively lower, while the asked quote will be higher than the quote in a newspaper or on a broker's quote machines.

⑤ Change. The change, in thirty-seconds, of the bid price from the price quoted for the previous trading day. Generally, the change is expressed in the same format as bid and asked prices. Here are two examples:

+⁵/₃₂	+ 5	+.5
−²¹/₃₂	− 21	−.21

In the following example, the quoted bid price ($136^{18}/_{32}$) for the $11^{1}/_{4}$ percent T-bond of February 2015 was $^{46}/_{32}$ lower (-46) than the previous day's bid (138).

Rate	Maturity	Bid	Asked	Change	Asked Yield
$11^{1}/_{4}$	Feb 15	136:18	136:20	-46	7.80

6   **Asked yield.** The annualized percentage return that an investor receives if the T-note or T-bond is purchased on the day of the quoted asked price and the bond is held to maturity (i.e., yield to maturity). The yield to maturity, as noted earlier in this chapter, is often referred to as the *equivalent coupon rate*. However, if the issue has a call provision and the bond is selling at a premium, the yield is *yield to call* rather than *YTM*. In the following quotation, the yield of 6.31 percent is the yield to call.

Rate	Maturity	Bid	Asked	Change	Asked Yield
10	May 05-10	130:20	130:24	-6	6.31

If this T-bond were not called on May 15, 2005, all future quotations for this issue would appear with the date of May 10 and the quoted yield would be the *YTM*.

Calculating Bond Dollar Prices

Like corporate and municipal bonds, T-note and T-bond prices are quoted as a percentage of par (equal to 100 percent of their face values) and are expressed in whole points and thirty-seconds (0.03125 point). Each whole point represents 1 percent of the issue's face value. For each $1,000 of face value, a full point is equal to $10, while a thirty-second equals 31.25 cents. For issues priced above par value of 100, the issue is said to be at a premium and is worth more than its face value. For issues priced below par, the issue is at a discount and is worth less than its face value. As an aid, Appendix A gives the decimal equivalents of thirty-seconds.

Two Examples: Calculating T-Bond Dollar Prices

Determine the dollar price of a $25,000 T-note quoted at a premium of $101^{20}/_{32}$ for a $100,000 T-bond quoted at a discount of $99^{1}/_{32}$.

1. A quote of $101^{20}/_{32}$ (also written as 101.20, 101:20, or 101-20) is equivalent to 101 full points and $^{20}/_{32}$ (0.625 points). The dollar price is:

$$\text{Price} = (\$25,000)\frac{101.625}{100}$$

$$= \$25,406.25$$

2. A quote of $99^{1}/_{32}$ (also 99.1, 99:1, or 99-01) is equivalent to 99 full points and $^{1}/_{32}$ (0.03125 points). The dollar price is:

$$\text{Price} = (\$100,000)\frac{99.03125}{100}$$

$$= \$99,031.25$$

Calculating Bond Yields

The methods used in calculating yields of T-notes and T-bonds are identical to those used in calculating yields of corporate and municipal bonds (see Chapter 2, Equation 2–3 or Equation 2–4).

Example: Calculating a T-Note's Yield to Maturity

On June 1, 1993, a T-note was quoted as:

					Asked
Rate	Maturity	Bid	Asked	Change	Yield
6³/₈	June 97n	105:00	105:02	+10	4.99

On the day of its quotation, the T-note had approximately 4 years until its maturity and was asked at a premium of 105:02 ($105^2/_{32}$). The annual yearly discount was:

$$AYD = \frac{100 - 105.0625}{4 \text{ years}}$$

$$= -1.266\%$$

Note that the *AYD* was negative for a T-note bought at a premium, and would be subtracted from the coupon rate. The yield to maturity (Equation 2–4) was:

$$YTM = \frac{2 \cdot (6.375 - 0.126)}{(100 + 105.0625)} \cdot 100\%$$

$$= 4.98\%$$

which was only 1 basis point below the published yield of 4.99 percent.

For T-bonds selling at a premium and having a call provision, the quoted yield is yield to call rather than yield to maturity.

Example: Calculating a T-Bond's Yield to Call

On June 1, 1993, a T-bond was quoted as:

Rate	Maturity	Bid	Asked	Change	Asked Yield
8	Aug 96-01	109:12	109:16	+14	4.77

On the day of its quotation, the T-bond had approximately 8 years and 2 months (8.17 years) until its maturity, but could be called 5 years earlier. The asked price was at a premium of 109:16 ($109^{16}/_{32}$). The annual yearly discount, based on the call date 3.17 years away, was:

$$AYD = \frac{100 - 109.5}{3.17 \text{ years}}$$

$$= -3.00\%$$

Note that the *AYD* was negative for a T-bond bought at a premium, and would be subtracted from the coupon rate. The yield to call (Equation 2–4) was:

$$YTC = \frac{2 \cdot (8.00 - 3.00)}{(100 + 109.5)} \cdot 100\%$$

$$= 4.77\%$$

and agreed with the published yield. If the yield to maturity were erroneously calculated instead, the yield would be in excess of 6.5 percent.

Auction Results

As it does with T-bills, the Treasury sells its newly issued T-notes and T-bonds by auction. The frequency is on a regular refunding cycle. Two-year T-notes are auctioned every 4 weeks and are issued usually on the last business day of the month. Five-year T-notes are auctioned quarterly near the end of February, May, August, and November. They are then issued on the first day of the next month. The Treasury's "minirefunding cycle" is currently a quarterly auction cycle of 4-year T-notes. The auctions generally occur near the end of March, June, September, and December for issue at the beginning of the month following the auction.

Prior to 1993, the standard quarterly **refunding cycle** consisted of sales of 3- and 10-year T-notes as well as the 30-year T-bond (the "**long bond**"). The auctions usually occur on consecutive days (Tuesday through Thursday) in February, May, August, and November. In 1993, to shorten the average maturity of its issues, the Treasury changed its auction cycle; T-bonds are now auctioned semiannually in February and August. Exhibit 3–5 illustrates the results of an auction of 2-year T-notes on June 22, 1993, as reported in *The Wall Street Journal*.

The published auction results generally contain the following information:

Amount sold
Average annual discount rate
Total bids (tenders) submitted
Amount of noncompetitive tenders
Average price (rate)
Coupon rate
Maturity date
CUSIP number

FLOWER BONDS

T-bonds that are owned by a person who dies become part of the decedent's estate. However, certain T-bond issues may, at the request of the estate's executor or administrator, be redeemed at

EXHIBIT 3–5
Published Two-Year T-Note Auction Results from **The Wall Street Journal.**

Here are the results of yesterday's two-year note auction:

All bids are awarded at a single price at the market-clearing yield. Rates are determined by the difference between that price and the face value.

Applications	$44,290,010,000
Accepted bids	$16,011,390,000
Bids at market-clearing yield accepted ...	52%
Accepted noncompetitively	$858,000,000
Auction price (rate)	99.933 (4.16%)
Interest rate	4⅛%
CUSIP number	912827L34

The notes are dated June 30, and mature June 30, 1995.

par value only if the Treasury is instructed to apply the proceeds to federal estate taxes. Because of the nature of these deeply discounted T-bonds, which have often been referred to as **flower bonds,** they were issued in minimum denominations of $500 and are no longer available as new issues.

T-bond quotations do not indicate which of the outstanding issues are the flower bonds. Nevertheless, they are easily identified by their lower-than-normal coupon rates. The three outstanding flower bond issues that still carry the federal estate tax provision are listed in Exhibit 3–6.

US TREASURY STRIPS—TREASURY ZERO COUPON BONDS

Merrill Lynch's TIGR and Other Animals

Historically, it was Merrill Lynch that, in August 1982, developed the first in a long line of Treasury zero coupon T-bonds. The company bought $500 million in already issued 30-year T-bonds (the 14s of 11/15/2011), placed them in an irrevocable trust with the Federal Reserve Bank of New York acting as custodian, and

EXHIBIT 3–6
Outstanding Flower Bonds.

Maturity Date	Coupon	Amount Outstanding*
5/15/1989–94	$4^{1}/_{8}\%$	$500
2/15/1995	3	320
11/15/1998	$3^{1}/_{2}$	1,000

* In millions of dollars.
Source: U.S. Treasury.

repackaged them by issuing "receipts" against all the $2.065 billion in the remaining 59 coupon payments of the underlying T-bonds plus the bond's $500 million principal.[4] Merrill Lynch marketed its new concept as **Treasury Investment Growth Receipts,** and these T-bonds are more commonly known as **TIGRs** (pronounced "tigers"). When TIGR certificates were issued to investors, they were actually imprinted with a drawing of a tiger in black ink on orange-colored paper.

For this 30-year T-bond, Merrill Lynch's new concept included a potential series of 60 separate zero coupon T-bonds—a different issue each time an interest coupon of the underlying T-bond came due (May 15 and November 15).

From the TIGR, other animals began to evolve. Second in line, Salomon Brothers marketed its **Certificates of Accrual on Treasury Securities (CATS),** which are now perhaps the best known of all the available Treasury-backed zeros. The TIGR begat the CATS. The CATS begat Lehman Brothers' LIONs (Lehman Investment Opportunity Notes). Other trademarked names followed, in an expanding "zoo": COUGAR (Certificate on Government Receipts) by A.G. Becker Peribas, GATOR, DOG, and EAGLE. Nonanimal names also were used. These included Treasury Receipts (TRs), created by First Boston; Treasury Bond Receipts (TBRs), by E.F. Hutton; Easy Growth Treasury Receipts (ETRs), by Dean Witter; and Generic Treasury Receipts (TRs), by Paine Webber. Like

---

[4] The earliest the 14s of 2011 can be called is November 15, 2006.

corporate and municipal zero coupon bonds, Treasury zeros are purchased at deep discounts and the original investment may increase severalfold because of interest compounding.

STRIPS

Originally, the US Treasury was unreceptive to the concept of brokerage firms stripping its T-bonds. However, it now sanctions the practice. On January 15, 1985, the Treasury announced its own version, called **Separate Trading of Registered Interest and Principal of Securities (STRIPS).** Issuance of STRIPS started with the February 6, 1985, sale of $6 billion of 10-year T-notes (11¼s of 2/15/1995) and the February 7 sale of $5.75 billion of 30-year T-bonds (11¼s of 2/15/2005). This issue was the first T-bond not to have a 5-year call feature, allowing the Treasury to repurchase its T-bond at par any time 25 years after issue.

Like other zeros, STRIPS are purchased at deep discounts, and the price depends on the maturity and interest rate. The value of any STRIPS is easily determined from published tables. Exhibit 3–7, from *The Wall Street Journal,* illustrates that STRIPS are quoted in almost the same manner as conventional T-notes and T-bonds (see Exhibit 3–4). The major differences are that (1) no coupon rate is given, because there are no coupons, and (2) the type of STRIPS is usually denoted by a letter code.

The following format is used:

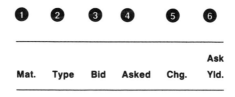

The columns used in the format are now described.

❶ **Maturity.** The date on which the underlying T-note or T-bond matures, expressed in a month-year format. T-notes and T-bonds usually mature on the 15th of the month.

EXHIBIT 3–7
STRIPS Quotations from **The Wall Street Journal.**

	U.S. TREASURY STRIPS				Ask	Nov 97	ci	80:01	80:04	−	6	5.10
Mat.	Type	Bid	Asked	Chg.	Yld.	Nov 97	np	79:29	80:00	−	6	5.14
Aug 93	ci	99:16	99:17	....	3.26	Feb 98	ci	78:29	79:00	−	6	5.13
Nov 93	ci	98:22	98:23	− 1	3.29	Feb 98	np	78:18	78:21	−	6	5.23
Feb 94	ci	97:27	97:27	− 1	3.37	May 98	ci	77:14	77:18	−	6	5.26
May 94	ci	96:30	96:30	− 1	3.48	May 98	np	77:03	77:07	−	6	5.35
Aug 94	ci	95:29	95:30	− 2	3.64	Aug 98	ci	76:00	76:04	−	7	5.37
Nov 94	ci	94:28	94:29	− 2	3.77	Aug 98	np	75:27	75:31	−	7	5.41
Nov 94	np	94:25	94:27	− 2	3.84	Nov 98	ci	74:21	74:25	−	7	5.46
Feb 95	ci	93:24	93:25	− 3	3.93	Nov 98	np	74:22	74:26	−	7	5.45
Feb 95	np	93:21 ·	93:23	− 3	3.98	Feb 99	ci	73:25	73:29	−	3	5.43
May 95	ci	92:20	92:22	− 3	4.05	Feb 99	np	73:24	73:28	−	3	5.43
May 95	np	92:21	92:23	− 3	4.03	May 99	ci	72:19	72:23	−	3	5.47
Aug 95	ci	91:23	91:25	− 3	4.03	May 99	np	72:15	72:19	−	3	5.51
Aug 95	np	91:21	91:23	− 3	4.07	Aug 99	ci	71:11	71:15	−	3	5.53
Nov 95	ci	90:15	90:17	− 4	4.20	Aug 99	np	71:09	71:13	−	3	5.55
Nov 95	np	90:14	90:16	− 4	4.21	Nov 99	ci	70:04	70:08	−	3	5.59
Feb 96	ci	89:00	89:02	− 4	4.42	Nov 99	np	70:04	70:08	−	3	5.59
Feb 96	np	88:31	89:01	− 4	4.44	Feb 00	ci	68:18	68:23	−	3	5.72
May 96	ci	87:20	87:23	− 4	4.58	Feb 00	np	68:14	68:18	−	3	5.76
May 96	np	87:21	87:24	− 4	4.57	May 00	ci	67:10	67:14	−	4	5.80
Aug 96	ci	86:09	86:12	− 5	4.71	May 00	np	66:29	67:01	=	4	5.89
Nov 96	ci	85:00	85:02	− 5	4.82	Aug 00	ci	66:08	66:12	−	4	5.82
Nov 96	np	84:30	85:00	− 5	4.84	Aug 00	np	65:29	66:02	−	4	5.89
Feb 97	ci	83:30	84:00	− 5	4.83	Nov 00	ci	65:02	65:07	−	4	5.86
May 97	ci	82:18	82:21	− 5	4.95	Nov 00	np	64:30	65:02	−	4	5.89
May 97	np	82:15	82:18	− 5	4.98	Feb 01	ci	63:27	63:31	−	4	5.93
Aug 97	cI	81:13	81:16	− 6	4.99	Feb 01	np	63:25	63:30	−	4	5.93
Aug 97	np	81:07	81:10	− 6	5.05	May 01	ci	62:17	62:22	−	4	6.01

❷ **Type.** The type of STRIPS. *The Wall Street Journal* uses the following letter codes to identify three different versions of the corpus:

bp   T-bond, stripped principal
ci   Stripped coupon interest
np   T-note, stripped principal

As an example, the following quotation is for the stripped coupons of a T-note.

Mat.	Type	Bid	Asked	Chg.	Ask Yld.
Feb 01	np	64:01	64:05	+1	5.89

Investor's Business Daily uses the letters b, a, and c, respectively, to identify the same three versions.

❸ Bid. The price in points at which a dealer has offered to buy the issue. The price, a percentage of par (100), is expressed in whole points and thirty-seconds (0.03125 point). Each whole point represents 1 percent of the issue's face value.

❹ Asked. The asked quote is the price at which the seller will sell the security. For STRIPS, the asked price is always higher than the bid.

For STRIPS having short maturities, the asked price will be very close to par (100). As the maturity lengthens, the asked price trades at a greater discount. For example, of three quotations in June, 1993, the first issue listed matures in two months and the asked price of 99:17 is $^{15}/_{32}$ below par.

Mat.	Type	Bid	Asked	Chg.	Ask. Yld.
Aug 93	ci	99:17	99:17	. . .	3.24
Feb 01	np	64:01	64:05	+1	5.89
Feb 23	bp	13:03	13:07	. . .	6.95

The example shows the trading at a very deep discount (13:07) because the maturity is almost 30 years away. At maturity, the investor of this STRIPS will receive $1/_{13.21875} \times 100$, or 7.6 times the original investment. The dollar price for STRIPS is determined in exactly the same manner as the dollar price for T-notes and T-bonds. For the last STRIPS, the purchase price for a $1,000 face value issue at maturity 30 years later will be 10×13.21875, or $132.19.

⑤ **Change.** The change in thirty-seconds of the bid price from the price quoted for the previous trading day. The change is generally expressed in the same format as that used for bid and asked prices.

⑥ **Asked yield.** The annualized percentage return an investor receives if the T-note or T-bond is purchased on the day of the quoted asked price and then held to maturity (i.e., yield to maturity). The longer the maturity, the greater the yield to maturity.

Chapter Four

Tax-Free Municipal Bonds

INTRODUCTION

The term **municipal bonds** is perhaps a misnomer, implying that it refers to bonds issued by *municipalities* (i.e., cities). In fact, municipal bonds, which are called **munis** for short, are issued by all levels of government other than the federal government: state, county, and local governments and their agencies. Such agencies include public school districts and higher education institutions, transportation facilities (bridges, tunnels, turnpikes), health facilities (hospitals), pollution and sewage or waste disposal authorities, housing authorities, and municipally owned utilities.

The most important reason for the attractiveness of municipal bonds to individual investors is that, in many states, they are *tax-free*.[1] This means that the semiannual interest is exempt from federal income taxes. The interest is also exempt from state and local taxation if the bondholder resides in the state of the issuing agency (making it triple-tax-free). Some states even exempt from state and local taxation the interest on munis of certain other states. Issues of the District of Columbia and US territories such as Puerto Rico and Guam, as well as bonds issued by local housing authorities operated by the Department of Housing and Urban Development (HUD) are also triple-tax-free in all states.

MUNICIPAL BOND ISSUES

Municipal bonds are issued for a variety of reasons. The majority involve allowing their issuers to borrow cash to fund various projects represented by many of the agencies mentioned earlier.

---

[1] Appendix B lists the tax status of municipal bonds in the different states.

116

On the other hand, some municipal bonds are issued solely for special situations, such as the sale of short-term securities as a "bridge loan" in anticipation of funds to be received later or seasonal cash-flow adjustments.

As fixed-income debt securities, tax-free munis have many of the characteristics of straight corporate bonds (Chapter 2), as well as Treasury notes and bonds (Chapter 3). A fixed rate of interest is paid semiannually until the maturity or call date. The market price moves in the opposite direction to that of market interest rates. When, as the saying goes, "A dollar was worth a dollar," and $1,000 was a lot of money, many municipal bonds were issued in a minimum face amount of $1,000. Currently, munis are generally issued in minimum denominations of $5,000. This change was instituted by issuers and underwriters in order to keep costs down by reducing the number of bonds issued.

Municipal bonds originally were available as **bearer bonds;** that is, they did not list the name and address of the owner, they did have coupons, and they were extremely negotiable (almost as negotiable as money, in fact). These features, coupled with their tax-free status, permitted many upper-income investors to take advantage of them as a very desirable tax shelter. Bearer bonds had their coupons clipped every 6 months, and the issuing agencies in most cases never knew who their bondholders were. This changed when Congress passed a law requiring that all municipal bonds with a maturity of more than 1 year and issued after July 1, 1982, be in registered form. Consequently, municipal bonds, like stock certificates, now have their owners' names on them, and the periodic interest payments are sent directly to the bondholders.

Tax-free securities fall into the following major categories:

• **General obligation (GO) bonds** are backed solely by the pledge of the issuer's full faith and credit for the payment of interest and principal. The funds received from the issue of these bonds have no specific allocation. They are for the issuer's general obligations.

• **Revenue bonds** are issued by agencies that produce revenue, such as bridges and turnpikes, utilities, sports complexes, waste and sewage disposal authorities, and pollution control agencies. The payment of interest and principal is based solely on the agency's ability to produce the revenue.

• **Municipal notes** are short-term obligations, usually with terms from 1 to 3 years, that are issued in anticipation of revenues that will be received from the sale of bonds, taxes, or other revenues.

READING MUNICIPAL BOND QUOTATIONS

While newspaper coverage of corporate bonds, as compared to stocks and mutual funds, is sparse, the coverage of municipal bonds is virtually nonexistent. This is because there are literally tens of thousands of issues. Among the few newspapers which do list municipal bonds are *The Wall Street Journal* and *Barron's*, both of which list them under the title "Tax-Exempt Bonds." An example is shown in Exhibit 4–1.

The format is as follows:

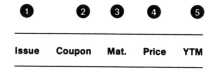

❶	❷	❸	❹	❺
Issue	Coupon	Mat.	Price	YTM

The columns used in the format are described in the following.

❶ **Issue.** The name of the political authority issuing the bond. The names are listed in alphabetical order. For example,

Issue	Coupon	Mat.	Price	YTM
P.R. G.O. Pub Imprvmnt	6.800	07-01-21	105½	6.39

is the quotation for a Puerto Rican GO bond intended to support public improvements.

❷ **Coupon rate.** The fixed annual coupon percentage rate, which is also called the **coupon yield.** With very few exceptions, interest is paid semiannually.

EXHIBIT 4–1
***Municipal Bond Quotations from* Barron's.**

TAX-EXEMPT BONDS

MUNI ISSUES

Friday, July 2, 1993

Obligations issued by a state or municipality whose interest payments are exempt from Federal, and possibly from local taxation as well.

Issue	Coupon	Mat.	Price	YTM
Adams Co Colo Ser 93A	5.875	04-01-14	102¼	5.69
Boston Mass Ref Ser B	5.750	02-15-23	98¾	5.84
Ca Comm Devlmnt Auth	5.500	10-01-14	98¼	5.64
Ca Comm Devp Auth-n	5.500	07-01-23	97⅝	5.66
Calif Dept Wtr Ser L	5.750	12-01-19	99⅞	5.76
Calif Hlth Fac	5.600	05-01-33	97¼	5.78
Chgo Emergency Tel	5.625	01-01-23	98⅛	5.76
Chgo Ill Genl Airpt	5.600	01-01-18	97	5.83
Frmington NM PCR 93A	5.875	06-01-23	101½	5.77
Franklin Co Ohio	5.750	05-15-20	99	5.83
Ill Ed Fac Auth Ser 85	5.700	12-01-25	98⅜	5.81
Intermountain Pwr Utah	5.500	07-01-20	96⅞	5.73
Jacksonville Elec Fla	5.500	10-01-13	98¾	5.60
Kansas Dept Trans	5.375	03-01-13	98	5.54
LA Wastewater System-n	5.700	06-01-23	100	5.70
LA Wastwater System-n	5.600	06-01-20	99⅝	5.63
Los Angeles Co MTA	5.625	07-01-18	99	5.70
Mass Bay Transp Auth-n	5.500	03-01-22	98	5.64
Mass G.O. Cons Loan	5.500	11-01-12	98⅝	5.62
Mich Pub Pwr Agcy Ref	5.500	01-01-13	98½	5.63
Northrn Ca Transm Agy	5.250	05-01-20	95⅛	5.60
NY Lcl Gvt Asst Ser92	6.250	04-01-18	104⅝	5.89
NYC Hlth & Hsp Ser 93A	5.750	02-15-22	100⅞	5.69
NYS Engy Res & Dev	6.000	03-15-28	101¾	5.88
NYS Urban Devel Corp	5.250	01-01-18	96	5.55
Oconee Co SC Ser 93	5.800	04-01-14	100¾	5.74
Ohio Muni Ele Gen Agy-n	5.375	02-15-24	97¼	5.56
Okla Bldg Bds 92 Ser A	5.200	07-15-16	96⅛	5.5
Omaha Pub Pwr Dist	5.500	02-01-17	98⅜	5.63
Orlando Expwy Auth	5.950	07-01-23	101	5.88
Orlando Expwy Auth 93	5.500	07-01-18	98⅜	5.62
P R Various G O	6.000	07-01-14	102⅜	5.80
P.R. Pub Bldg Ser M	5.500	07-01-21	97⅛	5.71
P.R. Pub Bldg Ser M	5.750	07-01-15	100⅜	5.73
Penn Higher Ed Asst	6.050	01-01-19	101½	5.94
Phoenix Civic Ariz	6.125	07-01-23	101⅞	5.99
PR G.O. Pub Imprvmt-n	5.500	07-01-13	98⅛	5.66
SC Pub Svc Auth	5.500	07-01-21	97⅜	5.69
Washn Pub Pwr Ser 9	5.700	07-01-17	99¼	5.76
Wisc Public Power	5.250	07-01-21	94	5.68

③ Maturity. The date on which the bond matures, expressed in a month-day-year format. The last two digits of the year are abbreviated. The following quotation is for a bond issued by the Charlotte, North Carolina, Hospital Authority that matures on January 1, 2020.

Issue	Coupon	Mat.	Price	YTM
Charlotte Hospital Auth NC	6.250	01-01-20	100$^1/_8$	6.24

④ Price. The closing price of the bond as a percentage of par. Like corporate bond prices, municipal bond prices are quoted as a percentage of par, equal to 100 percent of face value, and are generally expressed in whole points and eighths (0.125 point). Each whole point equals 100 basis points, and represents 1 percent of the bond's face value. For each $100 of face value, a full point is equal to $1, while an eighth equals 12.5 cents. Bond prices generally move in the opposite direction from changes in interest rates.

⑤ Yield to maturity. The yield the bond will have when held to maturity. It takes into account (1) the present value of all interest payments (and assumes that these interest payments are reinvested as the bond's coupon rate), and (2) the current price. It also assumes that, at maturity, all bonds are priced at par. If a bond was bought at a premium (priced above par value of 100), the premium paid is lost at maturity. For issues priced below par, the bond is bought at a discount and is worth less than face value.

Unlike most corporate bond tables, the above format does not include a bond's trading volume, bond rating, or whether it is backed by insurance against default. This information, however, is generally available from brokerage firms that actively trade bonds.

CALCULATING BOND YIELDS

Yield to Maturity

The methods used for calculating yields for municipal bonds are identical to those used for corporate bonds as well as Treasury notes and bonds (see Chapter 2, Equation 2–3 or Equation 2–4).

Example: Calculating the Purchase Price and Yield to Maturity of a Tax-Free Bond

On August 14, 1992, a Puerto Rican general obligation bond was quoted as follows:

Issue	Coupon	Mat.	Price	YTM
P.R. G.O. Pub Imprvmnt	6.800	07-01-21	105¹/₂	6.39

On the day of its quotation, the bond had approximately 29 years until maturity with a closing price of 105¹/₂. The equivalent dollar price to purchase a face value of $5,000 was:

$$Price = \frac{105.50}{100} \cdot \$5,000$$

$$= \$5,275.00$$

The annual yearly discount was:

$$AYD = \frac{100 - 105.50}{29 \text{ years}}$$

$$= -0.190\%$$

since the AYD is negative for a bond bought at a premium, and must be subtracted from the coupon rate. The yield to maturity for the bond is computed in the same manner as for straight corporate bonds. From Equation 2–4:

$$YTM = \frac{2 \cdot (6.80 - 0.190)}{(100 + 105.50)} \cdot 100\%$$

$$= 6.43\%$$

which is 4 basis points (0.04 percent) above the published yield of 6.39 percent.

Taxable Equivalent Yield

Because of the tax-free nature of municipal bonds, a bond's yield to maturity often does not reflect its true worth when taxes are taken into account. In states that have income taxes, the bond's **taxable equivalent yield** is the value often mentioned by bond sellers as an attractive advantage. The taxable equivalent yield (*TEqY*) is determined by the following equation:

$$TEqY = \frac{TExY}{1 - F + [S \cdot (1 - F)]} \tag{4-1}$$

where:

F = Investor's federal tax bracket (as a decimal)

S = Investor's state tax bracket (as a decimal)

$TExY$ = Tax-exempt yield (as a percentage)

The taxable equivalent yield, which is always higher than the tax-exempt yield, represents the yield that would have to be obtained before taxes to achieve the same yield as a tax-free bond.

Example: Calculating the Taxable Equivalent Yield of a Municipal Bond

A State of Delaware municipal bond has a coupon of 7¼ percent. For a Delaware resident who is in the 31 percent federal income tax bracket and the 7.7 percent state income tax bracket, the bond's taxable equivalent yield is:

$$TEqY = \frac{7.25\%}{1 - 0.31 + [(0.077)(1 - 0.31)]}$$

$$= \frac{7.25\%}{0.743}$$

$$= \mathbf{9.76\%}$$

This means that, for the Delaware investor, a yield of 9.76 percent on a fully taxable investment (such as stocks or corporate bonds) would be equivalent to a tax-exempt yield of 7¼ percent.

CALCULATING THE ACCRUED INTEREST

Accrued interest on a municipal bond, like accrued interest on all debt securities not sold as a discount, must be paid to the seller at the time of settlement. Accrued interest for a municipal bond is computed by the same basic formula as the one used for corporate bonds. All months are treated as if they each had 30 days. (See Chapter 2, Equation 2–1.)

MUNICIPAL BOND RATINGS

For municipal bonds, as for corporate bonds, bond rating firms assess the issuer's ability to (1) pay the interest and (2) repay the principal of a specific debt issue when due. The ratings used for corporate bonds by Moody's as well as by Standard & Poor's (see Exhibit 2–5) are also used for municipal bonds. For short-term notes, however, Moody's uses a separate system—Moody's Investment Grade (MIG) rating system. This system is summarized in Exhibit 4–2.

BOND INSURANCE

As an investment, municipal bonds for many years were regarded as second in line to Treasury securities in terms of safety. However, New York City's financial crisis in 1975 put it on the brink of default. The city's ability to pay its bondholders was in serious jeopardy until the New York State government bailed it out. The Washington Public Power Supply System (WPPSS), known as "Whoops," did default on certain bonds issued in the early 1980s. These events, combined with the ability of municipalities to obtain financial protection under federal bankruptcy law, caused many investors to reevaluate the safety of municipal bonds.

Since 1971, bond insurance has been available to insure the payments of periodic interest and principal at maturity from unforeseen economic conditions that could put the issuer in default. This insurance is purchased by the issuer, and the cost is passed to the purchaser of its bonds in the form of a slightly lower coupon rate as compared to other bonds of the same quality, maturity, and coupon, without insurance. Typically, insurance reduces a coupon by about 1/4 percent for AAA- and Aaa-rated bonds. This in turn causes insured bonds on the secondary market to sell at lower yields (i.e., higher prices) than they otherwise would.

Purchase of insurance for the life of a bond by the municipal agency is not obligatory, but it usually makes the bond more attractive to investors by removing one element of risk concerning

EXHIBIT 4–2
Moody's Municipal Note Ratings.

Rating	Definition
MIG 1	Best quality
MIG 2	High quality
MIG 3	Favorable quality
MIG 4	Adequate quality

Source: *Moody's Bond Record.*

the issuer's ability to pay interest and principal when due. The four major bond insurance firms are listed below.

American Municipal Bond Assurance Corporation (AMBAC)
Bond Investors Guaranty Insurance Company (BIG)
Financial Guarantee Insurance Corporation (FGIC)
Municipal Bond Insurance Corporation (MBIC)

Chapter Five

Government Agency Bonds

INTRODUCTION

Besides Treasury securities, such as T-bills, T-notes, and T-bonds, there is another group of government debt instruments. These do not have the same direct obligation as the Treasury has, to pay interest and principal. Once referred to as *federal agency bonds*, or simply *agencies* for short, these are now called *Government Sponsored Entity bonds*.

AGENCY ISSUES

Government agencies are quasi-official organizations that back home and farm mortgages, student loans, and banks. Agency securities have certain restrictions and disadvantages. Unlike Treasury securities, agency securities cannot be bought by individuals directly from the issuer. Individual investors are not able to purchase some agency securities because the minimum amounts are extremely high. The new issues that are available to individual investors must be bought from investment firms that act as underwriters for the agency that is issuing the securities. Many are denominated in $5,000 units, with $1,000 increments, but often the minimum purchase price is $25,000. Compared to T-bonds, agency bonds are traded in a less active market.

The major draw of agency bonds is their higher yields as compared to T-bonds with similar maturities. Obviously, the higher yields are offered to make the bonds more attractive to investors. However, an axiom that applies in many areas of investment is that higher yields carry higher risks. This axiom holds true for agency bonds. The interest of many agency securities, like the interest of Treasury securities, is exempt from state and local income taxes. Like T-bonds, agencies are not rated as to their investment quality. Furthermore, agency bonds are not registered with the Securities and Exchange Commission (SEC) because they are exempt by an act of Congress.

The term *bond* is often used in conjunction with agency securities, but actually the securities are available in two major forms: short-term notes sold at a discount (as T-bills are) and interest-bearing notes and bonds. Agency issues may be backed by several means:

- Collateral, usually cash, Treasury securities, and other acquired debt obligations
- De facto guarantee of the full faith and credit of the US government
- Guarantee by the Treasury
- The particular agency's right to borrow a limited amount of funds from the Treasury

Finally, there are agency securities that have no direct or indirect backing from the Treasury, or have no collateral at all. These agencies are classified as debentures, and the Treasury has never permitted any of them to default.

Although there are over two dozen different agency issues, only the most actively traded agencies are listed in the few newspapers that list them at all. These actively traded issues include:

Federal National Mortgage Association (FNMA)

Government National Mortgage Association (GNMA)

Student Loan Marketing Administration (SLMA)

Tennessee Valley Authority (TVA)

Federal Farm Credit Bank (FFCB)

Federal Home Loan Bank (FHLB)

Federal Land Bank

Farm Credit Financial Assistance Corporation (FCFAC)

Federal Home Loan Mortgage Corporation (FHLMC)

Asian Development Bank (ADB)

Export-Import Bank
Inter-American Development Bank (IADB)
World Bank
Resolution Funding Corporation

Some of these agencies are known by nicknames instead of by their alphabet soup letters. The Government National Mortgage Association, the best known, often goes by the name **Ginnie Mae.** The Federal National Mortgage Association is **Fannie Mae.** The Student Loan Marketing Administration is **Sallie Mae.** The lone male name belongs to the Federal Home Loan Mortgage Corporation, which is known as **Freddie Mac.** Fannie Mae is unique in that it is a government-sponsored corporation the stock of which is traded in the NYSE.

Agency bond issues can have noncallable maturities as high as 30 years, although 15-year maturities are the most common. Besides bonds, issued notes can range in maturity from 2 to 5 years, with $50,000 minimums.

READING PRICE QUOTATIONS

As illustrated by Exhibit 5–1, the format for quoting agency issues is essentially the same as for T-notes and T-bonds, and they are divided according to the issuing agency. For example, several issues of FNMA may be listed as follows:

①   ②   ③   ④   ⑤

FNMA				
Rate	Mat.	Bid	Asked	Yld.
11.15	6-95	116:30	117:10	4.56
8.65	7-99*	107:31	108:07	4.14
9.50	11-20	114:27	115:03	6.17

Note that the securities are listed in order of maturity. The columns used in the format are now described.

EXHIBIT 5–1
Government Agency Quotations from **The Wall Street Journal.**

GOVERNMENT AGENCY & SIMILAR ISSUES

Tuesday, June 22, 1993

Over-the-Counter mid-afternoon quotations based on large transactions, usually $1 million or more. Colons in bid-and-asked quotes represent 32nds; 101:01 means 101 1/32.

All yields are calculated to maturity, and based on the asked quote. * -- Callable issue, maturity date shown. For issues callable prior to maturity, yields are computed to the earliest call date for issues quoted above par, or 100, and to the maturity date for issues below par.

Source: Bear, Stearns & Co. via Street Software Technology Inc.

FNMA Issues

Rate	Mat.	Bid	Asked	Yld.
5.10	6-93	100:00	100:04	0.00
8.45	7-93	100:08	100:16	0.00
7.75	11-93	101:15	101:23	3.12
7.38	12-93	101:23	101:31	3.04
7.55	1-94	102:04	102:08	3.32
9.45	1-94	103:05	103:13	3.05
7.65	4-94	103:06	103:14	3.23
9.60	4-94	104:23	104:31	3.21
9.30	5-94	104:29	105:01	3.41
8.60	6-94	104:21	104:29	3.36
7.45	7-94	103:27	103:31	3.55
8.90	8-94	105:19	105:27	3.55
10.10	10-94	107:30	108:06	3.57
9.25	11-94	106:26	107:02	3.92
5.50	12-94	101:28	102:00	4.10
9.00	1-95	107:13	107:21	3.84
11.95	1-95	111:25	112:05	3.77
11.50	2-95	111:22	112:02	3.78
8.85	3-95	107:27	108:03	3.90
11.70	5-95	113:16	113:28	3.95
11.15	6-95	112:26	113:06	4.10
4.75	8-95	100:22	100:26	4.35
10.50	9-95	112:04	112:16	4.50
8.40	11-95*	101:16	101:20	3.99
8.80	11-95	109:06	109:14	4.56
10.60	11-95	113:06	113:14	4.57
9.20	1-96	111:18	111:26	4.25
7.00	2-96	106:07	106:15	4.36
7.70	2-96*	102:19	102:23	3.30
9.35	2-96	111:30	112:06	4.39
8.00	4-96*	103:13	103:17	3.43

Rate	Mat.	Bid	Asked	Yld.
0.00	10-19	14:01	14:09	7.54
9.65	8-20*	119:14	119:22	3.13
9.50	11-20*	120:04	120:12	3.24

Federal Farm Credit Bank

Rate	Mat.	Bid	Asked	Yld.
3.03	7-93	100:00	100:02	0.00
3.45	7-93	100:00	100:04	0.00
4.14	7-93	100:00	100:01	2.48
3.05	8-93	100:00	100:02	2.45
3.18	8-93	100:00	100:02	2.55
3.53	8-93	100:00	100:02	2.90
6.88	8-93	100:11	100:13	2.93
3.15	9-93	99:30	100:00	3.12
3.19	9-93	99:31	100:01	3.02
3.56	9-93	100:00	100:02	3.19
6.48	9-93	100:17	100:21	2.88
3.11	10-93	99:29	99:31	3.20
6.16	10-93	100:21	100:23	3.42

Federal Home Loan Bank

Rate	Mat.	Bid	Asked	Yld.
7.08	6-93	100:01	100:05	0.00
7.00	7-93	100:09	100:11	3.04
7.75	7-93	100:12	100:18	1.37
9.00	7-93	100:16	100:22	1.21
11.70	7-93	100:24	101:00	0.43
6.22	8-93	100:15	100:17	3.01
7.45	8-93	100:21	100:27	2.39
8.18	8-93	100:25	101:01	2.02
11.95	8-93	101:14	101:20	2.23
6.21	9-93	100:22	100:24	3.23
7.95	9-93	101:04	101:10	2.78
8.30	9-93	101:07	101:11	3.00
6.09	10-93	100:24	100:26	3.61
7.88	10-93	101:11	101:17	3.23
8.80	10-93	101:21	101:27	3.21
9.13	11-93	102:10	102:16	3.10
7.38	12-93	101:29	102:03	3.18
7.50	12-93	101:31	102:03	3.30

Rate	Mat.	Bid	Asked	Yld.
8.25	6-96	109:27	110:03	4.61
8.00	7-96	109:11	109:19	4.63
7.70	8-96	108:18	108:26	4.68
8.25	9-96	110:18	110:26	4.63
7.10	10-96	107:10	107:14	4.66
8.25	11-96	110:29	111:05	4.68
6.85	2-97	106:08	106:16	4.89
7.65	3-97	108:24	109:00	4.99
9.15	3-97	113:26	114:02	4.99
6.99	4-97	106:15	106:19	5.07
9.20	8-97	114:02	114:10	5.32
5.92	9-97*	100:19	100:27	2.12
5.26	4-98*	99:14	99:18	5.36
9.25	11-98	117:16	117:24	5.42
9.30	1-99	116:12	116:20	5.77
8.60	6-99	115:03	115:11	5.56
8.45	7-99	114:14	114:22	5.57
8.60	8-99	115:03	115:11	5.62
8.38	10-99	114:00	114:08	5.66
8.60	1-00	115:20	115:28	5.68
9.50	2-04	122:19	123:03	6.47

World Bank Bonds

Rate	Mat.	Bid	Asked	Yld.
11.63	12-94	110:13	110:17	4.18
8.63	10-95	108:13	108:17	4.62
7.25	10-96	107:00	107:08	4.82
8.75	3-97	112:14	112:22	4.94
5.88	7-97	102:19	102:27	5.09
9.88	10-97	117:12	117:20	5.21
8.38	10-99	113:24	114:00	5.69
8.13	3-01	112:19	112:21	6.04

❶ Rate. The stated annual percentage rate of interest, expressed as a two-place decimal.

❷ Maturity. The date on which the issue matures, expressed in a month-year format, with the year abbreviated to the last two digits. Callable issues are indicated by an asterisk (*), but the date shown is the maturity date. The following example is for a callable FNMA issue that matures in July 1999.

FNMA

Rate	Mat.	Bid	Asked	Yld.
8.65	7-99*	107:31	108:07	4.14

For maturity dates beyond 1999, 00 represents the year 2000. For the following entry, 11-20 represents a maturity date of November 2020.

FNMA				
Rate	Mat.	Bid	Asked	Yld.
9.50	11-20	114:27	115:03	6.17

❸ Bid. The price in points at which a dealer has offered to buy this issue. The price, a percentage of par (100), is expressed in whole points and thirty-seconds (0.03125 point). Each whole point represents 1 percent of the issue's face value.

Whole points and thirty-seconds can be separated either by a colon (as is done in *The Wall Street Journal*), a hyphen (as is done in *The New York Times*) or a period (as is done in *Investor's Business Daily*). When separated with a colon or a hyphen, the thirty-seconds are written as two-digit numbers from 00 to 32. When separated with a period, fractional thirty-seconds less than $^{10}/_{32}$ are written without leading zeros for 0 to 9.

❹ Asked. The asked quote is the price that the seller would like the buyer to accept. Agency securities are quoted on a bid-asked price basis, as are T-notes and T-bonds. The asked price is always higher than the bid quote, which corresponds to the commonsense practice whereby you (acting as the buyer) pay a higher price for the security compared with the price you would receive if you (now acting as the seller) immediately tried to sell the security. In the following example, the asked price (117:10) is higher than the bid price (116:30).

FNMA				
Rate	Mat.	Bid	Asked	Yld.
11.15	6-95	116:30	117:10	4.56

❺ Yield. The annualized percentage return an investor receives if the issue is purchased on the day of the quoted asked price and then held to maturity (i.e., yield to maturity). However, if the issue has a call provision and is selling at a premium, the yield is computed to the earliest call date.

Calculating Dollar Prices

Agency securities are quoted in the same manner as T-bonds, as a percentage of par (equal to 100) or face value. They are expressed in whole points and thirty-seconds (0.03125 point). For each $1,000 of face value, a full point is equal to $10, while a thirty-second equals 31.25 cents. As an aid, the decimal equivalents of thirty-seconds are given in Appendix A.

Calculating the Yield to Maturity

The methods used to calculate yields for agencies are identical to those used for corporate bonds, municipal bonds, and T-bonds. (See Chapter 2, Equation 2–3 or Equation 2–4.)

Example: Calculating the Purchase Price and Yield to Maturity of an FMNA Bond

On August 11, 1992, an FMNA bond was quoted as follows:

Rate	Mat.	Bid	Asked	Yld.
7.70	9-96	108:03	108:07	5.42

On the day of its quotation, the bond had approximately 4 years until maturity with an asked price of $108^7/_{32}$, which is equivalent to 108.21875. The dollar price to purchase a face value bond of $10,000 was:

$$\text{Price} = \frac{108.21875}{100} \cdot \$10,000$$

$$= \mathbf{\$10,821.88}$$

The annual yearly discount was:

$$AYD = \frac{100 - 108.21875}{4 \text{ years}}$$

$$= -2.055\%$$

since the annual yearly discount was negative for a bond bought at a premium, and had to be subtracted from the coupon rate. The yield to maturity for the FMNA bond is computed in the same manner as for straight bonds. From Equation 2–4:

$$YTM = \frac{2 \cdot (7.70 - 2.055)}{(100 + 108.21875)} \cdot 100\%$$

$$= \mathbf{5.42\%}$$

which agrees with the published yield.

Calculating the Accrued Interest

Accrued interest on an agency bond, like accrued interest on all debt securities not sold at a discount, must be paid to the seller at the time of settlement. Agency bonds are unlike T-bonds and T-notes in that their interest accrues as if every month had 30 days and the year had 360 days. This method is also used for corporate and municipal bonds. (See Chapter 2, Equation 2–1.)

Chapter Six

Futures Contracts

INTRODUCTION

A **commodity** is any item that can be bought or sold, for either immediate or future **delivery.** Historically, agricultural products such as grains and oilseeds (wheat, rye, soybeans, etc.), as well as livestock and meats (cattle, hogs, and pork bellies)—that is, the basic staples—were the original commodities. In time, the definition of *commodities* began to expand, and all the sectors listed with examples are now considered commodities.

Foods and fibers	Cocoa, sugar, coffee, cotton, orange juice
Metals	Gold, silver, platinum, copper, palladium
Petroleum products	Heating and crude oil, propane, gasoline
Interest rate instruments	CDs, T-bills, notes, and bonds
Currencies	Japanese yen, Swiss franc, Canadian dollar
Tradable market indexes	Stock indexes, commodity indexes, bond indexes

In **futures contracts,** the ability to contract now at a fixed price for future delivery performs two functions. First, if an investor is a hedger, risk is transferred to someone else. Second, the price is agreed to ahead of time.

In futures trading, there are two major positions: **long** and **short.** If you believe that the price of a particular commodity will increase before the contract expires, then you will buy a *long contract*, or simply "go long." If you do not transact the offsetting trade to close out the position before the delivery date, you must take delivery of the commodity contracted for and pay the full contract value of the commodity. This is not to say that if you did not close out a futures contract for live cattle before the delivery date, you would one day have 44,000 pounds of live cattle delivered to your front doorstep. All contracts have specific delivery specifications. If you became the proud owner of a herd of cattle, they would be placed in a stockyard and you would be charged storage fees until you sold them or moved them elsewhere.

On the other hand, if you feel that prices will decrease over time, then you will "go short," which is much the same as shorting a stock. Here you sell a given amount of a commodity in the hope of buying it back later, at a lower price. If you do not transact the offsetting trade to close out the position before the delivery date, then you must make delivery of the commodity contracted for and receive the full contract value of the commodity. If you do not physically own the specified amount of the commmodity contracted for, then you must purchase that amount on the open market at the prevailing cash or **spot price.** Usually, under these circumstances, you would realize a loss on the sale.

Speculators generally are not interested in taking delivery of the contracted commodity, and are interested in closing out their position and profiting from the difference in the buying and selling prices of the contract. Like stocks, which are also traded on margin, futures contracts are highly leveraged. The margin is simply a "good-faith" deposit as a guarantee for both buyer and seller. The amount of margin required depends on the type and number of contracts traded and is set by the exchange.

TICKER SYMBOLS AND DELIVERY MONTH SUFFIX CODES

Just as unique ticker symbols are used to identify the companies whose stocks are traded, especially when using quote machines, single-letter codes are added to the base commodity code to identify the contract's delivery (expiration) month, as follows:

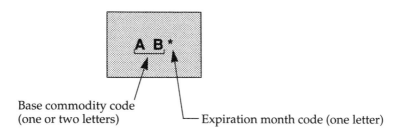

Base commodity code
(one or two letters)

Expiration month code (one letter)

Exhibit 6–1 lists the major domestic commodity contracts, along with some of their specifications and commodity codes. Exhibit 6–2 lists the monthly suffix codes that are used to identify the delivery months for futures contracts. Each commodity has a unique code, but the codes vary, depending on the exchange on which the contract is traded. Adding the proper contract month suffix code to the base commodity code allows complete specification of the type of contract and where it was traded.

For example, wheat futures contracts are traded on at least three exchanges: the **Chicago Board of Trade (CBOT),** the Kansas City Board of Trade (KC), and the Minneapolis Grain Exchange. A May wheat futures contract traded on these three exchanges would have contract codes of WK, KWK, and MWK, respectively.

READING FUTURES QUOTATIONS

As illustrated by Exhibit 6–3, quotations for futures contracts are typically given in the following format:

						Lifetime		Open
① Commodity (Exchange)—Contract Size; Unit Price								
Month	Open	High	Low	Settle	Change	High	Low	Interest
②	③	④	⑤	⑥	⑦	⑧		⑨
⑩ Estimated volume; previous day's volume, open interest, and change								

The columns used in the format are now described.

EXHIBIT 6–1
Futures Contract Specifications.

Commodity	Size	Contract Exchange	Code	Contract Months[1]	Minimum Price Change	Daily Limit (±)
Grains and Oilseeds						
Corn	5000 bu	CBOT	C	HKNUZ	$^1/_4$¢/bu	10¢/bu
Cotton	50,000 lb	CTN	CT	HKNVZ	0.01¢/lb	2¢/lb
Oats	5000 bu	CBOT	O	HKNUZ	$^1/_4$¢/bu	10¢/bu
Soybeans	5000 bu	CBOT	S	FHKNOUY	$^1/_4$¢/bu	3¢/bu
Soybean meal	100 tons	CBOT	SM	FHKNOUVZ	10¢/ton	$10/ton
Soybean oil	60,000 lb	CBOT	BO	FHKNOUVZ	0.01¢/lb	1¢/lb
Wheat	5000 bu	CBOT	W	HKNUZ	$^1/_4$¢/bu	20¢/bu
Wheat	5000 bu	KC	KW	HKNUZ	$^1/_4$¢/bu	25¢/bu
Wheat	5000 bu	MPLS	MW	HKNUZ	$^1/_4$¢/bu	20¢/bu
Foods and Fibers						
Cocoa	10 metric tons	CSCE	CC	HKNUZ	$1/mton	$88/mton
Coffee	37,500 lb	CSCE	KC	HKNUZ	0.02¢/lb	6¢/lb
Cotton	50,000 lb	CTN	CT	KHNUZ	0.01¢/lb	2¢/lb
Lumber	150,000 bd ft	CME	LB	FHKNUY	10¢/1000 bd ft	$5/1000 bd ft
Orange juice	15,000 lb	CTN	JO	FHKNUY	0.02¢/lb	5¢/lb
Sugar—world, No. 11	112,000 lb	CSCE	SE	HKNV	0.01¢/lb	$^1/_2$¢/lb
Sugar—domestic, No. 14	112,000 lb	CSCE	SB	FHKNUY	0.01¢/lb	$^1/_2$¢/lb
Livestock and Meats						
Cattle—feeder	50,000 lb	CME	FC	FHJKOUVY	2.5¢/cwt	1.5¢/lb
Cattle—live	40,000 lb	CME	LC	GJMOVZ	2.5¢/cwt	1.5¢/lb

	Contract size	Symbol	Exchange	Months	Minimum tick	Daily limit
Hogs	40,000 lb	LH	CME	GJMNOVZ	2.5¢/cwt	1.5¢/lb
Pork bellies	40,000 lb	PB	CME	GHKNO	2.5¢/cwt	2¢/lb
Metals						
Copper	25,000 lb	CU	COMEX	All	0.02¢/lb	20¢/lb
Gold	100 troy oz	GC	COMEX	All	10¢/troy oz	$75/troy oz
Palladium	100 troy oz	PA	COMEX	HMUZ	5¢/troy oz	$6/troy oz
Platinum	50 troy oz	PL	COMEX	FJNV	10¢/troy oz	$25/troy oz
Silver	5,000 troy oz	SI	COMEX	All	$1/2$¢/troy oz	$1.50/troy oz
Silver	1,000 troy oz	AG	CBOT	GJMOVZ	0.01¢/troy oz	$1/troy oz
Petroleum						
Crude oil—light	1,000 bbl	CL	NYMEX	All	1¢/bbl	$1.50/bbl
Gasoline—unleaded	42,000 gal	HU	NYMEX	All	0.01¢/gal	4¢/gal
Heating oil, No. 2	42,000 gal	HO	NYMEX	All	0.01¢/gal	4¢/gal
Propane	42,000 gal	PN	NYMEX	All	0.01¢/gal	4¢/gal
Interest Rates						
T-bills (90-day)	$1,000,000	TB	CME	HMUZ	1 pt	none
T-bonds	$100,000	US	CBOT	HMUZ	$1/32$ pt	3 pt
T-bonds	$50,000	XB	MCE	HMUZ	$1/32$ pt	3 pt
T-notes (6$1/2$–10 yr)	$100,000	TY	CBOT	HMUZ	$1/64$ pt	3 pt
Currencies						
Australian dollar	A$100,000	AD	CME	FHJMNUVZ	0.01¢/A$	150 pt
British pound	£62,500	BP	CME	FHJMNUVZ	0.02¢/£	400 pt
Canadian dollar	C$100,000	CD	CME	FHJMNUVZ	0.01¢/C$	100 pt
Deutsche mark	DM125,000	DM	CME	FHJMNUVZ	0.01¢/DM	150 pt
Japanese yen	¥12,500,000	JY	CME	FHJMNUVZ	0.0001¢/¥	150 pt

EXHIBIT 6–1 (concluded)

Commodity	Size	Contract Exchange	Code	Contract Months[1]	Minimum Price Change	Daily Limit (±)
Swiss franc	SFr125,000	CME	SF	FHJMNUVZ	0.01¢/SFr	150 pt
Indexes						
CRB	$500 × index	NYFE	CR	HMUZ	0.05 pt	18 pt
Major Market	$500 × index	CBOT	BC	All	0.05 pg	15 pt
Muni Bond	$1000 × index	CBOT	MB	HMUZ	$1/32$ pt	3 pt
NYSE Composite	$500 × index	NYFE	X	Next 3 mo	$1/16$ pt	None
S&P, 500	$500 × index	CME	SP	HMUZ	5 pt	Varies
US Dollar	$100 × index	FINEX	DX	HMUZ	0.01 pt	Varies
Value Line	$500 × index	KC	KV	HMUZ	0.05 pt	Varies

[1] Codes for contract months are defined in Exhibit 6–2.

Exchange Codes

CBOT	Chicago Board of Trade
CME	Chicago Mercantile Exchange
COMEX	Commodity Exchange (New York)
CSCE	Coffee, Sugar & Cocoa Exchange (New York)
CTN	New York Cotton Exchange
FINEX	Financial Exchange (New York)
KC	Kansas City Board of Trade
MCE	Mid-America Commodity Exchange
MPLS	Minneapolis Grain Exchange
NYFE	New York Futures Exchange
NYMEX	New York Mercantile Exchange

Unit abbreviations

bbl	barrel
bd ft	board foot
bu	bushel
cwt	hundredweight (100 lb)
gal	gallons
lb	pounds
oz	ounces

EXHIBIT 6–2
Standard Commodity Delivery Contract Month Suffix Codes.

Month	Code	Month	Code
January	F	July	N
February	G	August	O
March	H	September	U
April	J	October	V
May	K	November	Y
June	M	December	Z

❶ **Commodity, exchange, contract size, and unit price.** These entries tell what the commodity is, an abbreviation of the exchange on which it is traded, the size of one contract, and the units all prices are quoted by. As an example, the quotations below indicate that contracts for coffee futures are traded on the Coffee, Sugar & Cocoa Exchange (CSCE), that each contract consists of 37,500 pounds of coffee, and that all prices are quoted in cents per pound.

Coffee (CSCE)-37,500 lb; cents per lb

Month	Open	High	Low	Settle	Change	Lifetime High	Lifetime Low	Open Interest
July	58.80	60.00	57.00	59.80	+ .70	88.30	54.15	25,390
Mar94	63.30	64.15	61.50	64.15	+ .75	90.75	61.60	1,718

❷ **Month.** The contract's delivery month. The months are listed in order, with the nearest month first. The month cited here could also be the *spot month* if the delivery date is less than 30 days from the quote date. The actual date for delivery is specified by the exchange for each commodity. All delivery months are assumed to be in the current year unless the year follows the month in the listing.

EXHIBIT 6–3
Futures Contract Quotations from **The Wall Street Journal.**

Friday, June 18, 1993

Open Interest Reflects Previous Trading Day.

	Open	High	Low	Settle	Change	Lifetime High	Lifetime Low	Open Interest
GRAINS AND OILSEEDS								
CORN (CBT) 5,000 bu.; cents per bu.								
July	214½	216¾	214½	216¼	+ 1¼	286	211½	78,045
Sept	221	223¼	220½	223	+ 1¾	271½	217¾	41,943
Dec	229	232	229	231¾	+ 2	268½	225¼	91,725
Mr94	236¾	239¼	236¾	239	+ 2	256¼	232¾	12,790
May	242	244½	242	243¾	+ 2	260	238½	2,900
July	245	247½	245	247½	+ 2¼	263¼	241	3,808
Sept	242½	244	242½	243½	+ 1	251	240½	147
Dec	241½	245½	241½	244¾	+ 3½	255	238¾	2,356
Est vol 55,000; vol Thur 47,555; open int 233,714, +110.								
OATS (CBT) 5,000 bu.; cents per bu.								
July	131¾	133¾	131¾	132¾	....	163½	128¼	5,503
Sept	133¼	135¼	133¼	134	....	160½	129¾	1,968
Dec	137½	139	137¼	137¾	....	161	134	3,905
Est vol 2,000; vol Thur 1,882; open int 11,509, −181.								
SOYBEANS (CBT) 5,000 bu.; cents per bu.								
July	602½	606	600	605¼	+ 4	671	551	39,216
Aug	601½	606½	599½	605½	+ 5	655	551	20,158
Sept	601¾	606	599½	605½	+ 7	630	554	10,254
Nov	601	606½	599½	606	+ 7	620	555½	53,544
Ja94	608	612¼	606	611¾	+ 6½	620	576½	5,545
Mar	613½	617½	613	617½	+ 6½	627½	589¾	1,929
May	616	620½	615½	620¼	+ 6¼	630	592½	2,707
July	618	623	617½	622	+ 5½	633	594½	2,983
Nov	597	601½	596	598¾	+ 1¼	616	581½	2,454
Est vol 75,000; vol Thur 84,269; open int 138,790, +3,721.								

❸ Open. The price of the opening trade for the day, expressed in the base units for the commodity. The open is frequently not the same as the closing price of the previous day's trading. Certain events that affect commodity prices may have occurred overnight, and the market is getting its first chance to react. For example, the quote for July coffee had an opening price of 58.80. Since coffee is quoted in terms of cents per pound, this represents 58.80 cents per pound. The opening price, along with the other prices in the quotation, gives an indication of the trading activity for the day. However, not all newspapers publish the contract's opening price. The value of the contract is the **contract size** times the price. Here, the value of one contract of 37,500 pounds of coffee is then 37,500 lb × $0.5880/lb, or $22,050. Note that the price was converted from cents per pound to dollars per pound, as the total value of the contract is typically expressed in dollars.

From the opening price, contract prices then are free to change in minimum increments. As is summarized in Exhibit 6–1, each futures contract specification has a minimum fluctuation, or **tick**, that its price can move, as well as a maximum or daily limit by which the contract can change up or down from the previous trading day's close. For CSCE coffee contracts, the contract's price must move up or down in increments of 0.02 cents per pound. Each tick is equivalent to a dollar price of 37,500 lb × 0.02¢/lb, or $7.50. The maximum that the contract's trading price can change up or down from the previous day's close is 6 cents per pound, which corresponds to a dollar value of 37,500 lb × 6¢/lb, or $2,250. Here are some more examples:

Commodity	Contract Size	Tick	Daily Limit
CBOT wheat	5,000 bu	1/4¢/bu = $12.15	20¢/bu = $1,000
CME hogs	40,000 lb	2.5¢/cwt = $10.00	1.5¢/lb = $600
NYMEX propane	42,000 gal	0.01¢/gal = $4.20	4¢/gal = $1,680

④ **High.** The highest trade price for the day.

⑤ **Low.** The lowest trade price for the day.

⑥ **Settle.** The price of the day's last trade. This is analogous to a stock's closing price. In the example used earlier (see page 139), July coffee futures closed at 59.80 cents per pound and was only one tick (0.02 cents) below its high price of 60.00 for the day. The daily high, low, and settle prices give a good indication of the volatility of the market for the particular commodity on the given day.

⑦ **Change.** The change in the settle price from the previous day's settle price. The July coffee futures contract closed 0.70 cents higher than the previous day's close, which would be 59.80 − 0.70, or 59.10 cents a pound. Notice that the contract opened down (58.80) from the previous day's close of 59.10, and that the market forces for that day pushed the coffee price higher than the day before by 0.70 cents per pound.

⑧ Lifetime high and low.   The highest and lowest trading prices during the life of the particular contract, which may have started 9 months ago or even longer. Without a graph, this range gives some measure of the historical price range for the contract, such as whether or not the contract is currently trading at or near its contract high (or low).

⑨ Open interest.   The total number of contracts that are still outstanding, or have not been closed out. A contract is closed out by transacting an offsetting sale of an identical futures contract. The **open interest** gives a measure of interest, or contract activity, as well as the contract's liquidity. Large values near the contract's delivery date could make closing out the contract difficult, as the rules of supply and demand usually prevail. In the example above, there were 25,390 July coffee futures contracts still outstanding. As the expiration date nears, this number generally will decrease.

⑩ Estimated volume; previous day's volume, open interest, and change.   The last line gives the estimated total number of trades for all the active contracts for the commodity. This is followed by the volume of the previous trading day, for comparison. The open interest, like the volume, represents the total volume of all active contracts. The change in the open interest is from the previous trading day.

For example, the following represents all the Wednesday trades for active contracts for oats futures traded on the CBOT, as they might be reported in a newspaper on Thursday:

OATS (CBOT)-5,000 bu; cents per bu

Month	Open	High	Low	Settle	Change	Lifetime High	Low	Open Interest
May	142	142	$140^{1}/_{2}$	$141^{1}/_{2}$	$- \quad ^{1}/_{2}$	$177^{1}/_{4}$	126	394
July	$145^{1}/_{4}$	$145^{1}/_{4}$	$143^{1}/_{4}$	$144^{1}/_{4}$	. . .	$163^{1}/_{2}$	$129^{1}/_{2}$	8,376
Sept	145	145	144	$144^{1}/_{2}$	$- \quad ^{1}/_{4}$	$160^{1}/_{2}$	$133^{1}/_{2}$	991
Dec	147	$147^{1}/_{4}$	146	$146^{1}/_{2}$	. . .	161	$133^{1}/_{4}$	3,283

Est vol 1,000; vol Tues 723; open int 13,151, + 96

On Wednesday, the total estimated volume of all four active delivery months was 1,000 contracts, as compared to 723 contracts on the previous day (Tuesday). The open interest for all the CBOT futures contracts for oats was 13,151 at the close of Wednesday's trading, which was 96 higher than on Tuesday.

Chapter Seven

Options Contracts

INTRODUCTION

Options contracts are in the middle between the actual buying and selling of a security instrument, such as common stock or Japanese yen, and the trading of a futures contract. An options contract gives the holder simply the right, but not the obligation, to buy or sell an **underlying security,** with the following conditions:

1. The underlying security must be bought or sold at a specified price.
2. The holder must exercise the terms of the option contract by a given date. Otherwise the option expires and is worthless.

When handled properly, **options** can allow an investor to buy stocks at a lower price than would have been available on the secondary market. An option is an asset, the value of which diminishes with time. The closer the deadline for exercising the option, the less time there is for the value of the option to either increase or decrease as the buyer anticipates. Options contracts are traded on the New York Stock Exchange, the American Stock Exchange, the Philadelphia Stock Exchange, the Pacific Stock Exchange, and the Chicago Board of Options Exchange.

CALL AND PUT OPTIONS

Options can be broken down into two major types—**calls** and **puts**—and both can be either bought or sold.

Call options. A *call option* is the right, but not the obligation, to buy a specified amount of a security at a predetermined price on or before a stated date. The premium varies with the duration of the contract and with market activity. In general, shorter-term calls have smaller premiums.

Put options. A *put option*, the opposite of a call option, is the right, but not the obligation, to sell a specified amount of a security at a predetermined price on or before a stated date.

For both calls and puts, the holder pays a premium for the privilege of deciding whether or not to exercise the option. It must be reemphasized that the option holder is under no obligation to exercise the option. Five basic elements of any options contract are used for both calls and puts, as follows:

Underlying security. The **actuals** on which the option is traded. Options that are traded can be based on equities, or common stocks; on foreign currencies; or on tradable stock indexes. If equities or foreign currencies are listed as the underlying securities, the options, when exercised, are settled in actuals (i.e., the actual underlying securities). For stocks, a given number of stocks are traded, depending on the contract size.

Tradable indexes are a different ball game. A tradable index used as the underlying basis for an options (or futures) contract is a market basket of predefined stocks, bonds, or commodities. For example, the Major Market Index is a collection of 20 specific companies whose stocks are traded on the NYSE, and whose performance is intended to closely track movements in the Dow Jones Industrial Average. If the option for such an index is exercised, the settlement is in "cash" rather than in the physical delivery of 100 shares each of 20 different stocks. For the S&P 500 Index, this naturally could get absurd. This is in keeping with Berlin's first rule of business: "In God we trust; all others pay cash."

Contract size. The amount of the underlying security on which the option is traded. Generally, the amount of an underlying security that defines an options contract will depend on the type of underlying security, which is set by the exchange on which the particular option is traded. For common stocks as the underlying security, the contract size is 100 shares of a given company. For Swiss francs traded on the PHLX, it is 62,500 francs. Exhibit 7–1 summarizes the contract sizes of the major currency options contracts.

Striking (exercising) price. The predetermined per share price at which the underlying security may be bought or sold.

Expiration date. The deadline by which the option holder must exercise the option. The expiration date greatly affects the premium paid. As the **expiration date** nears, the option becomes less valuable, and the value of the premium decreases rapidly. Most options contracts are considered short-term, meaning that the maximum time before expiration is less than 9 months, and short-term options contracts expire at 11:59 PM Eastern time on the Saturday immediately following the third Friday (the last day of trading) of the expiration month. Options contracts on Long-Term Equity Anticipation Securities (LEAPS) are considered to be long-term, as the expiration is typically 18 to 30 months away. By convention, expiration is in January of the year named.

Some options contracts are specifically referred to as *European-style,* in that the contract can be exercised only on the last day of the contract. This is unlike *American-style* contracts, which permit the option to be exercised at any time.

Premium. The cost of the option that the buyer pays to the option's seller (or writer). The premium is separate from any commissions and miscellaneous charges imposed. As a general rule, a premium with call options increases with an increase in the market price of the underlying stock. With put options, a premium increases with a decline in the market price of the stock.

OPTION STRATEGIES

Both call and put options can be either bought or sold; thus there are four basic strategies.

Buying a call. The purchaser or holder of one call stock option contract has the option to buy 100 shares of company at

EXHIBIT 7–1
Contract Sizes of Currency Options Contracts (Philadelphia Stock Exchange).

Currency	Symbol	Contract Size
Australian dollar	AD	A$50,000
British pound	BP	£31,250
Canadian dollar	CD	C$50,000
European Currency Unit (ECU)	ECU	62,500 ECU
French franc	FF	Fr250,000
German deutsche mark	DM	DM62,500
Japanese yen	JY	¥6,250,000
Swiss franc	SF	SFr62,500

a given **strike price** no matter how high its market price may rise. If the strike price is $50 a share and the option holder exercises the option at any time prior to expiration, the option writer is obligated to sell 100 shares of the stock at $50 per share (for a total of $5,000) to the option holder, no matter how high the stock price may climb above the $50 strike price.

Exhibit 7–2a graphically shows the option holder's profit profile for buying a call option. For market prices at or lower than the contract's strike price (an **out-of-the-money** call) prior to expiration, the option holder incurs a loss equal to the amount of the premium.[1] When the market price of the underlying stock increases above the break-even point, the call option is generally profitable and is said to be an **in-the-money** call with opportunity for unlimited profit. When the two prices are equal, options are referred to as **at-the-money**.

Selling a call. In selling (writing) a call option, the option writer is obligated to sell (or deliver) the underlying security to the option holder at the strike price if the option is exercised,

---

[1] All examples exclude the cost of commissions paid to brokers. Unlike futures contracts, which involve a single "round-turn" commission fee, commissions are paid to brokers for buying and selling options contracts (like stocks). If the option expires worthless, or unexercised, no commission is paid.

EXHIBIT 7–2
Profit Profiles for Option Strategies.

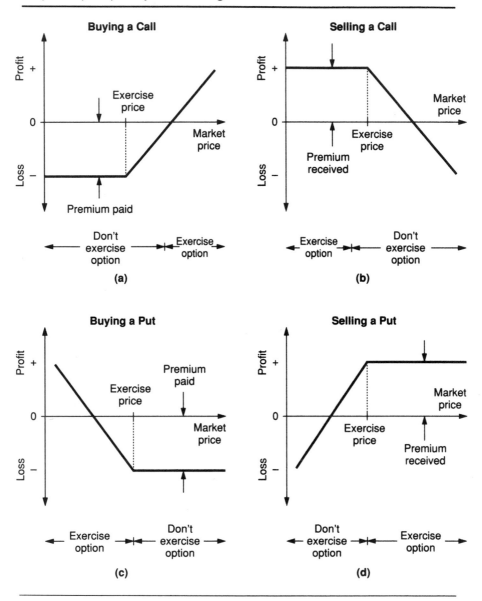

regardless of the underlying security's market price. Exhibit 7–2b illustrates the seller's profit profile for selling a call.

The option holder will not exercise the option to buy the underlying security for market prices less than the strike price. The option writer then keeps the premium paid by the option holder. As long as the option is not exercised, the option writer's profit is constant, and equals the premium paid. However, if market forces push the price of the underlying security above the strike price, the holder will exercise the option at the strike price. The holder then receives the underlying security that is now worth more than was paid for it.

If the option writer actually owns the underlying security, such as 100 shares of IBM stock for each contract, the option is said to be **covered**. On the other hand, if the security is not owned, then the option is said to be a **naked option**. Naked options can be financially costly to the option writer if the option is exercised, as the writer then has to buy the underlying security at the prevailing market price in order to cover the option and make delivery. In this situation, the writer's loss can be unlimited. Another choice available to the writer is "covering" (buying back) his or her position and terminating the obligation. Due to the costs involved, the transaction is less costly for the writer when the sold call is covered by the offsetting buy-back transaction.

Buying a put. The buyer of a put option contract has the right, but not the obligation, to sell the underlying security at the strike price. Here, the forecast is for lower market prices for the underlying security with the objective of buying cheap at some future time, while exercising the option contract to permit the sale of the security at a price higher than the strike price. The option holder's profit profile for buying a put is illustrated in Exhibit 7–2c.

As with call options, buying a put requires the payment of the premium to the option writer. If the price of the security is higher than the strike price, the option is not exercised and the option holder's loss is limited to the amount of the premium paid. If the market price decreases in value, the holder of the option has the right to buy the security in the secondary market and the opportunity to sell it at the higher strike price to the option writer.

Here, the holder's opportunity for profit is unlimited. When the market price is higher than the put option's strike price, the option is said to be an *out-of-the-money put*. Conversely, if the market price is less than the put option's strike price, the option is referred to as an *in-the-money put*.

Selling a put. The selling (writing) of a put option requires that the writer be obliged to sell the security to the option holder at the strike price, regardless of how low the market price of the security may fall. As shown by the profit profile of Exhibit 7–2d, the option writer keeps the premium paid by the option holder as profit if the market price equals or is greater than the strike price at expiration. However, the seller will sustain a loss on the trade if the market price is below the strike price and is unlimited. To minimize such losses, the seller of the put option can cover his or her position by buying back the option and terminating the obligation.

CONTRACT TICKER SYMBOLS

Just as unique ticker symbols are used on quote machines to identify the companies whose stocks are traded, a two-letter suffix code is added to the security's basic ticker symbol to identify the contract as either a call or a put, and also to indicate its contract expiration month and its striking price.

NYSE and AMEX Stocks and Stock Indexes

For NYSE and AMEX stocks as well as tradable indexes, option symbols are expressed in the following format:

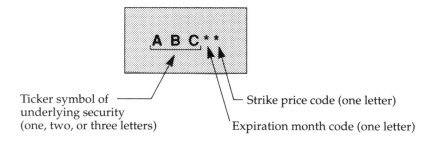

EXHIBIT 7–3
Ticker Symbols for Stock Index Options.

Stock Index	Symbol	Exchange
Bank Index	BKX	PHLX
Biotechnology Index	BTX	AMEX
Biotechnology Index	BGX	CBOE
Computer Technology Index	XCI	AMEX
Eurotop 100	EUR	AMEX
Financial Times–Stock Exchange 100 Index	FSX	CBOE
Gold/Silver Index	XAU	PHLX
Institutional Index (AM trading)	XII	AMEX
Institutional Index (PM trading)	PXP	AMEX
Japan Index	JPN	AMEX
Major Market Index	XMI	AMEX
National OTC Index	XOC	PHLX
NYSE Composite Index	NYA	NYSE
Oil Index	XOI	AMEX
Pharmaceutical Index	DRG	AMEX
Russell 2000 Index	RUT	CBOE
S&P 100 Index	OEX	CBOE
S&P 400 Mid Cap Index	MID	AMEX
S&P 500 Index (PM trading)	NPX	CBOE
S&P 500 Index (AM trading)	SPX	CBOE
Utility Index	UTY	PHLX
Value Line Index	VLE	PHLX
Wilshire Index	WSX	PSE

As discussed in Chapter 2, the ticker symbol used for stocks is a unique symbol assigned by the exchange on which the underlying security is traded. Tradable stock indexes have their own symbols and are summarized in Exhibit 7–3.

The one-letter codes for contract expiration months are standardized, with call and put options trading in three 4-month cycles. Exhibit 7–4 summarizes the letter codes used for all 12 expiration months. One-letter codes are also used for strike prices, which are at fixed dollar values in increments of $5. Exhibit 7–5 lists the letter codes used for option contracts for individual stocks and

EXHIBIT 7–4
Option Contract Expiration Month Letter Codes.

Call Options					
Cycle 1		Cycle 2		Cycle 3	
Code	Month	Code	Month	Code	Month
A	January	B	February	C	March
D	April	E	May	F	June
G	July	H	August	I	September
J	October	K	November	L	December

Put Options					
Cycle 1		Cycle 2		Cycle 3	
Code	Month	Code	Month	Code	Month
M	January	N	February	O	March
P	April	Q	May	R	June
S	July	T	August	U	September
V	October	W	November	X	December

stock indexes. The following examples show the use of strike price and expiration month contract codes for stock and index option contracts:

Option Symbol	Underlying Security (Symbol)	Option Type	Expiration Month	Strike Price
DDHJ	DuPont (DD)	Call	August	$50
SPXUT	CBOT S&P 100 (SPX)	Put	September	$400
XMIFI	AMEX Major Market Index (XMI)	Call	June	$345
UALWX	UAL (UAL)	Put	December	$130

OTC Issues

Ticker symbols for NASDAQ's OTC stocks generally have a four- or five-letter format (see Chapter 1). For options on some OTC

EXHIBIT 7–5
Strike Price Codes for Stock and Index Options.

Letter	Strike Prices	Letter	Strike Prices
A	5, 105, 205, etc.	M	65, 165, 265, etc.
B	10, 110, 210, etc.	N	70, 170, 270, etc.
C	15, 115, 215, etc.	O	75, 175, 275, etc.
D	20, 120, 220, etc.	P	80, 180, 280, etc.
E	25, 125, 225, etc.	Q	85, 185, 285, etc.
F	30, 130, 230, etc.	R	90, 190, 290, etc.
G	35, 135, 235, etc.	S	95, 195, 295, etc.
H	40, 140, 240, etc.	T	100, 200, 300, etc.
I	45, 145, 245, etc.	U	7.50
J	50, 150, 250, etc.	V	12.50
K	55, 155, 255, etc.	W	17.50
L	60, 160, 260, etc.	X	22.50

stocks, the stock's normal ticker symbol is shortened to the first two letters followed by the letter Q and the one-letter codes for the expiration month and for the strike price:

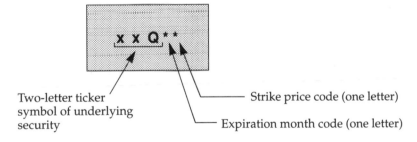

Two-letter ticker symbol of underlying security — Strike price code (one letter) — Expiration month code (one letter)

For example, the quote symbol for a put option contract for Apple Computer (AAPL), at a strike price of $45 and expiring in September, is written as:

AAQUI

Notice that Apple's ticker symbol (AAPL) is shortened to **AA** and is followed by the letter **Q** plus the expiration month code **U** (September call), and strike price code **I** ($45).

Currency Options

Ticker symbols for PHLX currency options have the same format as for stock and stock index options, as shown in the following example:

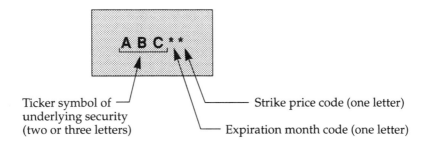

Ticker symbol of — underlying security (two or three letters)

Strike price code (one letter)

Expiration month code (one letter)

The ticker symbol is a two-letter code, with the exception of the **European Currency Unit (ECU)**,[2] which uses a three-letter code followed by the one-letter codes each for the expiration month and strike price.

For example, the quote symbol for a call option contract for 31,250 British pounds at a strike price of $160, expiring in July, is written as:

BPGL

Notice that the ticker symbol for British pounds is **BP** and is followed by the expiration month code **G** (July call), and the strike price code **L** ($160).

READING STOCK OPTION QUOTATIONS

Equity options quoted in newspapers have several formats. The format (shown in Exhibit 7–6) that is used in the *Chicago Tribune* divides the month cycles of puts and calls for each strike price.

---

[2] The ECU is equivalent to a combination of 10 currencies of European countries. It is discussed further in Chapter 9.

EXHIBIT 7–6

Stock Options Quotation Appearing in the **Chicago Tribune** *(August 27, 1992).*

Options

Chicago

Option & NY Close	Strike	Calls—Last			Puts—Last		
		Sep	Oct	Nov	Sep	Oct	Nov
AlexAl	25	3/8	3/4	r	r	r	r
AlianP	15	1-3/8	2-1/8	r	13/16	r	1-9/16
15-3/4	17-1/2	5/8	1-1/8	1-5/8	2-1/4	2-3/8	2-13/16
15-3/4	20	3/16	1/2	7/8	r	r	4-3/4
15-3/4	25	r	s	3/8	r	s	9-1/4
Amdahl	12-1/2	r	r	1-1/8	r	r	r
13-1/8	15	3/16	r	1/2	r	r	2-1/2
AInGrp	90	r	r	6-7/8	r	r	2-1/2
93-3/8	95	1-1/4	2-3/8	3-3/8	r	r	r
93-3/8	100	r	3/4	r	r	r	r
Amoco	45	6	r	r	r	r	r
50-7/8	50	1-1/2	r	2-5/8	3/8	r	1-3/8
50-7/8	55	r	1/8	r	r	r	r
BMCSft	40	r	r	r	3/8	r	r
46-1/4	45	r	r	r	r	r	4
46-1/4	50	7/8	1-13/16	r	r	r	r
46-1/4	55	5/16	s	1-13/16	r	s	r
46-1/4	60	s	s	7/8	s	s	r
46-1/4	70	s	s	7/16	s	s	r
Baxter	35	2-1/8	2-3/4	r	r	r	r
37	40	r	3/16	9/16	r	r	r
BioTcG	5	3/16	r	3/16	r	r	r
5	7-1/2	r	r	3/16	r	r	3/4
BlkDk	17-1/2	r	r	1-5/8	1/2	13/16	r
17-7/8	20	r	r	1/2	2-1/8	2-1/2	r
17-7/8	22-1/2	r	s	r	r	s	4-1/2
17-7/8	25	s	s	1/16	s	s	r
Boeing	35	2-3/8	3	3-3/8	5/16	11/16	15/16
37	40	1/4	7/16	7/8	3	3-3/8	3-1/4
37	45	1/16	r	3/16	r	r	8-1/8
37	50	s	s	r	s	s	13-1/8
BoisC	20	r	5/16	9/16	r	r	r
BostSc	20	r	r	1-3/8	r	r	r
CBS	180	r	s	r	1-1/8	s	r
192	185	r	r	r	2-1/4	r	r
192	190	6-1/8	r	r	4-1/2	r	8-1/2
192	195	3-3/8	6	r	6-1/8	r	r
192	200	2-3/16	r	r	r	r	r
192	210	r	r	3-1/8	r	r	r

The format is as follows:

❶	❷	❸			❹		
Option &	**Strike**						
NY Close	**Price**	**Calls—Last**			**Puts—Last**		
		Jan	Feb	Apr	Jan	Feb	Apr

The columns used in the format are now described.

❶ Stock and closing price. Stocks that have options contracts are listed alphabetically by the name of the company whose stock serves as the underlying security. The companies are usually separated according to the exchanges on which they are traded. Below the stock name is the closing market price for the previous day's trading on the NYSE. The closing price is repeated for each option that is listed for that company. As in conventional stock quotations, fractional dollars are expressed in eighths.

❷ Strike price. The dollar price at which the option is exercised. Generally the price is in whole dollars and is expressed in $5 increments for strike prices of $100 and less, in $10 increments for strike prices from $100 to $200, and in $20 increments for strike prices higher than $200. On occasion, depending on trading activity, smaller increments may be used, especially for strike prices between $100 and $150.

❸ Calls—last. The last price paid (i.e., the premium) for call options for the listed expiration months, expressed in the same dollar format as used for stock prices. There are usually three consecutive contract months, one for each contract cycle (Exhibit 7–4).

For the same contract month, the premium decreases as the strike price increases above the stock's market price. In cases in which the strike price is well above the current stock price, the premium is usually a fraction of a dollar and is often expressed in sixteenths. For calls having the same strike price, the premium increases with the expiration months that are further out. The contract loses its value as expiration nears. When a contract for a particular combination of strike price and expiration month is not traded that day, the letter r is used. If there is no contract for a given strike price and for the expiration month listed, the letter s is often used.

In the following quotation for IBM, for example, for strike prices above the current stock price of 85$\frac{1}{8}$ (an in-the-money call), say 90 to 100, the premium for an April call decreases from $\frac{1}{4}$ to $\frac{1}{16}$.

Option & NY Close	Strike Price	Calls—Last			Puts—Last		
		Apr	May	Jun	Apr	May	Jun
IBM 85$^{1}/_{8}$	75	r	10$^{1}/_{2}$	11$^{3}/_{4}$	r	$^{3}/_{8}$	1$^{1}/_{8}$
85$^{1}/_{8}$	80	5$^{1}/_{2}$	6$^{1}/_{4}$	7$^{5}/_{8}$	$^{1}/_{4}$	1$^{3}/_{16}$	2$^{9}/_{16}$
85$^{1}/_{8}$	85	1$^{7}/_{16}$	2$^{7}/_{8}$	4$^{3}/_{4}$	1$^{3}/_{8}$	3$^{3}/_{8}$	4$^{7}/_{8}$
85$^{1}/_{8}$	90	$^{1}/_{4}$	1$^{1}/_{8}$	2$^{3}/_{4}$	5$^{1}/_{4}$	6$^{3}/_{8}$	7$^{3}/_{4}$
85$^{1}/_{8}$	95	$^{1}/_{16}$	$^{7}/_{16}$	1$^{1}/_{2}$	10$^{3}/_{8}$	r	11$^{3}/_{4}$
85$^{1}/_{8}$	100	$^{1}/_{16}$	s	$^{13}/_{16}$	r	s	r

To buy a single June call option contract at a strike price of 90, the premium is 4³/₄. The option holder would pay 100 × $4.75, or $475.00 for the right to buy 100 shares of IBM stock at $85.125 a share at any time before the June call expired at 11:59 PM Eastern time on the Saturday immediately following the third Friday in June. The higher the premium, the more the stock market price must rise above the strike price to overcome the premium paid, before any profit is made. Time is of the essence, for as the expiration month approaches, the option becomes less and less valuable. If the option expires, the option holder in this example loses the $475.00 premium.

Any dividends that may be paid during the option contract are kept by the seller of the option. The payment of a stock dividend, especially if it is large, may affect the premium, because on the ex-dividend date, the stock's market will have been discounted or devalued to account for the dividend.

At a strike price of 85, the call is essentially at the money, and there is a 1⁷/₈-point premium. This makes sense, because if the call option were exercised, no one would sell you the option if you could buy stock at 85 by exercising the option and could then sell it immediately on the open market at 85¹/₈. A ¹/₈-point profit per share would be made by doing virtually nothing.

❹ Puts—last. The last price paid (i.e., the premium) for put options for the same three listed expiration months as for call options. For the same contract month, premiums move in the direction opposite to the direction of calls; they increase as the strike price increases above the stock's market price. For puts having the same strike price, the premium increases with the expiration months that are further out.

The other major format used for quoting stock options also involves an alphabetical listing, such as the one shown in Exhibit 7–7. This format is now used in both *The Wall Street Journal* and *Barron's*, and in fact, is now the more common of the two formats. The format is as follows:

❶	❷	❸	❹	❺	❻	❼	❽
Option	Sales (100s)	Open Int.	High	Low	Last	Net Chg.	Stock Close

The columns used in the format are now described.

❶ **Option.** The name, listed alphabetically, of the company whose stock serves as the underlying security. The companies are usually separated according to the exchanges on which they are traded. Following the stock name for each option contract are the expiration month (indicated by a three-letter abbreviation) and the strike price. The strike prices are listed in increasing order. A letter p qualifier following the strike price indicates that this contract is a put option; the absence of the p indicates a call option. In the examples below, the first quotation is for a call option for 100 shares of Time Warner with a September expiration at a strike price of 40 (contract symbol: TWXIH). The second quotation is for the put option with the same month and strike price (contract symbol: TWXUH).

Option	Sales (100s)	Open Int.	High	Low	Last	Net Chg.	Stock Close
TimeW Sep 40	469	3984	2	$1^{1}/_4$	$1^{3}/_8$	−	$^{3}/_8$	$38^{1}/_4$
TimeW Sep 40 p	407	699	3	$2^{1}/_4$	3	+	$^{7}/_{16}$	$38^{1}/_4$

EXHIBIT 7–7
***Stock Options Quotation from* Barron's.**

Expire date Strike price	Sales	Open Int.	Week's High	Low	Price	Net Chg.	N.Y. Close
AT&T Jul 60	1303	6651	3 1/2	2 1/2	2 1/2	− 1/4	62 1/4
AT&T Jul 60 p	1400	2432	3/8	1/8	1/4	− 3/16	62 1/4
AT&T Jul 65	1823	4645	1/2	3/16	3/16	− 1/8	62 1/4
AT&T Aug 60	217	191	4 1/8	3 3/8	3 3/4	+ 1/2	62 1/4
AT&T Aug 60 p	254	181	15/16	5/8	7/8	− 1/16	62 1/4
AT&T Aug 65	1758	805	1 1/4	5/8	13/16	− 1/16	62 1/4
AT&T Oct 60	397	4385	4 7/8	3 7/8	3 7/8	− 1/2	62 1/4
AT&T Oct 60 p	399	1124	1 9/16	1 1/4	1 3/8	− 1/8	62 1/4
AT&T Oct 65	619	3411	2	1 1/2	1 1/2	− 1/8	62 1/4
AT&T Jan 45	270	704	18 5/8	18	18 5/8	+ 1 1/4	62 1/4
AT&T Jan 55	337	894	9 1/2	8 3/4	9 1/4	+ 1 1/8	62 1/4
AT&T Jan 60	573	3289	5 7/8	5 1/8	5 1/8	− 1/4	62 1/4
AT&T Jan 65	446	2847	3 1/8	2 1/4	2 5/8	...	62 1/4
Amrtch Aug 80	256	267	2 1/4	1 15/16	1 15/16	+ 3/16	79 5/8
Amoco Jul 55 p	317	729	7/8	1/2	3/4	− 3/4	54 5/8
Atl R Jul 115 p	237	430	2 3/8	1 1/8	2 3/8	+ 15/16	113 5/8
Atl R Jul 120	250	2692	15/16	3/8	3/8	− 1/2	113 5/8
Atl R Jul 120 p	406	835	6 1/2	3 5/8	5 7/8	+ 1 5/8	113 5/8
Atl R Aug 120	391	138	2 1/16	1	1	− 7/8	113 5/8
Avon Aug 55 p	204	234	1 1/8	1	1 1/8	− 5/8	57
Avon Aug 60	333	354	1	3/4	1	+ 3/8	57
Avon Jan 55	955	2805	5 3/8	4 3/4	4 7/8	+ 3/8	57
Aztar Jul 10	956	2560	1/2	1/8	1/4	− 1/2	9 1/8
Aztar Aug 10	1022	2933	13/16	3/8	5/8	− 5/8	9 1/8
BMC Sft Jul 45	228	176	8 1/2	6 1/2	8 1/4	+ 2 3/8	54 3/8
BMC Sft Jul 45 p	336	312	11/16	1/4	1/4	− 1 1/2	54 3/8
BMC Sft Jul 50	378	306	4 3/4	3 1/4	4 5/8	+ 1 7/8	54 3/8
BMC Sft Jul 55	299	245	2 1/8	1 1/4	1 15/16	+ 1 3/16	54 3/8
BMC Sft Nov 60	401	436	4 3/4	4	4 3/4	+ 2 5/16	54 3/8
BankAm Jul 40 p	465	1388	3/16	1/16	1/16	− 3/16	44 7/8
BankAm Jul 45	3212	4444	1 7/16	11/16	3/4	...	44 7/8
BankAm Jul 45 p	2524	3430	1 3/8	5/8	3/4	− 7/8	44 7/8
BankAm Jul 55 p	300	200	9 7/8	9 7/8	9 7/8	− 3 3/8	44 7/8
BankAm Aug 40 p	463	402	1/2	5/16	3/8	− 3/16	44 7/8
BankAm Aug 45	216	301	2 3/8	1 3/8	1 3/4	+ 1/4	44 7/8
BankAm Aug 45 p	1228	1118	2 5/16	1 5/8	2	− 1/2	44 7/8
BankAm Aug 50	408	408	3/8	1/4	5/16	...	44 7/8
BankAm Oct 40	237	620	6 3/8	5 1/2	6 1/4	+ 7/8	44 7/8

❷ **Sales.** The number of option contracts traded (in 100s) in the last reporting period. In *Barron's*, this is a weekly sales figure. In the example above, 46,900 September 40 call contracts were traded and 40,700 put contracts were traded in the preceding week.

❸ **Open interest.** The total number of contracts that are still outstanding, or have not been closed out. A contract is closed out by transacting an offsetting sale of an identical option. In the example above, there were 3,984 September 40 call contracts still outstanding. To close out this position, the holder must sell a

September 40 call option. As the expiration date nears, this number generally will decrease.

④ **High.** The highest price (premium) paid for the option during the last week's trading.

⑤ **Low.** The lowest price (premium) paid for the option during the last week's trading.

⑥ **Last.** The last price (premium) paid for the option during the last week's trading.

⑦ **Net change.** The change in the premium from the previous week's trading.

⑧ **Stock close.** The stock's weekly closing market price on the NYSE.

OTHER CONTRACT QUOTATIONS

Besides stock options, other options contracts that are available include stock indexes, currencies, interest rates, and Treasury issues. The formats are essentially the same as the ones used for stock options, except that the contract size for the particular contract must be taken into account in computing costs.

Indexes

Unlike stock options, stock index options are cash transactions that do not relate to a particular number of shares. Rather, the size, or underlying value, of an index option contract is determined by the index multiplier and the level of the underlying index. Exercise prices and premiums are expressed in dollars, and the total exercise price or premium for a single option is the price multiplied by the appropriate index multiplier, which is usually 100.

Exhibit 7–8 shows weekly quotations for stock index options traded on the AMEX. The following example represents a Septem-

EXHIBIT 7–8
***Stock Index Options Quotation from* Barron's.**

AMERICAN EXCHANGE

INDEX OPTIONS

MajMkt Jul 340 p	334	866	3/8	3/16	5/16	–	3/16	355.82
MajMkt Jul 350	301	540	10 1/2	7 1/2	8 1/8	–	7/8	355.82
MajMkt Jul 350 p	1070	913	1 1/4	5/8	15/16	–	7/16	355.82
MajMkt Jul 355	1459	874	7 1/8	3 3/4	4	–	7/8	355.82
MajMkt Jul 355 p	1890	1268	2 1/2	1 3/8	2 1/4	–	3/8	355.82
MajMkt Jul 360	2809	1605	3 5/8	1 3/8	1 3/8	–	1 1/4	355.82
MajMkt Jul 360 p	1785	1119	5 1/4	2 7/8	4 7/8	–	1/8	355.82
MajMkt Jul 365	2831	1731	1 7/16	5/16	5/16	–	9/16	355.82
MajMkt Jul 365 p	899	1033	9	5 3/4	8 3/4	+	3/4	355.82
MajMkt Jul 375	1280	1606	1/8	1/16	1/16	–	1/8	355.82
MajMkt Aug 300 p	1808	1808	1/8	1/8	1/8		...	355.82
MajMkt Aug 345 p	340	306	2	1 3/4	1 7/8	–	1/2	355.82
MajMkt Aug 355	625	508	8 5/8	6 3/8	6 3/8	–	1	355.82
MajMkt Aug 355 p	645	695	5	4	5	–	1/4	355.82
MajMkt Aug 360	729	897	5 3/4	3 5/8	3 5/8	–	1 3/8	355.82
MajMkt Aug 360 p	762	807	7 5/8	6	7 1/4	+	1/2	355.82
MajMkt Aug 365	887	739	3 1/4	2 1/8	2 3/16	–	7/16	355.82
MajMkt Aug 365 p	600	706	10 1/2	8 3/4	10 1/2	+	1 7/8	355.82
MajMkt Aug 375	1916	1958	11/16	7/16	7/16	–	1/4	355.82
MajMkt Sep 300 p	465	1610	5/16	1/4	1/4	–	1/16	355.82
MajMkt Sep 325 p	225	1446	1	15/16	15/16	–	3/8	355.82
Oil Idx Jul 240 p	400	200	3/8	3/8	3/8	–	1/16	249.
Oil Idx Jul 250 p	238	182	3 1/4	1 5/16	3 1/4	+	1 1/8	249.
Oil Idx Jul 265 p	400	200	11 3/4	11 3/4	11 3/4	–	2 1/4	249.
InstOpen Jul 450	225	50	5 3/4	3 1/4	3 1/4	+	1/8	445.77
InstOpen Jul 450 p	300	175	4 1/8	3 3/8	4 1/8	–	1 3/4	445.77
InstOpen Jul 470 p	200	175	16 3/4	16 5/8	16 5/8	–	4 1/2	445.77
InstOpen Aug 470	2675	9950	1	13/16	13/16	+	1/8	445.77
InstOpen Aug 475	716	716	1/2	7/16	1/2		...	445.77
InstOpen Sep 475	750	1750	1 5/16	1 1/8	1 1/8	+	3/16	445.77

ber call for the S&P Mid Cap 400 Index with a strike price of 165 (contract symbol: MIDIM).

Option	Sales (100s)	Open Int.	High	Low	Last		Net Chg.	NY Close
MidCap Sep 165	510	1720	6 3/8	6	6	+	1 3/4	167.97

The last trade was for a premium of \$6. Coupled with a contract multiplier of 100, this means that the cost of the premium for one contract is 100 × \$6, or \$600. The option holder can exercise this option at any time and usually does so when the market price for the index level is greater than the strike price. The exercises for stock index options are always settled in cash, and the option writer is thus obligated to pay the option holder cash in an amount equal to the difference in dollars between the settlement value of the underlying index and the dollar value of the strike price. If this option were exercised when the current index level was 167.97, the holder would receive 167.97 − 165, or a difference of 2.97 points, which is equivalent to $2.97 × 100, or $297.00.

Currencies

Exhibit 7–9 shows quotations for currency options. The option for each currency is followed by a line giving the contract size and the basis for the quote. Exercise prices for currency options other than Japanese yen are stated in U.S. cents per unit of foreign currency. Exercise prices for Japanese yen options are expressed in hundredths of U.S. cents per unit. Following are examples of two contracts traded on the PHLX:

Option	Sales (100s)	Open Int.	High	Low	Last		Net Chg.	NY Close
62,500 German Marks-cents per unit.								
DMarkJul59	5	270	0.08	0.07	0.07	+	0.02	58.95
6,250,000 Japanese Yen-100ths of a cent per unit.								
JYenJul90 p	3	814	1.04	0.49	0.94	+	0.18	92.17

The first quotation is for a July 59 call for 62,500 German deutsche marks (DMs). The strike price of 59 means 59 cents per 1 DM. The last trade was for a premium of 0.07 (i.e., 0.07 cents), which means that the cost of the premium for one contract is 62,500 DM × $0.0007, or $43.75. The option holder can exercise this option at any time prior to expiration and buy 62,500 DM for 62,500 × 59 cents, or $36,875. Since the **spot price** (the cash price for immediate delivery) for DMs in New York closed at 58.95 cents per DM, the contract has a current value of 62,500 × $0.5895, or $36,843.75.

EXHIBIT 7-9
Quotations for Currency Options from **Barron's.**

Expire date Strike price	Sales	Open Int.	Week's High	Low	Net Price	Chg.	N.Y. Close
31,250 British Pounds-European Style.							
BPound Jul152½.	2	96	1.07	0.54	1.07+	0.42	150.86
BPound Aug155.	1	64	1.10	0.73	1.10	......	150.86
BPound Sep145 p	2	126	2.02	1.50	1.50-	1.65	150.86
BPound Mar142½ p	3	87	4.52	3.55	3.55-	1.20	150.86
31,250 British Pounds-cents per unit.							
BPound Jul145 p	6	1119	0.80	0.40	0.52-	0.78	150.86
BPound Jul147½ p	4	463	1.53	0.52	0.70-	1.00	150.86
BPoundJul150.	1	714	2.28	0.80	1.94+	1.32	150.86
BPoundJul150 p	2	575	2.35	0.90	1.00-	3.18	150.86
BPoundJul152½.	4	338	1.22	0.33	0.82+	0.42	150.86
BPoundJul155.	4	718	0.46	0.10	0.46-	0.14	150.86
BPoundJul157½.	1	324	0.15	0.13	0.13+	0.09	150.86
BPoundJul160.	2	900	0.06	0.06	0.06	......	150.86
BPound Aug142½ p	3	354	0.78	0.36	0.36-	0.66	150.86
BPound Aug147½ p	1	100	2.35	1.48	1.48-	0.04	150.86
BPoundAug152½.	8	556	2.05	1.24	1.85+	0.76	150.86
BPoundAug155.	5	575	1.29	1.05	1.29+	0.56	150.86
BPoundAug157½.	5	576	0.60	0.60	0.60+	0.37	150.86
BPound Sep140 p	3	772	0.54	0.53	0.53-	0.57	150.86
BPound Sep145 p	3	905	2.48	1.49	1.49-	1.51	150.86
BPound Sep147½.	3	242	4.70	4.10	4.70+	1.65	150.86
BPoundSep150.	3	261	4.10	2.63	4.10+	2.10	150.86
BPoundSep155.	9	708	1.65	1.35	1.60+	0.70	150.86
50,000 Canadian Dollars-European Style.							
CDollr Dec76.	1	108	0-12	0-12	0-12-	0-	77.63
CDollr Mar76½.	1	1270	0-	0-	0-	0-	77.63
CDollr Jun76.	1	108	0-	0-	0-	......	77.63
CDollr Aug75 p	15	1500	0-	0-	0-	......	77.63
CDollr Sep76½ p	6	650	0-	0-	0+	0-	77.63
250,000 French Francs-European Style.							
FFrancJul17¼ p	6	500	1.70	1.34	1.70+	0.38	174.30
FFrancJul17½.	5	500	1.42	1.42	1.42	......	174.30
FFrancJul18.	1	107	0.38	0.14	0.14-	0.46	174.30
FFrancSep17¼.	69	7233	3.90	3.90	3.90-	3.30	174.30
FFrancSep17¼ p	1	15311	4.10	4.10	4.10+	1.10	174.30
FFrancSep17½.	69	7150	2.78	2.44	2.44-	1.32	174.30
FFrancSep18¼.	65	29955	0.84	0.84	0.84-	0.46	174.30
FFrancDec16½.	11	3393	10.02	10.02	10.02-	1.18	174.30
FFrancDec16¾.	57	6000	8.42	8.42	8.42-	0.68	174.30
62,500 German Marks-European Style.							
DMarkJul56 p	1	270	0.08	0.07	0.07+	0.02	58.95
DMarkJul56½ p	3	125	0.09	0.04	0.05-	0.04	58.95
DMarkJul58 p	5	3668	0.42	0.30	0.33-	0.13	58.95
DMarkJul58½.	3	7350	0.85	0.78	0.78+	0.02	58.95
DMarkJul59.	5	510	0.48	0.42	0.42-	0.08	58.95

The second quotation is for a July 90 put for 6,250,000 Japanese yen. The p indicates a put (no letter is used for a call). Since options on yen are expressed in hundredths of U.S. cents per yen, the strike price of 90 means that the strike price is 90 × 0.01 cent, or 0.90 cent per yen. The last trade was for a premium of 0.94 (i.e., 0.000094 cent), and the cost of the premium for one contract is 6,250,000 × 0.000094 cent, or $587.50. The option holder at any time prior to expiration may exercise this option

EXHIBIT 7–10
Quotations for Futures Options from **The Wall Street Journal.**

FUTURES OPTIONS PRICES

Tuesday, June 22, 1993.

AGRICULTURAL

CORN (CBT)
5,000 bu.; cents per bu.

Strike Price	Calls–Settle Sep	Dec	Mar	Puts–Settle Sep	Dec	Mar
200	25	34½	....	⅝	1	....
210	18	26	....	2¾	3	2
220	12¼	19½	25½	7⅜	6	4¾
230	8¼	14½	18¼	13¼	11	8½
240	6¼	11⅛	15	21¾	17¾	15
250	4⅞	8¾	12	30	24¾	20½

Est vol 8,500 Mon 9,165 calls 1,319 puts
Op int Mon 93,526 calls 44,538 puts

SOYBEANS (CBT)
5,000 bu.; cents per bu.

Strike Price	Calls–Settle Aug	Sep	Nov	Puts–Settle Aug	Sep	Nov
575	45½	51¾	57½	2¾	6¾	10½
600	28½	36	43	10½	16⅝	21⅝
625	18	27½	33¼	25	32	37
650	12⅜	22½	26½	44	51½	54
675	8⅛	17½	21¼	....	....	74
700	6	14⅝	18¼	....	....	96½

Est vol 15,000 Mon 14,310 calls 5,-
945 puts
Op int Mon 109,516 calls 41,064 puts

160	3.05	5.60	7.80	0.55	1.10	1.30
165	0.50	2.55	4.50	3.00	3.05	3.00
170	0.10	0.80	2.25	7.60	6.30	5.75
175	0.00	0.25	0.95	12.50	10.75	9.45
180	0.00	0.15	0.35	17.50	15.65	13.85

Est vol 591 Mon 211 calls 310 puts
Op int Mon 12,768 calls 11,322 puts

LIVESTOCK

CATTLE-FEEDER (CME)
44,000 lbs.; cents per lb.

Strike Price	Calls–Settle Aug	Sep	Oct	Puts–Settle Aug	Sep	Oct
82	4.85	4.10	3.92	0.32	0.60	0.75
84	3.00	2.50	2.47	0.47	1.00	1.30
86	1.60	1.25	1.37	1.05	1.75	2.20
88	0.70	0.55	0.65	2.10	....	....
90	0.22	0.20	....	3.57	....	....
92	0.17	....	....	....	....	....

Est vol 278 Mon 40 calls 167 puts
Op int Mon 1,853 calls 7,340 puts

CATTLE-LIVE (CME)
40,000 lbs.; cents per lb.

Strike Price	Calls–Settle Jly	Aug	Oct	Puts–Settle Jly	Aug	Oct
70	....	3.57	....	....	0.17	0.47
72	....	1.97	2.70	0.07	0.55	0.95

5 YR TREAS NOTES (CBT)
$100,000; points and 64ths of 100%

Strike Price	Calls–Settle Aug	Sep	Dec	Puts–Settle Aug	Sep	Dec
10950	....	1-33	....	0-04	0-08	....
11000	....	1-08	....	0-09	0-13	....
11050	0-37	0-51	....	0-18	0-21	....
11100	0-20	0-33	....	0-33	0-32	....
11150	0-09	0-19	....	....	0-46	....
11200	....	0-12	....	....	....	....

Est vol 5,000 Mon 414 calls 662 puts
Op int Mon 33,812 calls 38,505 puts

EURODOLLAR (CME)
$ million; pts. of 100%

Strike Price	Calls–Settle Sep	Dec	Mar	Puts–Settle Sep	Dec	Mar
9600	0.54	0.28	0.27	0.03	0.22	0.33
9625	0.32	0.14	0.16	0.06	0.33	0.47
9650	0.13	0.06	0.08	0.12	0.50	0.63
9675	0.03	0.02	0.04	0.27	0.71	0.84
9700	0.01	0.01	0.02	0.50	0.95	1.07
9725	.0004	.0004	0.01	0.74	1.19	....

Est. vol. 42,307;
Mon vol. 9,077 calls; 16,742 puts
Op. int. Mon 557,770 calls; 696,480 puts

LIBOR – 1 Mo. (CME)
$3 million; pts. of 100%

Strike Price	Calls–Settle Jly	Aug	Sep	Puts–Settle Jly	Aug	Sep
9625	0.50	0.45	0.40	.0004	0.01	0.02

Reprinted by permission of *The Wall Street Journal*, © 1993 Dow Jones & Company, Inc. All Rights Reserved Worldwide.

and sell ¥6,250,000 for 6,250,000 × 0.90 cent, or $56,250.00. Since the spot price in New York closed at 0.9217 cent per yen, the contract has a current value of 6,250,000 × 0.9217 cent, or $57,606.25.

OPTIONS ON FUTURES

Options on futures contracts are very much like other options, except that they give the holder the right but not the obligation to buy or sell a futures contract. Many commodities (discussed in Chapter 6) also allow options trading. Exhibit 7–10 shows a typical futures options quotation.

Chapter Eight

Mutual Funds

INTRODUCTION

Many investors simply do not have either the time or the patience to try to pick the one super stock that will outperform the market. Though many sophisticated programs are now available for use on personal computers, stock picking is still part art and part luck. Rather than trying to put all their eggs in one basket, investors generally try to diversify by buying a variety of stocks that are consistent with their investment goals. More than 3,000 different **mutual funds** allow individual investors to invest indirectly in the stock (and bond) markets established by investment companies that pool the resources of many investors to create entities that might be called *stock clubs*. In a mutual fund, the investors share a **portfolio** that may combine stocks, bonds, CDs, T-bills, and virtually any other instruments that meet the fund's objectives.

Individuals invest in mutual funds by buying shares in the fund from the investment company, either directly or through brokers. The return on the fund's portfolio (less any management fees, etc.) is distributed to the investors in proportion to the number of shares held in the fund. Because mutual funds make it easy to own a large and diverse portfolio with a relatively modest investment, they have always been popular with individual investors.

FUND TYPES

To be precise, **investment company** is a broad term that includes mutual funds as one of its types. Mutual funds are themselves divided into several categories and, regardless of their objectives, are referred to as **open-end funds.** Open-end funds place no pre-determined upper limit upon the total number of shares its investors can own. Because mutual fund shares are redeemable, the fund can sell or redeem any number of its fund's shares without limit.

Stock and Bond Funds

Open-end mutual funds invest primarily in stocks, bonds, or some combination of the two. In many cases, a stock fund with short-term reserves of cash may also invest in short-term **money market**-type securities: CDs, T-bills, etc. Mutual funds are generally classified on the basis of their investment objectives, which are stated on each fund's **prospectus.**

These investment objectives can be grouped into categories as follows:

Growth funds	Investment for long-term growth of invested capital and future income.
Aggressive growth funds	Investment for maximum capital gains.
Growth and income funds	Investment for significant income along with long-term growth.
Balanced funds	Investment objectives generally overlap. The funds generally require (1) stability of net asset value and (2) a balanced portfolio of stocks and bonds, typically 60/40.
Bond funds	Bond funds are further classified on the basis of the bond type that makes up the major portion of their portfolios. The fund classifications include corporate, high-yield, government, mortgage-backed, and tax-exempt.
International and global funds	Investment in stocks and bonds of foreign firms, governments, or geographical regions. *Global funds* include foreign and US stocks and bonds, while *international funds* exclude US issues.
Gold funds	Investment in domestic and foreign companies that mine gold and other precious metals.
Other funds	Investment in funds that have industry-specific or sector companies (e.g., chemicals only); asset allocation funds that diversify among various investment instruments; index funds that match a particular index, such as the S&P 500; funds that

invest in other funds; socially conscious funds that choose investments solely on the basis of ideals of ethics and morality; and commodity funds that involve professionally managed portfolios of futures contracts.

Money Market Funds

Money market funds invest solely in short-term money market instruments: CDs, **repurchase agreements (repos, or RPs),**[1] T-bills, banker's acceptances, commercial paper, letters of credit, and other notes of indebtedness. These funds can be divided into the following:

General-purpose
Municipal tax-exempt (federal only)
US government

Closed-End Funds

Closed-end funds are the other broad category of investment companies. A closed-end fund maintains a constant number of shares, which are traded on exchanges in a manner identical to the trading of common stocks. Closed-end funds are often referred to as *publicly traded funds*.

READING MUTUAL FUND QUOTATIONS

Open-End Funds

Open-end mutual funds may rank behind stocks as the second most frequently quoted securities. The formats in which they are quoted vary widely in newspapers, but a number of items are

---

[1] A *repurchase agreement (repo, or RP)* is a short-term (generally less than 1-week) instrument through which a fund purchases the underlying security from a well-established securities dealer or a bank that is a member of the Federal Reserve System. At the time of purchase, the bank or dealer agrees to repurchase the underlying security at the same price plus a specified amount of interest.

common to all newspapers that quote these funds. The format used in the *Chicago Tribune* (Exhibit 8–1) is the simplest, and is typical of the formats published in many local daily newspapers. The format is as follows:

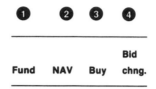

			Bid
Fund	**NAV**	**Buy**	**chng.**

The columns used in the format are now described.

❶ **Fund family.** The "family name" of the fund is bold-faced, and the names are listed in alphabetical order. Underneath are listed the various funds that are offered by the family, which are often abbreviated. In the example, two funds are listed for Fidelity Investments (Balanced Fund and Magellan Fund).

	NAV	**Buy**		**Bid** **chng.**
Fidelity Invest:				
Balance	12.76	N.L.	+	.03
MagIn	63.97	65.95	+	.30
FinHorGvt	11.16	11.42	+	.02

If only a single fund is listed for a fund family, the fund is not boldfaced. The last line in the example cites a fund that is separate from the two funds sold by Fidelity Investments.

❷ **Net asset value.** The **net asset value (NAV)** is the closing price per share. For all open-end funds, this is the dollar price at which the fund will buy (redeem) shares from investors. It is sometimes listed as the *bid price* and is obtained by dividing the fund's net assets by the total number of shares issued, as follows:

$$NAV = \frac{MV + C - L}{N} \qquad \text{(8-1)}$$

where:

C = Fund's cash reserve of cash equivalent positions (in dollars)

L = Fund's liabilities (in dollars)

MV = Market value of all stocks in the fund's portfolio at the end of the trading day (in dollars)

N = Number of shares issued by the fund

The example shows that Fidelity's Magellan Fund, as quoted for August 26, 1992, will redeem fund shares from investors at $63.97 a share for all redemptions received on August 27.

	NAV	Buy	Bid chng.
Fidelity Invest:			
Magln	63.97	65.95	+ .30

Unlike other markets with current bids and offers, mutual fund prices become effective after the close of the business day. The price goes out of existence until its next computation. When dividends are paid on a given date, as with stocks, the fund's NAV will always drop by the amount of the dividend paid.

❸ **Buy price.** The dollar price per share at which the fund sells shares to investors—the price at which the investor buys shares. The buy price is sometimes listed as the *asked price.* Funds that do not impose a sales charge, or **load,** are called **no-load mutual funds,** and are usually indicated by the letters NL (i.e., no load) for the buy price. No-load funds buy and sell fund shares at the same price. In the following example, shares of Fidelity's Balanced Fund have been bought or sold for $12.76 a share on the previous trading day.

	NAV	Buy	Bid chng.
Fidelity Invest:			
Balance	12.76	NL	+ .03

For funds that impose a sales charge, the buy (or asked) price is always higher than the bid (NAV) price. It does not make economic sense for a fund to be able to redeem shares at a higher price than the investor paid for them if both transactions could have occurred on the same day. The spread between the NAV and the buy price is the load that is charged for purchase.

❹ **Bid change.** The change in the NAV (or bid price) from the previous day.

A format that includes significantly more information is the one used by *The Wall Street Journal,* as shown in Exhibit 8–2. The data are supplied by both the National Association of Securities Dealers and Lipper Analytical Services Inc. This format is as follows:

❶   ❷   ❸   ❹   ❺   ❻   ❼

Fund	Inv. Obj.	NAV	Offer Price	NAV Chg.	-Total Return-			
					YTD	4 wks	1 yr	R

The columns used in the format are now described.

❶ **Fund family.** The family name of each fund is bold-faced, and the names are listed in alphabetical order. Underneath

EXHIBIT 8–1

Mutual Fund Quotations Appearing in the Chicago Tribune *(August 27, 1992).*

Mutual funds

Wednesday, August 26, 1992

```
AAL Mutual:              Cambridge Fds:            Equitable Funds:
  Bond p  10.44 10.96+ .01   CapGrA  13.98 14.79+ .09   BalB !   15.09 15.09+ .04
  CaGr p  14.17 14.88+ .06   CapGrB! 14.01 14.01+ .09   GvScB !  10.28 10.28+ .02
  MuBd p  10.65 11.18+ .01   GvinA   14.33 15.04+ .02   GrinB !  13.83 13.83+ .04
AARP Invst:                  GvinB ! 14.33 14.33+ .02   GrinF p  13.74 14.50+ .04
  CaGr    30.07 NL + .27     GwthB ! 13.65 13.65+ .18   GwthF p  19.19 20.25+ .14
  GiniM   16.09 NL + .03     GwthA   13.65 14.44+ .18   GwthB !  17.12 17.12+ .12
  Gthinc  28.40 NL + .14     CapitolEq 9.92 NL + .03    STWF p    9.02  9.30+ .01
  HQ Bd   16.32 NL + .03     CapitolFI 10.62 NL ......  STWB !    9.04  9.04+ .01
  TxFBd   17.80 NL + .06   Capstone Group:             TxEB !   10.68 10.68+ .01
ABT Funds:                   CshFr   10.21 10.72+ .07   EqStrat  33.81 NL + .16
  Emrg p  10.29 10.80+ .07   Fd SW   16.77 17.61+ .07 Evergreen Funds:
  FL TF   10.85 11.39+ .01   Gvtinc   4.80  4.80......  Evgrn    13.04 NL + .04
  Gthin p 10.02 10.52+ .04   MedRs   17.26 18.12+ .10   Found    11.52 NL + .06
  Utiln p 12.89 13.53+ .04   PBHG     8.99  9.44+ .10   LtdMk    19.62 NL + .06
AHA Funds:                   Trend   13.87 14.56+ .05   MuniF    10.34 NL + .02
  Balan   12.14 NL + .05     Cardnl  12.90 14.10+ .05   Retire   10.86 NL + .02
  Full    10.71 NL ......    CrdnlGv  8.92  9.34......  TotRtn   19.54 NL + .07
  Lim     10.55 NL + .01     CarilCa 12.39 13.04+ .01   ValTm    13.35 NL + .13
AIM Funds:                   CrnOHTE  9.61 10.06− .01   ExcelMld  2.49  2.61− .01
  AdiGv p  9.90 10.21......  Cnt Shs 22.95 NL + .11     ExcHY p   7.52  7.90− .01
  Chart p  8.20  8.68+ .04   ChartBC 11.71 11.74+ .06   FAM Val  17.87 17.87+ .04
  Const p 11.88 12.57+ .13   Chestnt 125.74 NL +1.17    FBL BIC ! 16.31 16.31+ .09
  CvYld p 12.72 13.35+ .08 Citibank IRA-CIT:           FBL Gth ! 12.43 12.43− .03
  HiYld p  5.72  6.01......  Balan f  2.78 NL ......  FFB Lexicon:
  IntlE p  8.95  9.47+ .05   Equit f  2.96 NL ......    CapApp   10.33 NL + .05
  LimMA p 10.23 10.33+ .01   Incom f  2.48 NL ......    FxInc    10.55 NL + .01
  Sumit    9.32 ... + .06    ShtTr f  1.90 NL ......    IntGv    10.42 NL + .01
  TF Int  10.53 10.86......  Clipper 50.12 50.12+ .24   FFB Eq   12.33 12.65+ .10
  Weing p 16.03 16.96+ .13 Colonial Funds:             FFBNJ    10.46 10.95......
AIM Funds C:                 CalTE    7.29  7.65− .01 FMB Funds:
  AgrsvC p 14.29 15.12+ .15  FedSec p 10.88 11.42+ .01  DivEC p  10.92 11.56+ .06
  GoScC p 10.33 10.85+ .02   IntEq p 15.11 16.03− .03   DivE !   10.93 NL + .06
  GrthC p 13.50 14.29+ .12   MI TE    6.83  7.17− .01   IntGC p  10.24 10.61+ .01
  HYldC p  9.54 10.02− .03   MN TE    7.12  7.48......  IntG !   10.24 NL + .01
  IncoC p  8.16  8.57+ .01   NY TE    7.01  7.36......  MITF !   10.20 10.68......
  MuBC p   8.30  8.71+ .03   OhTE     7.22  7.58......  MiTF !   10.20 NL ......
  TeCtC p 10.66 11.19+ .02   Smiln p 12.14 12.88+ .07 FPA Funds:
  UtilC p 13.88 14.69+ .03   US Id p 20.19 21.42+ .09   Capil    14.95 15.99+ .13
  ValuC o 17.66 18.69+ .10   ConTE A  7.32  7.69− .01   Nwinc    10.76 11.27+ .01
```

are listed the various funds that are offered by the family, which are often abbreviated. If only a single fund is listed for a fund family, the fund is not boldfaced. Here are some examples:

	Inv. Obj.	NAV	Offer Price	NAV Chg.	YTD	4 Wks	1 Yr	R
						-Total Return-		
First Omaha:								
Equity	G&I	10.54	NL	+0.03	+6.2	+1.0	NS	. . .
Fxdinc	BND	10.41	NL	−0.03	+7.1	+2.0	NS	. . .

EXHIBIT 8–2

Mutual Fund Quotations from Tuesday's Issue, **The Wall Street Journal.**

Monday, June 21, 1993
Ranges for investment companies, with daily price data supplied by the National Association of Securities Dealers and performance and cost calculations by Lipper Analytical Services Inc. The NASD requires a mutual fund to have at least 1,000 shareholders or net assets of $25 million before being listed. Detailed explanatory notes appear elsewhere on this page.

	Inv. Obj.	NAV	Offer Price	NAV Chg.	— Total Return — YTD	4 wks	1 yr	R
AAL Mutual:								
Bond	BND	10.64	11.17	+0.03	+6.1	+1.4	+11.3	C
CaGr	GRO	14.95	15.70	+0.07	+2.4	−0.5	+10.6	D
MuBd	GLM	11.05	11.60	+0.02	+5.6	+1.0	+11.1	D
AARP Invst:								
CaGr	GRO	32.96	NL	+0.05	+2.7	−2.6	+16.1	C
GiniM	BND	16.09	NL	+0.02	+4.5	+0.9	+9.1	E
GthInc	G&I	31.27	NL	+0.16	+7.0	+0.7	+15.8	B
HQ Bd	BND	16.68	NL	+0.05	+6.6	+1.9	+12.6	B
TxFBd	ISM	18.40	NL	+0.02	+6.9	+1.6	+13.2	A
ABT Funds:								
Emrg	CAP	12.85	13.49	−0.11	+0.5	−3.4	+34.6	A
FL HI	MFL	10.44	10.96	+0.01	+7.2k	+1.6k	NA	..
FL TF	MFL	11.32	11.88	+0.01	+6.6	+1.4	+12.4	D
Gthin	G&I	10.78	11.32	+0.04	+1.5	−1.0	+12.1	D
Utilin	SEC	13.69	14.37	+0.05	+9.4	+2.3	+21.2	C
Acc Mortg	BND	12.36	NL	+0.03	+4.8	+1.1	+8.2	E
Acc Sht Int	BST	12.41	NL	+0.01	+3.7	+0.5	+7.4	C
AHA Funds:								
Balan	S&B	12.60	NL	+0.05	+5.3	+0.1	+13.6	C
Full	BND	10.69	NL	+0.02	+6.9	+1.7	+12.0	C
Lim	BST	10.49	NL	...	+3.1	+0.5	+5.8	C
AIM Funds:								
AdjGv p	BST	9.89	10.20	...	+2.4	+0.3	+5.0	D
Agrsv p	SML	19.56	20.70	−0.06	+5.6	−0.2	+45.7	A
Chart p	G&I	8.81	9.32	+0.05	+3.7	+1.0	+12.7	D
Const p	CAP	15.23	16.12	−0.02	+2.1	−2.2	+34.1	A
CvYld p	S&B	14.80	15.54	+0.08	+5.2	+0.4	+24.7	A
GoSc p	BND	10.32	10.83	+0.02	+4.7	+1.1	+8.6	E
Grth p	GRO	11.63	12.31	+0.02	−5.3	−1.4	+5.6	E
HiYld p	BHI	5.88	6.17	+0.01	+9.6	+2.1	+14.4	E
HYldC p	BHI	9.88	10.37	+0.02	+10.8	+1.9	+17.7	B
Inco p	BND	8.48	8.90	+0.02	+9.5	+2.2	+15.8	A
IntlE p	ITL	10.09	10.68	−0.11	+12.6	−1.6	+8.4	B
LimM p	BST	10.19	10.29	...	+2.3	+0.2	+5.5	D
MuB p	GLM	8.51	8.93	+0.01	+6.0	+1.4	+12.1	C
Sumit	GRO	9.67	NA	+0.06	+0.3	−0.4	+16.7	C
TeCt p	SSM	11.03	11.58	+0.01	+6.4	+1.4	+12.0	C
TF Int	IDM	10.82	11.15	+0.01	+4.4	+0.9	+9.2	D
Util p	SEC	14.23	15.06	+0.08	+9.2	+3.6	+18.4	D
Valu p	G&I	19.33	20.46	+0.07	+6.0	+0.4	+25.9	A
Weirg p	GRO	16.42	17.38	+0.08	−5.3	−0.5	+7.4	E
AMF Funds:								
AdjMtg	BST	10.00	NL		+2.5	+0.4	+4.5	D
IntMtg	BND	9.99	NL	+0.01	+5.5	+1.2	+10.3	D
IntlLiq	BST	10.89	NL	...	+3.5	+0.4	+7.5	C
MtgSc	BND	11.38	NL	+0.01	+3.5	+0.9	+7.5	E
ASM Fd	G&I	9.73	NL	+0.02	+6.9	+1.8	NA	..
ASO Funds:								
Balance	S&B	11.78	12.34	+0.05	+8.4	+0.8	+15.3	B
Bond	BND	11.27	11.80	+0.02	+6.9	+1.2	+12.8	B
Equity	CAP	14.25	14.92	+0.08	+10.2	+0.7	+18.6	C
LtdMat	BST	10.77	11.05	+0.02	+4.3	+0.9	+7.9	B
RegEq	CAP	16.52	17.30	−0.04	+0.9	−0.7	NA	..
Acornin	ITL	12.92	12.92	−0.07	+20.9	+2.2	NS	..
AcornF	SML	63.15	63.15	−0.12	+14.2	+0.4	+39.8	A
AdsnCa p	G&I	22.24	22.93	+0.10	+6.7	+0.6	+20.5	A
AdvCapl Bal	S&B	10.34	NL	+0.02	+0.9	−0.4	NA	..
AdvCapl Ret	BND	10.55	NL	+0.02	+8.7	+2.8	NS	..

Here, two funds are listed for First Omaha (the Equity Fund and the Fixed Income Fund).

On occasion, one or more letter codes may follow the fund's name. The letter codes generally are explained near the beginning of the tables, but two of them deserve special attention here. The letter p following the fund name signifies the fund charges distribution costs, particularly if it is a 12b-1 type fee. The letter r indicates that the fund charges a commission for redemption of its shares, called a **back-end load.** The charges are spelled out in the fund's prospectus.

② **Investment objective.** The fund's investment objective is based on the goals stated in its prospectus. *The Wall Street Journal* uses three-letter abbreviations for 27 different classifications, which are defined by Lipper Analytical Services. These classifications include the following:

Stock funds

CAP	Capital appreciation fund
EQI	Equity fund
G&I	Growth and income fund
GRO	Growth fund
ITL	International (non-US) fund
SEC	Sector fund
SML	Small company growth fund
WOR	World fund

Bond funds

BHI	High-yield fund
BIN	Intermediate and long-term fund
BND	General US taxable fund
BST	Short-term fund
WBD	World fund

Municipal bond funds

STM	Short-term fund
IDM	Intermediate-term fund

GLM   General municipal fund
MCA   California-only municipals
MFL   Florida-only municipals
DMA   Massachusetts-only municipals
DNY   New York-only municipals
MNJ   New Jersey-only municipals
MOH   Ohio-only municipals
MPA   Pennsylvania-only municipals
SSM   All other single-state municipals
HTM   High-yield fund
ISM   Insured, all maturities, all issuers

Combination stock and bond funds

S&B   Blended fund

❸ Net asset value. The NAV is the closing price per share. For all open-end funds, this is the dollar price at which the fund will buy (redeem) shares from investors.

❹ Offer price. The dollar price per share at which the fund sells shares to investors; that is, the price at which the investor buys shares. In some quotations it is listed as the asked price. Funds that do not impose a sales charge, or *load*, are called *no-load mutual funds*, and are usually indicated by the letters NL for the buy price, as shown in the following example:

	Inv. Obj.	NAV	Offer Price	NAV Chg.	-Total Return- YTD	4 wks	1 yr	R
First Omaha:								
Equity	G&I	10.54	NL	+0.03	+6.2	+1.0	NS	. . .
Fxdlnc	BND	10.41	NL	−0.03	+7.1	+2.0	NS	. . .

For funds that impose a load, the offer price (the buy or asked price) is always higher than the bid (the NAV).

❺ Net asset value change. The change in the NAV from the previous day.

6 **Total return statistics.** Depending on the day, *The Wall Street Journal* provides different statistics from those provided by Lipper Analytical Services for the total return of each listed fund, as follows:

Monday   Year to date only
Tuesday   Year to date, 4-week, and 1-year performances
Wednesday   Year to date, 13-week, and 3-year
            performances
Thursday   Year to date, 26-week, and 4-year
            performances
Friday   Year to date, 39-week, and 5-year
            performances

This format indicates that the example given next is the Tuesday edition, as the total return yield statistics include the 4-week and 1-year performance yields. NA means that the yield is not available due to incomplete price, performance, or cost data. NS means that the particular fund did not exist at the start of the performance period.

	Inv. Obj.	NAV	Offer Price	NAV Chg.	-Total Return- YTD	4 wks	1 yr	R
First Omaha:								
Equity	G&I	10.54	NL	+0.03	+6.2	+1.0	NS	...
FxdInc	BND	10.41	NL	−0.03	−7.1	−2.0	NS	...
FPDiv Ast	BND	12.99	13.60	+0.04	+4.9	+1.1	NA	...
FirPrEqt	G&I	10.24	NL	+0.01	−2.5	−1.6	+8.3	E

Here, neither of the First Omaha funds existed at the start of the 1-year performance period, while the 1-year return statistic was not available at press time for the third entry.

7 **Rank.** How the fund ranks in comparison to other funds with the same investment objective. Each day's ranking, provided by Lipper Analytical Services, is based on the longest performance period for that day, as follows:

Monday	No ranking given
Tuesday	1 year
Wednesday	3 years
Thursday	4 years
Friday	5 years

With the exception of the year-to-date statistics, which are based on January 1, performance periods begin either on the closest Thursday or at month-end, for periods greater than one year.

The single-letter codes used for the rankings represent quintiles. An A shows that the fund's performance for the time period ranked in the upper 20 percent of all the funds that had the same investment objective; a B represents the second highest 20 percent (60 to 79 percent); a C represents the third highest 20 percent; a D represents the second lowest 20 percent; and an E represents the bottom 20 percent. The following example indicates that the particular growth and income (G&I) fund, although it had an 8.5 percent total return for the last year, nevertheless ranked in the bottom 20 percent of all the growth and income stocks tracked.

	Inv.		Offer	NAV	-Total Return-			
	Obj.	NAV	Price	Chg.	YTD	4 wks	1 yr	R
FirPrEqt	G&I	10.24	NL	+0.01	−2.5	−1.6	+8.3	E

On Mondays (Exhibit 8–3), the three "total return" columns are changed for each fund. The format is:

❶   ❷

	Inv.		Offer	NAV	%Ret	Max Initl	Total Exp	
	Obj.	NAV	Price	Chg.	YTD	Chrg.	Ratio	R

The columns used in the format are now described.

❶   **Maximum initial charge.** The maximum percentage sales commission (load) that is outlined by the fund's prospectus. For no-load funds, this is zero. The following entry indicates that

EXHIBIT 8–3
Mutual Fund Quotations from Monday's Issue, The Wall Street Journal.

	Inv. Obj.	NAV	Offer Price	NAV Chg.	%Ret YTD	Max Initl Chrg.	Total Exp Ratio	R
GvSc	BND	10.02	10.52	...	+5.8	4.750	1.200	..
HiInc t	BHI	5.29	5.55	+0.01	+10.6	4.750	1.030	..
IncOp	BND	8.12	8.52	+0.01	+6.0	4.750	2.020	..
LtdM r	BST	7.40	7.59	−0.01	+3.4	2.500	NA	..
MuLtd r	STM	7.64	7.84	...	+4.2	2.500	NA	..
Rsrch t	G&I	13.07	13.87	−0.10	+6.3	5.750	0.840	..
Sect	SEC	16.20	17.19	−0.16	−4.9	5.750	1.670	..
Spec t	CAP	10.21	10.83	−0.05	+12.4	5.750	1.530	..
TotRet t	S&B	13.04	13.69	−0.05	+9.4	4.750	0.840	..
Util	SEC	7.39	7.76	−0.01	+12.2	4.750	0.650	..
WldGv	WBD	12.46	13.08	−0.01	+8.3	4.750	1.530	..
WldTot	WOR	10.22	10.73	−0.05	+5.4	4.750	1.840	..
MuBd r	GLM	11.34	11.91	...	+9.6	4.750	0.570	..
MuHy r	HYM	9.31	9.77	...	+5.0	4.750	1.000	..
MuAL t	SSM	10.65	11.18	...	+6.7	4.750	1.080	..
MuAR r	SSM	10.17	10.68	...	+6.8	4.750	0.180	..
MuCA r	MCA	5.82	6.11	...	+6.7	4.750	0.390	..
MuFL	MFL	10.33	10.85	...	+8.3	4.750	0.050	..
MuGA t	SSM	10.87	11.41	...	+6.3	4.750	1.080	..
MuMD t	SSM	11.61	12.19	+0.01	+5.5	4.750	1.140	..
MMA t	DMA	11.61	12.19	...	+5.5	4.750	1.080	..
MuMs r	SSM	9.65	10.13	...	+6.7	4.750	0.000	..
MuNY	DNY	11.09	11.64	...	+6.8	4.750	0.530	..
MuNC t	SSM	12.06	12.66	...	+5.6	4.750	1.070	..
MuSC t	SSM	12.34	12.96	...	+6.1	4.750	1.120	..
MuTN t	SSM	10.64	11.17	...	+5.8	4.750	1.140	..
MuVA t	SSM	11.84	12.43	...	+5.6	4.750	1.080	..
MuWV t	SSM	11.79	12.38	...	+6.0	4.750	1.150	..
MFS Lifetime:								
CapG t	CAP	14.16	14.16	−0.08	−1.1	0.000	2.240	..
EmgG	SML	16.07	16.07	−0.14	+5.4	0.000	2.330	..
Gold t	SEC	6.34	6.34	−0.01	+30.7	0.000	4.090	..
Gmtg	BND	7.07	7.07	...	+5.2	0.000	1.950	..
GvSc t	BND	10.24	10.24	−0.01	+5.5	0.000	2.160	..
HiInc t	BHI	6.26	6.26	...	+12.4	0.000	2.230	..
Intmd	BIN	8.97	8.97	−0.02	+5.0	0.000	2.200	..
MuBd	GLM	8.93	8.93	+0.01	+8.0	0.000	2.030	..
Sect	SEC	14.60	14.60	−0.15	−5.3	0.000	2.370	..
TotRt	S&B	11.04	11.04	−0.03	+6.2	0.000	2.230	..
WldE t	WOR	14.44	14.44	−0.05	+7.0	0.000	2.910	..
MIM Funds:								
BdInc	BND	9.26	9.26	−0.03	−0.3	0.000	2.800	..
StkInc	S&B	10.02	10.02	−0.13	−4.4	0.000	2.600	..
StkGr	GRO	10.55	10.55	−0.11	−5.5	0.000	2.900	..
StkAp	CAP	15.44	15.44	−0.27	+4.0	0.000	2.700	..

the fund is a no-load fund in two places: the offer price is marked by NL, and the maximum initial charge is zero.

	Inv. Obj.	NAV	Offer Price	NAV Chg.	%Ret YTD	Max Initl Chrg.	Total Exp Ratio	R
FirPrEqt	G&I	10.23	NL	−0.11	−2.6	0.000	0.760	. . .

EXHIBIT 8–4
Weekly Mutual Fund Quotations from **Barron's.**

52-Week High	Low	Fund Name	Week's High	Low	Close NAV	Week's Chg.	LATEST DIVIDEND Dividend Inc.+Cap. Gains	Record Date	Payment Date	12 MTH Inco. Divs.	Cap. Gain
		Kent Funds:									
11.84	10.06	ExpEq nx	11.72	11.61	11.67 + .15		.005	6-25-93	7-06-93	.055	....
10.37	9.92	FxdIn nx	10.37	10.34	10.37 + .01		.0425	6-25-93	7-06-93	.34	....
10.91	9.97	IdxEq nx	10.80	10.66	10.66 − .05		.015	6-25-93	7-06-93	.135	....
12.15	9.78	IntlEq n	11.84	11.70	11.70 ...		.01	12-31-92	1-15-93	.01	....
10.04	9.95	LtMat nx	9.97	9.95	9.97 − .01		.035	6-25-93	7-06-93	.2775	....
10.37	10.00	MedTE nx	10.32	10.30	10.31 − .01		.03	6-25-93	7-06-93	.20	....
...	...	MI Mun	...	...	... ...						
11.01	9.96	ValEq pnx	10.92	10.78	10.78 − .07		.0225	6-25-93	7-06-93	.1805	....
		Keystone:									
16.59	15.73	CusB1 tx	16.20	16.16	16.19 − .03		.098	6-25-93	7-06-93	1.176	....
16.93	15.86	CusB2 tx	16.66	16.61	16.66 − .27		.33	6-25-93	7-06-93	1.36	....
5.10	4.52	CusB4 t	5.10	5.05	5.10 + .06		.12	5-25-93	6-04-93	.50	....
10.25	9.44	CusK1 t	10.13	10.05	10.05 − .02		.10	4-23-93	5-06-93	.40	.24
8.36	6.75	CusK2 t	8.31	8.21	8.21 + .01		.03+.40	11-30-92	12-15-92	.03	.40
24.79	22.58	CusS1 tx	24.52	24.21	24.21 − .13		.07	6-25-93	7-06-93	.28	.69
9.84	8.14	CusS3 t	9.58	9.46	9.46 + .01		....+.73	11-30-92	12-15-92	....	.73
7.42	5.19	CusS4 te	7.37	7.33	7.34 − .53		....+.65	6-25-93	7-06-93	....	.69
6.69	5.85	Intl t	6.60	6.56	6.57 − .05		.04	11-30-92	12-15-92	.04	....
23.03	12.45	KPM t	23.03	21.28	23.03 + 1.88		.05	9-30-92	10-15-92	.05	....
11.62	10.96	TxETr t	11.50	11.48	11.50 + .03		.0467	....	6-01-93	.6358	.13
8.43	7.86	TaxFr t	8.36	8.35	8.36 + .02		.0349	....	6-01-93	.4825	.11
		Keystone America:									
10.13	8.62	AuInc fp	9.22	9.13	9.22 + .06		.0448	....	6-01-93	.6693	.12
9.35	8.31	AuSTI fp	8.43	8.36	8.43 ...		.0224	....	6-01-93	.3531	....
9.97	9.75	CAPIF	9.87	9.85	9.87 + .01		.0371	....	6-01-93	.4808	....
10.03	9.80	CPI2B t	9.90	9.88	9.90 + .02		.0309	....	6-01-93	.4077	....
13.44	11.68	EinA	13.11	13.02	13.02 + .01		.06	5-25-93	6-04-93	.24	.53
11.27	10.49	FtxA	11.20	11.18	11.20 + .04		.054	....	6-01-93	.6345	.10
16.15	11.01	GIOA	16.15	15.98	16.09 + .23		....				
10.51	9.98	GvSA x	10.43	10.42	10.43 − .03		.064	6-25-93	7-06-93	.74	.63
27.42	18.45	HrtEGrA	26.33	26.20	26.27 + .73		....	....	....	....	....
24.59	20.34	HrtGrA	23.69	23.31	23.31 − .11		....	....	....	....	....
9.50	9.07	ImdA x	9.47	9.44	9.47 ...		.054	6-25-93	7-06-93	.648	....
17.43	13.87	OmegaA	17.20	17.05	17.05 + .09		....+.15	11-30-92	12-15-92	....	2.23
11.73	10.72	PtxA	11.70	11.68	11.70 + .04		.056	....	6-01-93	.6517	.02
7.89	6.76	StcA x	7.89	7.78	7.89 + .08		.059	6-25-93	7-06-93	.748	....
10.73	10.16	TxFA x	10.56	10.53	10.56 − .01		.051	6-25-93	7-06-93	.614	.27
9.48	8.56	WrldBA x	9.35	9.30	9.32 − .16		.15	6-25-93	7-06-93	1.24	.69
9.95	9.78	KIARF p	9.93	9.90	9.93 + .03		.0401	....	6-01-93	.5283	....
		Kidder Group:									
12.08	12.00	ARM GvA	12.08	12.08	12.08 ...		.0394	....	5-28-93	.2893	....
13.34	11.82	AstAllB	13.15	12.98	12.98 − .05		.015	3-24-93	3-26-93	.094	.002
13.98	12.28	GlbEqA	13.66	13.55	13.59 + .10		....+.241	12-29-92	12-31-92	....	.241
12.82	11.95	GlbFxA	12.72	12.66	12.68 + .03		.0488	....	5-28-93	.3622	....
15.08	14.60	GvtA t	15.00	14.96	15.00 + .03		.073	....	5-28-93	1.024	....
12.73	12.24	IntFIA	12.68	12.66	12.68 + .02		.0588	....	5-28-93	.8001	.093
28.58	26.44	KPE t	27.79	27.63	27.63 + .06		.136	6-08-93	6-10-93	.573	....
13.23	11.42	KBIntEq np	13.12	13.03	13.05 + .05		.02	....	12-29-92	.02	....
18.76	16.87	LMH n	18.56	18.38	18.38 − .08		.37	12-28-92	1-04-93	.37	....

② Total expense ratio. The percentage ratio of the fund's total operating expenses for the fiscal year to the fund's average net assets. These expenses include many asset-based charges such as advisor management fees, 12b-1 fees, and distribution fees. The following quotation indicates that the fund spends 0.76 percent of its average net assets for the year for total operating expenses. As a general rule, the lower the number, the better.

	Inv. Obj.	NAV	Offer Price	NAV Chg.	%Ret YTD	Initl Chrg.	Exp Ratio	R
FirPrEqt	G&I	10.23	NL	−0.11	−2.6	0.000	0.760	...

A third variation in how mutual funds are quoted is illustrated by Exhibit 8–4, which is taken from *Barron's*. As a weekly newspaper, *Barron's* provides additional information that is not often found in other newspaper tables. This additional information includes:

52-week high and low NAV.

Weekly high and low NAV.

Information on the latest dividend—record and payment dates, and the amount of the dividend plus the amount of any capital gains.

Amounts of cash dividends paid and any capital gains distributed during the last 12 months. This information is useful in calculating the fund's total return.

Money Market Funds

Summaries for money market funds are generally printed separately from the quotations for mutual funds. I use the term *summaries*, rather than *quotations*, because the data listed for money market funds are simply statistics, not the actual traded market quotes that are given for stocks, bonds, commodities, foreign exchange, and so forth. Financial papers as well as local newspapers publish summaries for money market funds on a weekly basis. Local papers that have Sunday editions, usually print money market fund summaries on Sundays. *The Wall Street Journal* (Exhibit 8–5) usually

EXHIBIT 8–5
Money Market Quotations from The Wall Street Journal.

MONEY MARKET MUTUAL FUNDS

The following quotations, collected by the National Association of Securities Dealers Inc., represent the average of annualized yields and dollar-weighted portfolio maturities ending Wednesday, June 23, 1993. Yields don't include capital gains or losses.

Fund	Avg. Mat.	7Day Yld.	Assets
AALMny	72	1.99	82
AARP HQ	48	2.11	260
AIMCsh	58	2.33	60
AIM MM	60	2.19	117
AIMMMC	63	2.42	77
ASO Pr	60	2.52	479
ASO US	42	2.50	315
AccUSGov	45	2.65	27
ActAsGv	73	2.48	516
ActAsMny	68	2.64	3650
Aetna MM	54	3.34	69
AlexBwn	49	2.53	1246
AlxBTr	49	2.46	654
AlgerMM	74	2.91	125
AllaCpRs	75	2.34	2147
AliaGvR	66	2.24	1827
AlliMny	74	2.35	1634
AmAAdTr	43	3.02	115
AmAAdMM	60	3.16	2613
AmCRes	58	2.04	281
AmExDDiv	83	2.66	16441
AmExGv	84	2.62	3676
AmPerCsh	72	2.66	176
AmPerTrs	52	2.45	163
AmbMMF	42	2.63	314
AmbTreas	67	2.55	307
AmbMMI	42	2.63	266
Amcore Gv	68	2.67	94
ArchUSTr	52	2.35	1
ArchFd	52	2.42	45
AMF St Lq	14	2.71	147
AutCsh	58	2.74	1014
AutGvt	49	2.63	3464
AuGvSvc	54	2.70	407
AutTreasC	47	2.45	278
BB&T UST Tr	54	2.68	77
BT InstCash	39	3.02	1570
BT Inst Trsy	43	2.86	176

Fund	Avg. Mat.	7Day Yld.	Assets
GrtHallPr	73	2.48	871
GrdCsFd	23	2.58	286
GrdCsMg	24	2.12	36
HTInsgtCs	36	2.63	296
HTInsgtGv	37	2.51	263
HanvCsh	77	2.66	738
HanvGov	72	2.56	428
HanvUSTr	50	2.42	1066
HanvTreas	67	2.46	511
Harbor	68	2.64	48
HelmsTresOnA	73	2.99	61
HrtgCsh	23	2.36	930
HIMrkDv	66	2.47	351
HIMrkUS	57	2.46	119
HIMrkUST	70	2.39	221
HIIrdGovt	50	2.43	229
HmestdDiv	61	2.64	23
HorznPr	55	3.16	15989
HorznTr	48	2.91	2623
Hummer	41	2.41	155
IAATrMM	31	2.04	32
IAIMnyMktFd	58	2.73	33
IDS CshM	49	2.24	1002
IDS PLA	35	2.21	67
IMGLiq	49	2.44	122
IndCaGv	35	2.21	271
IndCaMM	46	2.27	300
IndOnPr	47	2.51	345
IndOnUS	48	2.52	199
InfnAlGv	67	2.84	52
InfnCCR Inst	81	3.14	237
InfCCR	81	2.39	334
InstFdGFd	67	3.04	1456
InstFdGFdT	55	3.01	345
InstFdGTCs	70	3.09	1121
InstFdGTFd	50	2.99	1346
InstFdGTmp	66	3.05	7687
InstFdGTrs	57	2.92	1479

Fund	Avg. Mat.	7Day Yld.	Assets
ReserveFd	47	2.27	1391
RetirGv	46	1.51	44
RetireInvTr	57	2.48	29
RimcoTrs	39	2.54	83
RIMCOPrm	75	3.20	254
RiverUSGv	18	2.75	105
RiversdeCap	57	2.51	146
RdSqMM	58	2.80	724
RdSqUS	53	2.79	380
RshFGI	41	2.24	656
Rshmre	32	2.37	58
SBSF MM	73	2.50	14
SEICshTrea	46	2.90	48
SEI CsPrB	59	2.70	2
SEI CsFd	56	2.60	25
SEI CshGvII	53	2.92	613
SEI CsMM	57	2.90	228
SEI CsPr	59	3.00	2033
SEI LqGv	50	2.74	494
SEI LqPr	63	2.77	1219
SEI LqTr	49	2.73	2346
SEI CsTrIIA	57	2.80	377
SEI CsTrIIB	57	2.50	8
STIPrQuTr	60	2.70	443
STIUSGvTr	61	2.57	447
Safeco f	46	2.38	131
SalomonUST	66	2.78	42
SchbValAdv	76	2.89	514
SchwbGv	75	2.60	1699
SchbMM	74	2.55	7194
Schb UST	80	2.47	243
ScudCshin	55	2.48	1135
Scud UST	72	2.49	308
SecurityCsh	68	2.28	38
SelectGv	4	2.48	7
SelectIn	15	2.62	48
SeligCsh Gvt	38	2.18	17
SeligCshPrA	36	2.39	176
SentinelUST	59	2.15	69
SevnSea f	61	3.03	3350
SvnSeaGv	61	2.88	135
ShmtPrTr	47	2.63	228
SLB MMP	29	1.53	183

Fund	Avg. Mat.	7Day Yld.	Assets
FMPACsh	53	1.46	22
FN Netwk	59	1.58	35
FMMASv	44	1.52	99
FMPASvc	53	1.86	338
FMMNIn	66	2.15	172
FMCTSvc	51	1.63	125
FdOHMuII	70	1.79	133
FedTxF c	48	1.78	1433
FldCapRsMu	52	1.52	111
FldInTxEx	43	2.10	2245
FldCA	41	1.67	509
FldCT	32	1.57	289
FldDlyTE	42	1.74	467
FldMA	37	1.32	552
FldMI	60	1.63	166
FldNJ	59	1.51	347
FldNY	60	1.59	551
FldOH	56	1.77	241
FldSpCA	39	2.21	905
FldSpCT	31	1.91	139
FldSpNJ	58	1.74	324
FldSpNY	60	1.74	444
FldSpPA	61	1.90	217
FldTxEx	48	1.86	2793
FldSpFL	34	2.21	211
FldSpMA	35	1.62	343
FldSpMu	59	2.13	1704
FInclTxFr	45	1.68	65
FtInvTax	31	1.47	22
FtPraTE	49	1.65	186
FrkCal	17	1.61	662
FrkNYTE	27	1.31	50
FrkTx c	29	1.69	164
Free CA	31	1.64	78
FreeTE	47	1.50	262
FtBostInTE	56	2.32	23
FirstUnTFI	34	1.79	252
FirstUnTFT	34	2.00	59
FundmentTF	41	.96	6
Gab OC TE	24	1.78	106
GalxyTE	60	1.64	227
GnTxEx	85	1.79	361
GnCalMu	21	2.07	609
GnNYMu	60	1.54	570

publishes money market summaries on Thursdays, using the data supplied by the NASD for the week ending each Wednesday.

The general format is as follows:

① ② ③ ④

Fund	Mat.	7 Day yld.	Assets

The columns used in the format are now described.

❶ Fund. The name of the fund. The funds are listed in alphabetical order, and the names are usually abbreviated.

❷ Maturity. The average number of days until maturity of the fund's portfolio. Although not always indicative of the future direction of interest rates, a higher-than-average maturity generally reflects the fund manager's view of interest rate movements. A higher-than-average maturity may be indicative of a decline in interest rates, so that the fund manager wanted to lock in rates for a longer-than-average term. Conversely, a short maturity may be indicative of interest rates that may rise soon, so that the fund manager wishes to be able to roll over significant portions of the portfolio quickly.

In the following example, the average maturity for Aetna Money Market Fund's portfolio for the week was 54 days. This would have to be compared with other funds, to determine its meaning in terms of the market as a whole.

Fund	Mat.	7 Day yld.	Assets
Aetna MM	54	3.34	69

❸ 7-day yield. The percentage yield for the previous 7 days. This figure does not take into account any management fees or other costs. Virtually all money market funds are no-load, but management fees are deducted. Although the stated rate is for the previous week, the inference is that if the stated rate remained the same for a year, the accrued interest would equal that percentage of the total funds invested.

❹ Assets. The total of the fund's assets (in millions of dollars). In many local newspapers, this figure is omitted. In the following example, the 69 means that the fund had $69 million in assets.

EXHIBIT 8–6
Money Market Quotations from **Barron's.**

Money Market Fund	Assets (Mil $)	Days Average Maturity	7-day Average Yield(%)	30-day Average Yield(%)	7-day Compound Yield(%)
TAXABLE MONEY FUNDS					
AAL Money Market Fund kr	81.5	71	1.97	2.02	1.99
AARP High Quality Money Fund r	258.7	45	2.12	2.12	2.14
ACM Instit Res/Government Port k	86.3	54	3.05	3.06	3.10
ACM Instit Res/Prime Port k	87.5	63	3.18	3.14	3.23
AMCORE Vintage US Govt Obligs k	92.5	66	2.68	2.67	2.72
ASO Outlook Group Prime MMF	483.8	54	2.53	2.51	2.56
ASO Outlook Group Treas MMF	335.0	43	2.50	2.50	2.53
Aetna Money Market Fund k	70.4	54	3.34	3.34	3.40
Alex Brown Cash Res/Prime Series k	1247.4	49	2.53	2.54	2.56
Alex Brown Cash Res/Treas Series k	646.0	48	2.47	2.46	2.50
Alex Brown/Instit Prime Series	26.0	49	2.85	2.86	2.89
Alex Brown/Instit Treas Series k	79.3	48	2.76	2.74	2.80
Alger Money Market Portfolio k	124.8	71	2.91	2.90	2.95
Alliance Capital Reserves	2129.4	73	2.36	2.34	2.39
Alliance Government Reserves	1802.2	69	2.24	2.26	2.26
Alliance Money Reserves	1631.2	74	2.36	2.35	2.39
Ambassador MMF/Fiduciary k	313.4	41	2.63	2.63	2.66
Ambassador MMF/Investor k	257.0	41	2.63	2.63	2.66
Ambassador US Treas/Fiduciary k	306.0	63	2.55	2.55	2.58
American AAdvantage MMF/Instit Cl	2656.2	58	3.17	3.19	3.22
American AAdvantage MMF/Mileage Cl	20.8	58	2.92	2.94	2.96
American AAdvantage US Treas MMF	105.0	26	2.96	3.00	3.00
American Capital Reserve Fund	254.0	60	2.04	2.02	2.06
American Express Daily Dividend	16348.9	81	2.67	2.65	2.71
American Express Govt & Agencies	3647.4	81	2.63	2.63	2.66
American Performance Cash Mgt k	194.0	60	2.63	2.66	2.66
American Performance US Treasury k	170.2	34	2.46	2.45	2.49
Arch MM/Investor Shares k	46.1	66	2.44	2.42	2.47
Arch MM/Trust Shares kr	592.1	66	2.67	2.65	2.71
Arch Treasury MMP/Investor Shares k	1.3	48	2.36	2.34	2.39
Arch Treasury MMP/Trust Shares kr	183.1	48	2.60	2.58	2.63

Fund	Mat.	7 Day yld.	Assets
Aetna MM	54	3.34	69

Money market summaries appearing in *Barron's* (Exhibit 8–6) are supplied by *Donoghue's Money Fund Report. Barron's,* unlike other publications, gives separate listings for general and tax-free money market funds. For both types, the general format is as follows:

Money Market Fund	Assets (Mil $)	Days Average Maturity	7-day Average Yield (%)	30-day Average Yield (%)	7-day Compound Yield (%)
Fidelity Cash Reserves	10021.6	88	3.33	3.44	3.38

The major differences between *Barron's* format and the format provided by NASD is that, in addition to the 7-day yield, two other yields are quoted in *Barron's:* a *30-day yield*, which represents a long-term measure of return on investment, and a *7-day compound yield*. The latter yield, sometimes called the *effective 7-day yield*, is the yield obtained after reinvesting and compounding interest earned. Of the two 7-day figures, the compound yield is the more meaningful.

Closed-End Funds

Closed-end funds are generally quoted weekly, and by only a few papers. For example, every Monday *The Wall Street Journal* lists quotations for closed-end funds separately from its larger list of open-end funds, as is illustrated in Exhibit 8–7. The funds are divided as to type: general equity, specialized equity, world, dual-purpose, convertible securities, bond, loan participation, world income, national municipal bond, and single-state municipal bond funds. The shares of closed-end funds, like stock shares, are traded either on an exchange or over the counter.

The format used in *The Wall Street Journal* is as follows:

①	②	③	④	⑤	⑥

Fund Name	Stock Exch.	NAV	Market Price	Prem/Disc	52-week Market Return
Adams Express	N	20.40	20³/₄	+1.7	20.1
Engex	A	12.16	9⁵/₈	−20.8	13.2
Z-Seven	O	15.68	16³/₄	+3.6	−14.5

EXHIBIT 8–7

***Closed-End Fund Quotations from* The Wall Street Journal.**

CLOSED END FUNDS

Friday, June 18, 1993

Unaudited Net Asset Values (NAV) of closed end funds, reported by the companies as of Friday's close. Each quote includes the closing stock exchange price or dealer-to-dealer asked price of each fund's shares, with the percentage of difference. For equity funds, the final column shows the 52-week percentage change in stock market price plus dividends. For bond funds, the final column shows dividends paid from income in the last 12 months, as of the prior month-end, as a percentage of the stock market price. The figure doesn't include capital gains distributions. N-New York Stock Exchange. O-Over-the-Counter. A-American. M-Midwest.

Fund Name	Stock Exch	NAV	Market Price	Prem /Disc	52 week Market Return
General Equity Funds					
Adams Express	N	20.40	20¾	+ 1.7	20.1
Baker Fentress	N	21.51	18	−16.3	8.5
Bergstrom Capital	A	87.41	96	+ 9.8	−6.2
Blue Chip Value	N	7.87	8¼	+ 4.8	12.8
Central Securities	A	15.73	14⅞	− 5.4	59.3
Charles Allmon Tr	N	10.49	10	− 4.7	7.0
Engex	A	12.16	9⅝	−20.8	13.2
Gabelli Equity Tr	N	11.13	10¾	− 3.4	16.1
General American	N	25.05	23⅞	− 4.7	−0.6
Inefficient Mkt	A	11.27	9½	−15.7	1.9
Jundt Growth	N	14.69	14⅛	− 3.8	6.7
Liberty All-Star	N	10.32	10⅞	+ 5.4	16.2
Morgan Gren Sm Cap	N	11.69	10¾	− 8.0	5.2
NAIC Growth	O	N/A	9½	N/A	−0.7
Royce Value Trust	N	13.31	13	− 2.3	22.8
Salomon SBF	N	15.36	13⅜	−12.9	6.6
Source Capital	N	41.78	48⅜	+15.8	13.0
Spectra	O	18.59	16½	−11.2	25.5
Tri-Continental	N	a27.67	24¾	−10.6	0.4
Z-Seven	O	15.68	16¼	+ 3.6	−14.5
Zweig	N	11.26	12⅞	+14.3	12.6
Specialized Equity Funds					
ASA Limited	N	cv47.60	44⅝	− 6.3	5.4
Alliance Glob Env	N	10.80	9⅝	−10.9	−7.2
Anchor Gold & Curr	M	5.77	5¾	− 0.3	29.6
BGR Prec Metals	T	cy12.46	11⅜	− 8.7	68.5
C&S Realty Income	A	8.75	9⅛	+ 4.3	28.6
Central Fd Canada	A	c4.52	4 15/16	+ 9.2	25.6
Counsellors Tandem	N	17.25	15¼	−11.6	24.3
Delaware Gr Div	N	14.15	13⅞	− 1.9	N/A
Dover Regional Fin	O	7.64	6½	−14.9	52.9
Duff Phelps Ut Inc	N	10.07	10½	+ 4.3	12.8
Emerging Mkts Tel	N	15.70	14¾	− 6.1	−0.8
First Financial	N	15.83	14¼	−10.0	57.0
Global Health Sci	N	11.31	10	−11.6	−12.4
H&Q Healthcare Inv	N	17.41	17⅞	+ 2.7	−6.4
H&Q Life Sci Inv	N	12.59	11⅞	− 5.7	−20.8
Patriot Global Dvd	N	14.85	14½	− 2.4	N/A
Patriot Pre Dvd II	N	13.12	12¼	− 6.6	19.6
Patriot Prem Divd	N	10.76	10½	− 2.4	21.6
Patriot Select Dvd	N	17.06	18⅜	+ 7.7	19.6
Petroleum & Res	N	31.48	28⅜	− 9.9	12.0
Pilgrim Reg Bk Shs	N	a12.23	11⅜	− 7.0	12.2
Preferred Inc Mgt	N	a14.06	14⅜	+ 2.2	N/A
Preferred Inc Opp	N	a12.98	13⅝	+ 5.0	18.3

Fund Name	Stock Exch	NAV	Market Price	Prem /Disc	12 Mo Yield 5/28/93
Amer Adj Rate '97	N	c9.61	9⅝	+ 0.2	6.9
Amer Adj Rate '98	N	c9.66	9⅝	− 0.4	7.1
Amer Adj Rate '99	N	c9.59	9⅝	+ 0.4	N/A
Amer Govt Income	N	c8.76	9⅜	+ 7.0	8.7
Amer Govt Port	N	c11.08	11¾	+ 6.0	9.4
Amer Govt Term Tr	N	c9.68	10⅛	+ 4.6	8.6
Amer Oppty Income	N	c10.85	11⅝	+ 7.1	9.5
Amer Str Income	N	c15.52	16¼	+ 4.7	8.3
Amer Strat Inc II	N	c14.65	15⅝	+ 6.7	N/A
Amer Strat Inc III	N	c14.22	15⅛	+ 6.4	N/A
American Cap Bond	N	ab20.86	20½	− 1.7	8.0
American Cap Inc	N	a8.11	8⅛	+ 0.2	10.3
BlckRk 1998 Term	N	c10.27	9⅞	− 3.8	7.6
BlckRk 1999 Term	N	c9.56	9⅞	+ 3.3	N/A
BlckRk 2001 Term	N	c9.58	9½	− 0.8	N/A
BlckRk Adv Term	N	c10.68	10¼	− 4.0	8.3
BlckRk Income Tr	N	c8.91	9⅛	+ 2.4	9.8
BlckRk Inv Qual Tm	N	c9.79	9¾	− 0.4	8.2
BlckRk Strat Term	N	c9.71	9¾	+ 0.4	8.7
BlckRk Target Term	N	c10.64	10¼	− 3.7	8.1
Bunker Hill Income	N	16.70	16	− 4.2	8.6
CIGNA High Income	N	7.55	8⅝	+14.2	11.5
CIM High Yld Secs	N	8.12	8¼	+ 1.6	9.4
CNA Income Shares	N	c10.97	11⅞	+ 8.2	9.5
Circle Income	O	c12.25	11½	− 6.1	7.9
Colonial Int High	N	6.78	7	+ 3.2	10.6
Colonial Intrmkt I	N	11.86	11⅝	− 2.0	9.2
Current Inc Shares	N	13.99	13⅝	− 2.6	7.6
Dean Witter Govt	N	9.60	8⅞	− 7.6	7.8
Dreyfus Str Govt	N	10.95	11¼	+ 2.7	7.9
Duff&PhelpsUtilCor	N	14.72	14⅝	− 0.6	N/A
Excelsior Income	N	c19.43	17⅞	− 8.0	7.2
First Boston Inc	N	8.92	9¼	+ 3.7	9.7
First Boston Strat	N	10.33	10⅜	+ 0.4	10.2
Fortis Securities	N	10.15	11⅛	+ 9.6	9.2
Franklin Multi-Inc	N	c11.21	10¾	− 4.1	8.9
Franklin Princ Mat	N	cN/A	7⅞	N/A	7.4
Franklin Univ Tr	N	cN/A	9¼	N/A	8.0
Ft Dearborn Income	N	17.08	17⅛	+ 0.3	7.3
Hatteras Income	N	a16.63	18¼	+ 9.7	8.0
High Inc Adv III	N	7.08	7	− 1.1	12.7
High Income Adv II	N	6.51	6⅜	− 2.1	14.0
High Income Adv Tr	N	5.88	6¼	+ 6.3	13.4
High Yield Income	N	a7.70	8¼	+ 7.1	10.8
High Yield Plus	N	8.78	9	+ 2.5	9.6
Hyperion 1997 Tm	N	c9.05	9½	+ 5.0	N/A
Hyperion 1999 Tm	N	c8.08	8⅜	+ 3.7	N/A
Hyperion 2002 Tm	N	c9.01	9¼	+ 2.7	N/A
Hyperion 2005 Inv	N	c9.43	9⅛	− 3.2	N/A
Hyperion Total Rtn	N	c10.70	11	+ 2.8	11.5
INA Investments	N	19.60	17⅞	− 8.8	7.7
Inc Opp 1999	N	a9.47	9¼	− 2.3	N/A
Inc Opp 2000	N	a10.02	9½	− 5.2	N/A
Independence Sq	O	18.60	18⅜	− 1.2	8.1
InterCap Income	N	18.80	20½	+ 9.0	8.6
J Hancock Income	N	17.25	17⅝	+ 2.2	8.0
J Hancock Invest	N	22.87	23¾	+ 3.8	8.0
Kemper High Inc Tr	N	9.13	9¾	+ 6.8	9.9

The columns used in the format are now described.

❶ Fund name.   The name of the fund. Funds are listed in alphabetical order.

❷ Stock exchange.   The exchange on which the fund's shares are traded. As previously mentioned, closed-end funds are frequently referred to as *publicly traded funds*. The letter codes used for the exchanges are: N for the NYSE, A for AMEX, O for the OTC market, and M for the Midwest Stock Exchange.[2]

❸ Net asset value.   The NAV in dollars is the value obtained by dividing the fund's net assets by the total number of shares issued. With closed-end funds, unlike open-end funds, the NAV is not the fund's per share market price.

❹ Market price.   The fund's closing per share price, as traded on the exchange or from dealer-to-dealer asked prices. As in conventional stock tables, the market price is quoted in whole dollars and eighths. It is often compared to the fund's NAV.

❺ Percent premium or discount.   The percent difference between the NAV and the market price. If the percent difference is positive, the stock price is higher than the NAV and is trading at a premium; if the stock market price is lower than the NAV, the percent difference is negative and trades at a discount. As with the premium and discount terminology used for bonds, the NAV of a closed-end fund is considered the par value. In the following quotation, the Engex fund is trading at a discount ($9^5/8$), relative to the NAV of 12.16 by 20.8 percent.

---

[2] In 1993, the Midwest Stock Exchange became the Chicago Stock Exchange and *The Wall Street Journal* now uses the letter C. In addition, those fund shares traded on the Toronto Stock Exchange are now added and symbolized by the letter T.

Fund Name	Stock Exch.	NAV	Market Price	Prem/Disc	52-Week Market Return
Engex	A	12.16	$9^5/_8$	−20.8	13.2

The percent premium or discount is determined by using the following equation:

$$\% \text{ Premium (discount)} = \frac{MP - NAV}{NAV} \cdot 100 \qquad (8\text{--}2)$$

where:

    MP = Fund market price per share (in dollars)

    NAV = Fund net asset value (in dollars)

❻ 52-week market return. For equity funds, this is the 52-week percentage change in the stock's market price plus dividends. For bond funds, the last column heading is changed to "12-Month Yield," and it represents the yield of the dividends paid as of the end of the previous month (not including capital gains distributions), as a percentage of the stock market price.

Example: Calculating a Fund's Percentage Premium (or Discount)

For the first example listed on page 184, the Adams Express fund has a net asset value of 20.40 and a closing market price as traded on the NYSE of $20^3/_4$. Because the stock's market price is higher than the NAV the percent premium is calculated as follows (Equation 8–2):

$$\% \text{ Premium} = \frac{20.75 - 20.40}{20.40} \cdot 100$$

$$= 1.72\%$$

This answer agrees with the quoted value when rounded to one decimal place.

CALCULATING THE FUND'S TOTAL RETURN

Over a given time period, the total return on a single share for the investment in a given mutual fund can be determined from Equation 8–3, which is as follows:

$$\% \text{ Total return} = \frac{(NAV_2 - NAV_1) + D + CG}{NAV_1} \cdot 100 \qquad (8\text{–}3)$$

where:

CG = Capital gains paid (in dollars)

D = Dividends paid (in dollars)

NAV_1 = Net asset value at some initial time period, or at purchase (in dollars)

NAV_2 = Net asset value 1 year later (in dollars)

Example: Determining a Mutual Fund's Total Return

Suppose that, as of December 31, the shares in a given mutual fund had a net asset value of $10.28, and 1 year later, the NAV was $9.93. Also, during this period, a total of $1.91 per share was realized in capital gains, and $0.16 was paid in the form of dividends from net investment income. Over this period, the fund's net return is calculated as follows (Equation 8–3):

$$\% \text{ Total return} = \frac{(\$9.93 - \$10.28) + \$0.16 + \$1.91}{\$10.28} \cdot 100$$

$$= 16.7\%$$

Just as there may be capital gains, a fund may experience a capital loss. When a capital loss occurs, the total return can be a negative value.

USING MORNINGSTAR REPORTS

Just as Standard & Poor's and Value Line publish analyses of stocks, several companies publish analyses of mutual finds. Chicago-based Morningstar Inc.[3] publishes *Morningstar Mutual Funds* every 2 weeks, providing detailed analyses of approximately 1,240 open-end mutual funds. Its companion, *Morningstar Closed-End Funds*, covers approximately 280 closed-end funds.

Exhibit 8–8 illustrates the single-page report format used in *Morningstar Mutual Funds*. At the top of each page, the official name of the fund is listed. This is followed by several major pieces of information for the most recent quarter, highlighting the fund's investment objective, percent maximum load, percent yield, assets (in millions of dollars), and net asset value. It should be pointed

---

[3] Morningstar Inc., 53 West Jackson Blvd., Chicago, IL 60604.

EXHIBIT 8–8

Mutual Fund Report for the Putnam Fund for Growth & Income from Morningstar Mutual Funds.

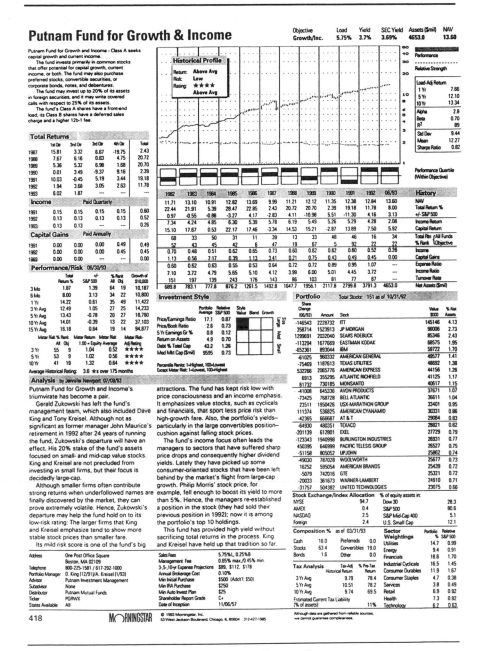

Reprinted by permission of Morningstar, Inc., Chicago, IL.

out that the percent yield here is not the same as the percent total return. Morningstar calculates percent yield as dividing the income for the last 12 months by the NAV. In contrast, the total return is based on the change in the NAV plus dividends and capital gains distributions, divided by the NAV (Equation 8–3).

The remainder of the analysis for each fund can be divided into the following areas:

Investment criteria.   A description of the fund's primary investment objective and policies as stated in its prospectus. Events such as a change in investment advisor, objective, or fund name are also mentioned here.

Quarterly total return, income, capital gains, and performance risk statistics.   The fund's total return is tabulated by quarter and by year, for the current year and the last 5 years. The same is true for dividends paid (income) and capital gains distributions, except that only the previous 2 years are included with the current year.

Performance risk for various time periods is based on several measurements, which are to be described.

Percent total return.   The percent total return is calculated by Equation 8–3.

Spread.   The second measure is the **spread** between the fund's total return and the return achieved by a given market index. The indexes used for equities and for bonds are as follows:

Equities   S&P 500 Stock Index
            Morgan Stanley Europe, Australia, Far East Index
            (EAFE)
            Wilshire 4500
Bonds   Lehman Brothers Government/Corporate Bond
            Index

A positive number is taken to mean that the fund outperformed the particular index by a given percentage. For the Putnam Fund for Growth & Income, the risk for a 3-year period relative to the S&P 500 is 1.05 percent. The fund's total return of 12.49 percent outperformed the S&P 500 by 1.05 percent. The total return for the S&P 500 was 12.49 − 1.05, or 11.44 percent.

Percentile rankings also indicate how a given fund ranks (1) in relation to all funds tracked by Morningstar and (2) in relation to all funds with the same objective. Here, a 1 is taken to represent the highest, or best, percentile, while 100 is the lowest, or worst. The Putnam Fund for Growth & Income ranked in the top 27 percent of all funds tracked by Morningstar for the 3-year period, and ranked in the top 25 percent of growth and income funds only.

The method of risk calculation involves using the current rate on 3-month (90-day) T-bills for comparison, because an investor can expect no risk from a T-bill. By definition, returns of a fund less than that of a T-bill are viewed as negative; returns greater than T-bills are positive.

For each month the return on the T-bill is subtracted. Only the negative returns are then added up by the number of months in the rating period (not the number of months with negative returns) to arrive at the average monthly loss. The following table gives an example for a given 6-month rating period.

Month	Fund Return	T-Bill Return	Difference
1	2.30	1.00	+1.30
2	−1.45	1.05	−2.50 (Negative)
3	4.35	1.10	+3.25
4	6.00	1.05	+4.95
5	−3.00	1.00	−4.00 (Negative)
6	−0.50	1.10	−1.60 (Negative)

$$\text{Average monthly loss} = \frac{\text{Total of 3 negative returns}}{\text{Months in rating period}}$$

$$= \frac{-8.10}{6}$$

$$= -1.35$$

The average monthly loss is then compared to the losses of all equity (or bond) funds, depending on the fund's objective. A group average is computed and set equal to 1.00. The relative number expresses in percentage points how risky the fund is relative to the average fund (1.00). For the Putnam Fund for Growth & Income report shown in Exhibit 8–8, the risk for a 3-year period is 0.52, meaning that this fund is 52 percent less risky than the average equity fund over this period. The smaller the number, the lower the risk.

The final four measures are based on a least-squares regression of the fund's excess total returns (for a 36-month period) with the same market index used earlier.

Alpha (α). A fund's risk-adjusted performance is measured by **Alpha (α)**. Alpha represents the difference between a fund's actual returns and expected performance, given its level of risk as measured by *beta (β)*. Alpha is expressed as an annualized percentage and is calculated from the following equation:

$$\alpha = AR - \beta \cdot (IR - TBR) - TBR \qquad (8\text{--}4)$$

where:

β = Fund's beta coefficient

AR = Fund's actual percentage return

IR = Index's percentage return

TBR = T-bill's percentage return

A positive value is indicative of performance better than expected; a negative value indicates underperformance.

Example: Calculation of a Fund's Alpha (α)

Assume that T-bills returned 7 percent, the S&P's 500 stock index returned 12 percent, and a fund's beta (β) was 1.2 for a given time period. During this period the fund actually returned 15 percent. The excess market return was 12 − 7, or 5 percent, while the expected return of the fund was (5 percent × 1.2) + 7 percent, or 13 percent. The fund's alpha was calculated as follows (Equation 8–3):

$$\alpha = 15\% - (1.2) \cdot (12\% - 7\%)$$

$$= 2\%$$

This means that the fund performed 2 percent better than expected, considering its beta coefficient.

Beta (β). As with stocks, beta measures the responsiveness of a fund to a given market index, and indicates the fund's volatility. In terms of the least-squares regression coefficients, it is equivalent to the slope of the line. By definition, the beta of the comparison market, such as the S&P's 500, is 1.00. In contrast, if a fund has a beta of 1.2, this means that the fund is expected to perform 20 percent better than the market when the market is up and 20 percent worse than the market when it is down. As with stocks, betas of less than 1.00 are usually preferred.

R-squared (r^2). A fund's percentage movements that result from movements in the index are measured by R-squared (r^2). In terms of a least-squares regression, this is the square of the correlation coefficient. Expressed as a percentage, R-squared values can range from 0 to 100. Index funds will have R-squared values close to 100, as they correlate highly with the index it mirrors.

Standard deviation (SD or σ).   The risk or volatility of a fund's total return is measured by the standard deviation (SD or σ). Unlike α, β, and r^2, which rely on a fund's performance in relation to a particular market index, the SD is fund-specific. It measures the volatility of short-term fluctuations, no matter what the cause, from the historical average return on the fund. Information about SDs can be used to compare the relative risk of different securities. For mutual funds, this is often expressed as a percentage of the fund's historical mean value. For example, at the end of 1992, Vanguard's Windsor Fund (a growth and income fund) had an SD of 16.5 percent, while the Linder Dividend Fund (a balanced fund) had an SD of 6.6 percent. Since the Windsor Fund had the higher SD, it also had the greater degree of risk.

Analyst's evaluation.   In this section the analyst (whose name is given along with the date this analysis was made) gives an opinion on the economic state of the fund. The purpose of the analysis is to interpret and enhance the numerical data appearing in the report.

Historical perspective.   The historical perspective includes two graphs. The top is a line graph showing the fund's performance over the previous 12 years or starting with the fund's inception year, if less than 12 years. The vertical axis, which uses a logarithmic scale, represents the fund's net asset value, adjusted for all income and capital gains distributions. The logarithmic scale is used so that identical percentage changes in the NAV will occupy the same vertical distance on the graph.

The bottom line represents the fund's relative strength. Its purpose is to demonstrate the performance of the particular fund relative to the market as a whole. Its value is simply the ratio of the fund's NAV relative to that of another series, usually a broad market index such as the S&P 500. A rising relative strength denotes that the fund in question is performing better than the market, while a declining line indicates that the fund is being outperformed by the general market.

A bar graph illustrates the historical fluctuations of the fund's net assets.

Ratings box. The ratings box provides three pieces of information, as follows:

1. *Return.* An overall assessment of a fund's historical total returns (low, below average, above average, or high). The return is relative to other funds in the same class.
2. *Risk.* Morningstar's overall assessment of a fund's risk level relative to others in its class.
3. *Rating.* A fund's historical risk-adjusted return relative to others in its class. Funds are ranked in one of five categories: highest, above average, neutral, below average, and lowest. This rating serves as one of the first parameters for evaluation.

Operations data. This section contains information concerning the fund's operations. The data given include: the addresses and phone numbers of the fund, the fund advisor, the distributor, and the portfolio manager (with the year he or she began managing the fund); the number of shareholders; management fees and other fees; minimum initial purchase and minimum subsequent purchases; the date of inception; the NASDAQ ticker symbol; phone switch privileges; and a shareholder report rating. The latter is Morningstar's evaluation of the quality of the report sent by a fund to its shareholders on a scale from F to A+ (the highest rating). Morningstar reserves the special honor of an F rating for reports that are strongly misleading or plainly dishonest.

Style box. The style box is designed to enable the investor to make an accurate determination of a fund's investment objectives. It is divided into nine squares, with different axes for equity funds and bond funds (Exhibit 8–9). For equity (or stock) funds, the style box utilizes market capitalization to show the size of companies in which the fund invests according to the group definitions used on the vertical axis, as follows:

Small (S)   Less than $1 billion
Medium (M) $1 billion to $5 billion
Large (L)   More than $5 billion

EXHIBIT 8–9
Style Boxes for Equity and Bond Funds from **Morningstar Mutual Funds.**

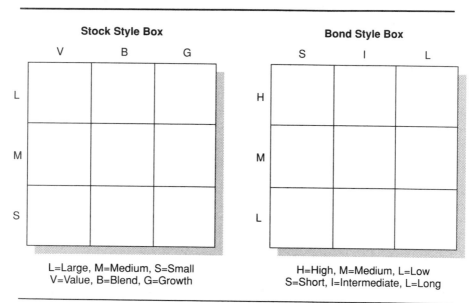

| Stock Style Box | | | | Bond Style Box | | |

L=Large, M=Medium, S=Small
V=Value, B=Blend, G=Growth

H=High, M=Medium, L=Low
S=Short, I=Intermediate, L=Long

Reprinted by permission of Morningstar, Inc., Chicago, IL.

The horizontal axis focuses on the following three investment styles as major objectives:

Value (V)   Combined P/E and P/B ratio[4] less than 1.75

Blend (B)   Combined P/E and P/B ratio between 1.75 and 2.25

Growth (G) Combined P/E and P/B ratio greater than 2.25

For bond (or fixed-income) funds, the vertical axis represents the bond risk in terms of its bond rating (Standard & Poor's)[5] using the following three groups:

---

[4] P/E is the price/earnings ratio (explained in Chapter 1). P/B is the price/book value ratio.

[5] Bond rating criteria are summarized in Exhibit 2–5.

Low (L)	Below BBB
Medium (M)	Between BBB and AA
High (H)	AA and above

The horizontal axis represents the average maturity of the fund's portfolio in three ranges, as follows:

Short (S)	Less than 4 years
Intermediate (I)	4 to 10 years
Long (L)	10 years and longer

Top 30 holdings in portfolio. This section lists the fund's top 30 stocks in order of capitalization, with data concerning weighting and the number of shares owned. Also included is the total number of stocks in the portfolio.

Portfolio breakdown. The final section describes the portfolio's diversification by industrial sector and by type of security (stocks, bonds, cash, preferred stocks, convertible bonds, and other). Included are data about the portfolio's overall P/E and P/B ratios.

Chapter Nine

The Dollar and Foreign Exchange

INTRODUCTION

The US dollar is the principal international medium of exchange and is a key reserve currency of almost every nation. Over half of the world's trade is dollar-denominated. Virtually every nation, corporation, and investor has a stake in the value of the dollar. This chapter discusses the measures by which the US dollar is measured, in addition to several measures of money and interest rates.

FOREIGN EXCHANGE

Spot Rates

Newspapers often list the exchange rates of the currencies of many countries relative to the US dollar. These individual rates are referred to as **bilateral exchange rates.** As illustrated in Exhibit 9–1, the bilateral exchange rate for a particular country's currency can take either of the following two forms:

The US dollar equivalent of one unit of the country's currency.

The number of units of a country's currency per one US dollar.

There is no uniform method for expressing an exchange rate. Of the two forms, the second is the more commonly used and is referred to as **European terms,** because Europeans (and the Japanese) tend to consider currency exchange rates as the price of

EXHIBIT 9–1
Foreign Exchange Rates from **The Wall Street Journal.**

CURRENCY TRADING

EXCHANGE RATES

Thursday, June 24, 1993

The New York foreign exchange selling rates below apply to trading among banks in amounts of $1 million and more, as quoted at 3 p.m. Eastern time by Bankers Trust Co., Telerate and other sources. Retail transactions provide fewer units of foreign currency per dollar.

Country	U.S. $ equiv. Thur.	Wed.	Currency per U.S. $ Thur.	Wed.
Argentina (Peso)	1.01	1.01	.99	.99
Australia (Dollar)	.6676	.6737	1.4979	1.4843
Austria (Schilling)	.08328	.08397	12.01	11.91
Bahrain (Dinar)	2.6522	2.6522	.3771	.3771
Belgium (Franc)	.02850	.02878	35.09	34.75
Brazil (Cruzeiro)	.0000202	.0000204	49504.95	48948.01
Britain (Pound)	1.4690	1.4725	.6807	.6791
30-Day Forward	1.4658	1.4691	.6822	.6807
90-Day Forward	1.4594	1.4628	.6852	.6836
180-Day Forward	1.4518	1.4552	.6888	.6872
Canada (Dollar)	.7792	.7811	1.2834	1.2803
30-Day Forward	.7782	.7801	1.2850	1.2819
90-Day Forward	.7763	.7782	1.2882	1.2850
180-Day Forward	.7733	.7751	1.2932	1.2901
Czech. Rep. (Koruna)				
Commercial rate	.0343997	.0345304	29.0700	28.9600
Chile (Peso)	.002561	.002549	390.52	392.28
China (Renminbi)	.174856	.174856	5.7190	5.7190
Colombia (Peso)	.001495	.001495	668.95	668.95
Denmark (Krone)	.1526	.1544	6.5525	6.4784
Ecuador (Sucre)				
Floating rate	.000539	.000539	1856.01	1856.01
Finland (Markka)	.17430	.17658	5.7372	5.6631
France (Franc)	.17391	.17573	5.7500	5.6905
30-Day Forward	.17331	.17509	5.7700	5.7112
90-Day Forward	.17234	.17403	5.8025	5.7462
180-Day Forward	.17119	.17285	5.8415	5.7855
Germany (Mark)	.5857	.5912	1.7075	1.6915
30-Day Forward	.5834	.5888	1.7142	1.6983
90-Day Forward	.5794	.5849	1.7259	1.7101
180-Day Forward	.5750	.5803	1.7391	1.7232
Greece (Drachma)	.004301	.004339	232.50	230.45
Hong Kong (Dollar)	.12878	.12892	7.7652	7.7570
Hungary (Forint)	.0113122	.0111235	88.4000	89.9000
India (Rupee)	.03205	.03205	31.20	31.20
Indonesia (Rupiah)	.0004793	.0004793	2086.51	2086.51
Ireland (Punt)	1.4305	1.4431	.6991	.6930
Israel (Shekel)	.3641	.3650	2.7465	2.7396
Italy (Lira)	.0006486	.0006547	1541.88	1527.44
Japan (Yen)	.009187	.009174	108.85	109.00

Country	U.S. $ equiv. Thurs.	Wed.	Currency per U.S. $ Thurs.	Wed.
30-Day Forward	.009187	.009174	108.85	109.00
90-Day Forward	.009188	.009175	108.84	108.99
180-Day Forward	.009201	.009189	108.68	108.83
Jordan (Dinar)	1.4682	1.4682	.6811	.6811
Kuwait (Dinar)	3.3118	3.3118	.3020	.3020
Lebanon (Pound)	.000577	.000577	1732.00	1732.00
Malaysia (Ringgit)	.3864	.3868	2.5880	2.5855
Malta (Lira)	2.6042	2.6042	.3840	.3840
Mexico (Peso)				
Floating rate	.3214917	.3214917	3.1105	3.1105
Netherland (Guilder) ..	.5222	.5272	1.9150	1.8968
New Zealand (Dollar) .	.5371	.5387	1.8619	1.8563
Norway (Krone)	.1387	.1401	7.2098	7.1390
Pakistan (Rupee)	.0371	.0371	26.95	26.98
Peru (New Sol)	.5154	.5154	1.94	1.94
Philippines (Peso)	.03738	.03738	26.75	26.75
Poland (Zloty)	.00005888	.00005902	16983.00	16942.00
Portugal (Escudo)	.006181	.006243	161.79	160.19
Saudi Arabia (Rival) ..	.26665	.26665	3.7503	3.7503
Singapore (Dollar)	.6114	.6134	1.6356	1.6302
Slovak Rep. (Koruna) .	.0343997	.0345304	29.0700	28.9600
South Africa (Rand)				
Commercial rate	.3016	.3028	3.3156	3.3021
Financial rate	.2129	.2115	4.6970	4.7285
South Korea (Won)	.0012450	.0012435	803.21	804.20
Spain (Peseta)	.007683	.007754	130.16	128.96
Sweden (Krona)	.1279	.1299	7.8186	7.6963
Switzerland (Franc) ...	.6596	.6638	1.5161	1.5065
30-Day Forward	.6585	.6626	1.5186	1.5093
90-Day Forward	.6567	.6608	1.5228	1.5134
180-Day Forward	.6552	.6592	1.5263	1.5170
Taiwan (Dollar)	.038255	.038285	26.14	26.12
Thailand (Baht)	.03951	.03951	25.31	25.31
Turkey (Lira)	.0000936	.0000939	10683.76	10644.00
United Arab (Dirham)	.2723	.2723	3.6725	3.6725
Uruguay (New Peso)				
Financial	.250312	.250312	4.00	4.00
Venezuela (Bolivar)				
Floating rate	.01131	.01133	88.40	88.26
— — —				
SDR	1.38794	1.38573	.72049	.72164
ECU	1.14670	1.15740	....	....

Special Drawing Rights (SDR) are based on exchange rates for the U.S., German, British, French and Japanese currencies. Source: International Monetary Fund.

European Currency Unit (ECU) is based on a basket of community currencies.

z-Not quoted.

foreign currency. On the other hand, the Americans and the English prefer the opposite. Very often when exchange rates are quoted on television—on CNN or CNBC broadcasts, for instance—the dollar is quoted in European terms, with the exception of the British pound. Regardless of which form is used, either is the reciprocal of the other. Knowing one form, the investor can immediately determine the other by using the following formula:

$$\frac{\text{U.S. dollar equivalent}}{\text{1 Currency unit}} = \frac{1}{\text{Currency unit/1 U.S. dollar}} \quad (9\text{–}1)$$

The rates quoted in newspapers are usually applicable for transactions greater than $1 million between banks at a specific time during the day, such as noon or 3:00 PM. For individuals who buy foreign-denominated traveler's checks or change their dollars into foreign currency (locally or abroad), the exchange rate will be several percentage points higher than the quoted interbank rate. Very often, newspapers print qualifier codes or statements, generally for the purpose of pointing out that a given rate is the country's official rate, that the rate is a floating rate, or that one rate applies only to financial transactions (interbank) while another rate applies only to commercial transactions.

As in Exhibit 9–1, which shows foreign exchange rates taken from *The Wall Street Journal*, most newspapers use a two-day quotation format for bilateral foreign exchange rates. The quotation format shown gives the exchange rate for the current day as well as the closing rate for the previous day's trading.

	US $ equiv.		Currency per US $	
Country	Fri.	Thurs.	Fri.	Thurs.
Belgium (Franc)	.03072	.03086	32.55	32.40

The Friday rate at 3:00 PM Eastern time for Belgian francs was such that each franc was worth less than the day before: 3.072 cents versus 3.086 cents. Consequently, the dollar became weaker in terms of Belgian francs.

Other papers, such as the *Chicago Sun Times* (Exhibit 9–2), give only a single day's quotation, and give it in European terms.

EXHIBIT 9–2
Foreign Exchange Rates from the Chicago Sun Times.

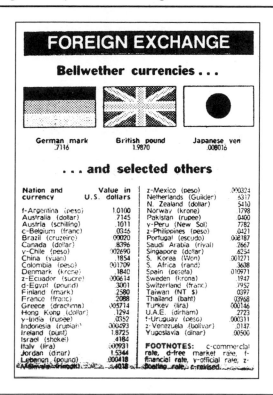

Once the exchange rate is known, determining how many dollars a given number of units of currency will bring, or how many units of currency a set number of US dollars will be worth, becomes a simple matter.

Example: Converting Dollars into Belgian Francs

In the previous quotation, the Belgian franc on May 7, 1993, was quoted at BFr32.55 to the dollar (European terms). In terms of equivalent dollars, each franc would then be worth (from Equation 9–1):

$$\text{Equivalent dollars} = \frac{1}{32.55 \text{ Fr} / \$}$$

$$= \$0.03072 \text{ per franc}$$

To find out how many Belgian francs would be received if an investor were exchanging \$2.5 million at the quoted interbank rate, you multiply the exchange rate in European terms (BFr32.55 per dollar) by the dollar amount to be exchanged, as follows:

$$\text{Belgian francs} = (32.55 \text{ BFr}/\$) \cdot (\$2,500,000)$$

$$= \textbf{BFr81,375,000}$$

If, on the other hand, only the dollar equivalent of one Belgian franc is known (\$0.03072 per franc), the same result is found by calculating as follows:

$$\text{Belgian francs} = \frac{\$2,500,000}{\$0.03072 / \text{BFr}}$$

$$= \textbf{BFr81,375,000}$$

If \$2.5 million were exchanged the day before, the exchange rate was 32.40 francs to the dollar, so that each franc would be worth more. This results in the equivalent of 81 million francs.

Besides aiding in the straight exchange of currency, foreign exchange rates are also helpful in determining the share value of foreign stocks, which are quoted in terms of local currency units.

Example: Finding the Dollar Price per Share of KLM

On a particular day the closing price of KLM (Koninklijke Luchvaart Maatschappij), as traded on the Amsterdam Stock Exchange, was quoted at Dfl40.30 (guilders). On the same day the exchange rate was Dfl1.8050 per dollar, or $0.5540/Dfl. The dollar price per share of KLM was then determined as follows:

Dollar price per share = (Dfl40.30) · ($0.5540/Dfl)

= **$22.33**

rounded off to the nearest cent.

In the equations used in the preceding two examples (see page 202 and this page), the denominations of the currencies and exchange rates were included in the calculations. This serves several purposes. For one, it helps to show on a dimensional basis that the particular equation makes sense. Second, the included dimensions help the investor to correctly determine whether one number should be multiplied by another or whether division is required. In the second example the intention is to determine the answer in dollars. The dimensions on the right-hand side of the equation must also be in dollars. When guilders (Dfl) are multiplied by the exchange rate expressed in dollars per guilder ($/Dfl), we then have, in dimensional form: Dfl × $/Dfl, such that Dfl cancels and only the dollar sign remains.

Forward Rates

The majority of the rates given in Exhibit 9–1 are for spot transactions. Besides spot exchange rates, the rates of the world's major economic countries, such as Canada, France, Great Britain, Germany, Japan, and Switzerland, also include what is termed the

forward rate, meaning that banks will provide delivery of certain foreign currencies at a guaranteed exchange rate at some future time. Some papers, such as *Investor's Business Daily*, give forward rates for 30, 60, and 90 days, while *The Wall Street Journal* uses times periods of 30, 90, and 180 days. Using forward rates, banks and their customers can try to limit their risk to fluctuations in the exchange rates. This is similar to futures trading on certain foreign currencies, except that delivery is required.

The forward rates are placed immediately below the current rate for the country, as shown in the following example:

Country	US $ equiv.		Currency per US $	
	Fri.	Thurs.	Fri.	Thurs.
Britain (Pound)	1.5710	1.5795	.6365	.6331
30-day forward	1.5673	1.5757	.6380	.6346
90-day forward	1.5599	1.5683	.6411	.6376
180-day forward	1.5498	1.5574	.6452	.6421

As a general rule, the dollar equivalent will be worth less further into the future. Here, the British pound is quoted at $1.5673 if delivery is taken 30 days later instead of being worth $1.5710 currently. For delivery in 90 days, the pound is worth even less ($1.5599).

Cross Rates

Exhibits 9–1 and 9–2 give only bilateral currency exchange rates with the US dollar. What is the exchange rate between the British pound and the Swiss franc? If the exchange rates relative to the dollar of any two currencies are known, it is possible to determine the exchange rate between the two currencies. This exchange rate is termed a **cross rate,** defined as an exchange rate between two currencies, neither of which is the US dollar.[1]

---

[1] This assumes that the domestic currency is the US dollar. The exchange cross rates that appear in the *Financial Times*, for example, assume that the British pound is the domestic currency.

Example: Determining the Exchange Rate between British Pounds and Swiss Francs

On May 7, 1993, the exchange rates between the US dollar and the British pound (£), and between the US dollar and the Swiss franc (SFr) were quoted by Telerate as:

$1 = £0.63633   or   £1 = $1.5715

$1 = SFr 1.4290   or   SFr 1 = $0.69979

The value of SFr1 in terms of British pounds is determined as follows:

SFr1 = (SFr1) · ($0.69979/Sfr) · (1£/$1.5715)

    = £0.44530

On the other hand, the value of £1 in terms of Swiss francs is calculated as follows:

£1 = (£1) · ($1.5715/£1) · (SFr 1/$0.69979)

    = **SFr 2.2457**

This series of calculations can be summarized by the following cross-rate formula:

$$\text{Swiss franc price of 1 British pound} = \frac{\text{Swiss franc price of \$1}}{\text{British pound price of \$1}}$$

$$= \frac{\$1.4290}{0.63633}$$

$$= \text{SFr 2.2457}$$

The generalized cross-rate formula is:

$$\frac{\text{Currency A price of}}{\text{1 unit of Currency B}} = \frac{\text{Currency A price of \$1}}{\text{Currency B price of \$1}} \quad (9\text{--}2)$$

The previous example forms the basis for construction of a simple table that shows the exchange rate between any two currencies. This example is concerned with the currencies of three countries: Switzerland, Great Britain, and the United States. Being concerned only first with the bilateral rate between the US dollar and the British pound, we can form a 2-by-2 table that gives the exchange rate between collars and pounds, as follows:

	Dollar ($)	Pound (£)
United States ($)	. . .	1.5715
Great Britain (£)	0.63633	. . .

The currencies in the countries listed in the first column can be expressed in the denomination of the country that corresponds to the top row. When the same country matches up (row and column), there is a trivial 1-to-1 relationship. Instead of writing this 1-to-1 relationship as 1.0, very often we either omit it or represent it by a series of dots (. . .). For example, the intersection between British pounds and US dollars produces the number 0.63633, as shown in the following:

	Dollar ($)	Pound (£)
United States ($)	. . .	1.5715
Great Britain (£)	**0.63633**	. . .

This means that $1 = £0.63633.

This process can be expanded by adding the Swiss franc, as follows:

	Dollar ($)	Pound (£)	Franc (SFr)
United States ($)	. . .	1.5715	0.69979
Great Britain (£)	0.63633	. . .	0.44530
Switzerland (SFr)	1.4290	2.2457	. . .

The bottom row shows that there are SFr1.4290 to the dollar and SFr2.2457 to the British pound. Eliminating the need for an investor to calculate these cross rates, the cross-rate table is a method whereby the exchange rates between a number of currencies may be easily compared. *The Wall Street Journal* and London's *Financial Times* publish tables of currency exchange cross rates. An example is shown in Exhibit 9–3.

In general, given N currencies including the dollar, the number of cross rates may be calculated as follows:

$$\text{Number of cross rates} = \frac{N(N-1)}{2} \qquad (9\text{--}3)$$

For the cross-rate table in Exhibit 9–3, there are nine currencies (including the dollar), so that there are eight (i.e., 9 − 1) different dollar rates and (9 × 8)/2 = 36 cross rates. Although there are 9 × 9 = 81 entries, and nine trivial cross rates, each with a value of 1.0, the remaining 81 − 36 − 9 = 36 are reciprocals of the cross rates.

EUROPEAN CURRENCY UNIT

The **European Currency Unit (ECU)** is the official composite currency unit for the European Monetary System (EMS), which was established in 1979 to promote exchange-rate stability among the European currencies of EMS members. The ECU has been defined as a market basket of the national currencies of the member countries of the European Economic Community (EEC) (Exhibit 9–4).

EXHIBIT 9–3
Currency Exchange Cross Rates from **The Wall Street Journal.**

Key Currency Cross Rates
Late New York Trading June 24, 1993

	Dollar	Pound	SFranc	Guilder	Yen	Lira	D-Mark	FFranc	CdnDlr
Canada	1.2833	1.8852	.84622	.67031	.01180	.00083	.75165	.22322	
France	5.7490	8.445	3.7910	3.0029	.05287	.00373	3.3673		4.4799
Germany	1.7073	2.5080	1.1258	.89177	.01570	.00111		.29697	1.3304
Italy	1540.6	2263.1	1015.86	804.67	14.169		902.33	267.97	1200.5
Japan	108.73	159.72	71.698	56.793		.07058	63.685	18.913	84.73
Netherlands	1.9145	2.8124	1.2624		.01761	.00124	1.1214	.33301	1.4919
Switzerland	1.5165	2.2277		.79211	.01395	.00098	.88824	.26379	1.1817
U.K.	.68074		.44889	.35557	.00626	.00044	.39872	.11841	.53046
U.S.		1.4690	.65941	.52233	.00920	.00065	.58572	.17394	.77924

Source: Telerate

The weight of each currency in the ECU is the percentage share of the US dollar equivalent of the prescribed amount of that currency. Because of fluctuations in exchange rates, the value of the ECU relative to the dollar also changes. As illustrated by Exhibit 9–1, the value of the ECU is often given in foreign exchange-rate tables.

The composition of the ECU changes periodically. The currencies that make up the ECU are reviewed every 5 years, or when a new member joins the EEC. The revisions that follow these reviews are made in an effort to restore the original proportion of each currency in the ECU. The ECU has been accepted as a currency in its own right, and many bonds issued by the member countries are denominated in ECUs.

The dollar value of the ECU is determined by first multiplying the current EMS weight of each currency by the corresponding current exchange rate for that currency, and then adding the 10 values to obtain the total dollar value of one ECU.

EXHIBIT 9-4
European Currency Unit (ECU)
Component Currencies.

Country	Currency Unit	Current EMS Weight
Germany	Deutsche mark	DM 0.719
France	Franc	FFr 1.31
Great Britain	Pound	£ 0.0878
Netherlands	Guilder	Dfl 0.256
Italy	Lira	L 140.0
Belgium	Franc	BFr 3.71
Denmark	Krone	Kr 0.219
Ireland	Punt	IR£ 0.00871
Greece	Drachma	Dr 1.15
Luxembourg	Franc	LuxFr 0.14

Source: Federal Reserve System.

Example: Calculating the Dollar Value of One ECU

On March 11, 1989, the dollar per unit exchange rates for the ten EMS currencies (as obtained from *The Wall Street Journal*) were as follows:

Germany	$0.5228/deutsche mark
France	$0.1546/franc
Great Britain	$1.6670/pound
Netherlands	$0.4639/guilder
Italy	$0.000713/lira
Belgium	$0.02496/franc
Denmark	$0.1344/krone
Ireland	$1.4020/punt
Greece	$0.006134/drachma
Luxembourg	$0.02496/franc

The EMS weight from Exhibit 9–4 for Germany was 0.719, so that the equivalent dollar amount for the portion of the DM's value that makes up the ECU is then calculated as follows:

$$\text{Equivalent dollars} = (\text{EMS weight}) \times (\text{exchange rate})$$

$$= (\text{DM } 0.719) \times (\$0.5228/\text{DM})$$

$$= \mathbf{\$0.3759}$$

In similar fashion, this calculation is carried out for the remaining nine currencies, as follows:

Country	Currency Unit	Current EMS Weight	Current Exchange Rate ($/Unit)	Equivalent Dollars
Germany	Deutsche mark	DM 0.719	0.5228	$0.3759
France	Franc	FFr 1.31	0.1546	$0.2025
Great Britain	Pound	£ 0.0878	1.6670	$0.1464
Netherlands	Guilder	Dfl 0.256	0.4639	$0.1188
Italy	Lira	L 140.0	0.0007173	$0.1004
Belgium	Franc	BFr 3.71	0.02496	$0.0926
Denmark	Krone	Kr 0.219	0.1344	$0.0294
Ireland	Punt	IR£ 0.00871	1.4020	$0.0122
Greece	Drachma	Dr 1.15	0.006134	$0.0071
Luxembourg	Franc	LuxFr 0.14	0.02496	$0.0035
Total			1 ECU	$1.0888

On March 11, 1988, 1 ECU was worth $1.0888 (or $1 equaled 0.9184 ECU).

SPECIAL DRAWING RIGHTS

In the late 1960s, neither gold nor major foreign currencies were available in sufficient quantities to support the growing volume of international transactions. In 1967, an agreement was reached among the industrial and developing countries to create an artificial currency called *Special Drawing Rights* (*SDR*). These are credits extended to importing countries and are monitored by the **International Monetary Fund** (**IMF**). Each country has a credit quota, depending on the volume of its exports and imports. Unlike foreign currency and ECUs, SDRs are exchanged only among central banks but are also readily converted into other currencies.

The value of one SDR was initially based on 16 major currencies, each having a different weight depending on its volume in international trade. In 1981, the composition was changed, and the SDR is now a weighted average of five currencies: the US dollar, the German deutsche mark, the French franc, the British pound, and the Japanese yen. Of these, the US dollar has the most influence, comprising over 40 percent of the SDR's value. SDRs are often quoted with the ECU in foreign exchange-rate tables, as illustrated in Exhibit 9–1.

Appendix A

Decimal Equivalents of Thirty-Seconds

Thirty-Seconds	Decimal Equivalent	Thirty-Seconds	Decimal Equivalent
1	0.03125	17	0.53125
2	0.0625	18	0.5625
3	0.09375	19	0.59375
4	0.125	20	0.625
5	0.15615	21	0.65625
6	0.1875	22	0.6875
7	0.21875	23	0.71875
8	0.25	24	0.75
9	0.28125	25	0.78125
10	0.3125	26	0.8125
11	0.34375	27	0.84375
12	0.375	28	0.875
13	0.40425	29	0.90625
14	0.4375	30	0.9375
15	0.46875	31	0.96875
16	0.5	32	1.0

Tax Status of Municipal Bonds by State

Despite their name, municipal bonds are not tax-free in all states. Some states allow the interest from bonds of other states to be tax-free. The following list summarizes the tax status of municipal bonds for each state.

State	Own Bonds Tax-Exempt	Bonds of Other States Tax-Exempt	State	Own Bonds Tax-Exempt	Bonds of Other States Tax-Exempt
Alabama	x		Montana	x	x
Alaska	x	x	Nebraska	x	
Arizona	x		Nevada	x	
Arkansas	x		New Hampshire	x	
California	x		New Jersey	x	
Colorado			New Mexico	x	
Connecticut	x		New York	x	
Delaware	x		North Carolina	x	
Florida	x	x	North Dakota	x	
Georgia	x		Ohio	x	
Hawaii	x		Oklahoma		
Idaho	x		Oregon	x	
Illinois			Pennsylvania	x	
Indiana	x	x	Rhode Island	x	
Iowa			South Carolina	x	
Kansas			South Dakota	x	x
Kentucky	x		Tennessee	x	
Louisiana	x	x	Texas	x	x
Maine	x		Utah	x	x

State	Own Bonds Tax-Exempt	Bonds of Other States Tax-Exempt	State	Own Bonds Tax-Exempt	Bonds of Other States Tax-Exempt
Maryland	x		Vermont	x	x
Massachusetts	x		Virginia	x	
Michigan	x		Washington	x	x
Minnesota	x		West Virginia	x	
Mississippi	x		Wisconsin		
Missouri	x		Wyoming	x	x

Glossary

accrued interest Interest due, either from issue date or from the last interest payment (coupon) date to the present, on an interest-bearing security. The buyer of the security pays the quoted dollar price plus accrued interest.

actuals Physical commodities, as opposed to futures contracts.

ADR see *American Depository Receipt*.

alpha (α) A statistic that measures a mutual fund's risk-adjusted performance. Alpha represents the difference between a fund's actual returns and its expected performance, given its level of risk as measured by beta (β). Alpha is expressed as an annualized percentage. A positive value is indicative of performance better than expected; a negative value indicates underperformance. See also *beta*.

American Depository Receipt (ADR) A US security representing ownership of a specified number of ordinary shares of a foreign company traded either on the NYSE, on the AMEX, or over the counter. The physical shares are held by an agent or a foreign branch of an American bank (an ADR bank). The custodian bank is usually an office of an American bank in the country of the company that issued the ADR. If not, the custodian bank is then the bank geographically closest to the foreign company.

AMEX The American Stock Exchange. Also abbreviated as ASE.

arrears Overdue payments, which are frequently charged when the dividend on a preferred stock is omitted.

ASE The American Stock Exchange. See also *AMEX*.

asked price The price at which a broker has offered to buy securities.

at-the-money option An option selling at its strike price.

back-end load A commission charged for redemption of the shares of a mutual fund.

basis point One one-hundredth of 1 percent (0.01 percent).

bearer bond A bond issued without the name and address of the bondholder on it. The bond also has interest-bearing coupons attached to it.

beta (β) An index of volatility in the return of an asset relative to a given market portfolio. Beta is a measure of systematic risk. See also *alpha*.

bid price The price that a broker has offered to pay for securities.

bid cover The ratio of the amount bid in Treasury auctions to the amount accepted.

Big Board The New York Stock Exchange (NYSE).

bilateral exchange rates Currency exchange rates between two currencies.

block Ten thousand shares of stock.

bonds Long-term interest-bearing debt instruments.

book value The value at which a debt security is shown on the holder's balance sheet. Also called *shareholder's equity*.

calls Options that give a holder the right, but not the obligation, to buy underlying securities at a specified price during a fixed time period.

call date The date at which the issuer may redeem part or all of a bond's issue before its maturity date.

callable bonds Bonds that the issuer has the right to redeem prior to maturity by paying a specified call price.

CATS Certificates of Accrual on Treasury Securities. Zero coupon Treasury bonds, originally sold by Salomon Brothers. See also *zero coupon bonds*.

CBOE The Chicago Board of Options Exchange.

CBOT The Chicago Board of Trade.

CDs See *certificates of deposit*.

certificates of deposit (CDs) Time deposits with a specific maturity, evidenced by certificates.

closed-end funds Investment funds with a limited number of shares. The shares of closed-end funds are traded on a stock exchange.

closing price The last trade price for a security at the close of the trading day.

commercial paper Unsecured short-term promissory notes issued by the leading industrial, finance, and bank holding companies.

commodities Items that can be bought or sold, for either immediate or future delivery. Historically, agricultural products such as grains and oilseeds as well as livestock and meats were the original commodities. In time, foods and fibers, metals, petroleum products, currencies, interest rate instruments, and tradable market indexes also came to be considered commodities.

common stocks (or **common shares**) Instruments that represent ownership of a corporation. The owner of common shares is a residual claimant—the last one to receive assets if the firm is liquidated.

competitive bid A bid tendered in a Treasury auction for a specific number of securities at a specific yield or price.

contract size The amount of a commodity that forms the basis for a futures contract.

conversion price The effective price paid for common stock when the stock is obtained by converting either convertible preferred stock or convertible bonds.

conversion ratio (*CR*) The number of shares of common stock, adjusted for stock splits, that may be obtained by converting a convertible bond.

conversion value (*CV*) The current value of the total shares into which a bond can be converted.

convertible bonds Bonds that are exchangeable at the option of the holder for common stock of the issuing company.

coupon yield The annual rate of interest paid on a bond's face value, which the bond's issuer promises to pay the bondholder. Also, a certificate attached to a bond evidencing interest due on a payment date.

covered option An option in which the seller owns the underlying security.

cross rate The exchange rate between two currencies, neither of which is the currency of the home country.

cum-rights A term meaning "with rights." A stock selling with rights attached.

current yield Coupon payments on a security as a percentage of the security's market price.

CUSIP The Committee of Uniform Securities Identification Procedures.

debentures Bonds secured only by the general credit of the issuer.

debt securities IOUs created through loan-type transactions—commercial paper, bank CDs, bills, bonds, and notes.

deep discount A market price far below the face value of a bond.

delivery The month in which a futures contract expires and delivery may be taken or made.

discount A trading price that is lower than the issue's par value.

discount bonds Bonds selling below par.

discount securities Non-interest-bearing money market instruments that are issued at a discount and redeemed at maturity for full face value; for example, a US Treasury bill.

ECU See *European Currency Unit.*

Dow Jones Industrial Average (DJIA) A price-weighted stock market barometer of 30 "blue chip" stocks traded on the NYSE. Over most of its history the DJIA was composed solely of industrial stocks, but there now are exceptions.

Dow Jones Transportation Average (DJTA) A price-weighted stock market barometer of 20 transportation industry stocks traded on the NYSE. Prior to 1970, the DJTA was called the Dow Jones Railroad Average.

Dow Jones Utilities Average (DJUA) A price-weighted stock market barometer of 15 utility industry stocks traded on the NYSE. It is a leading indicator of interest rate changes.

equities A term commonly used to refer to shares of common or preferred stocks.

equivalent bond yield The annual yield on a short-term, non-interest-bearing security, calculated so as to be comparable to yields quoted on coupon securities.

equivalent coupon rate A T-bill's annualized rate of return if it is held to maturity and calculated on the amount *invested*, not on the face value of the T-bill. The yield quote is based on the T-bill's asked quote. This yield is also known as either the *asked yield* or the *annual percentage rate.* As the annual percentage rate, it can be directly compared to the stated annual interest rates of other fixed-rate investments, such as CDs, which are not quoted at a discount.

European Currency Unit (ECU) The official composite currency unit for the European Monetary System (EMS), established in 1979 to promote exchange-rate stability among the European currencies of EMS members. The ECU is a basket of the national currencies of the member countries of the European Economic Community (EEC).

European terms Exchange rates in which the number of units of a country's currency is given in terms of $1.

ex-dividend A term meaning "without dividend." A stock selling without the rights to the recently declared dividend.

ex-rights A term meaning "without rights." A stock selling without rights attached.

exercise price The price at which an option holder may buy or sell the underlying security. Also called *striking price* or *strike price*.

expiration date The last date on which the holder of an option may exercise the option.

face value The value of a bond that appears on the face of the bond, unless otherwise specified. The amount paid at maturity. Also called *par*.

Fannie Mae The Federal National Mortgage Association (FNMA).

FHLMC See *Freddie Mac*.

FINEX The Financial Exchange, a futures exchange.

fixed-income securities Securities that provide a fixed rate of interest paid over their life. These include CDs, T-bills, notes, and bonds, as well as corporate and municipal bonds.

flat A situation in which a bond trades without accrued interest.

flower bonds T-bonds that are acceptable at par in payment of federal estate taxes when owned by the decedent at the time of death.

FNMA See *Fannie Mae*.

forward rate A rate at which banks will provide future delivery of certain foreign currencies at a guaranteed exchange rate at a specified future time.

Freddie Mac Federal Home Loan Mortgage Corporation (FHLMC).

futures contracts Investment contracts that agree to deliver specified quantities of a commodity at a specified time and price.

futures market A market in which contracts for future delivery of a commodity or security are bought and sold.

general obligation (GO) bonds Municipal securities secured by the issuer's pledge of its full faith, credit, and taxing power.

Ginnie Mae Government National Mortgage Association (GNMA).

GO bonds See *general obligation bonds*.

IMM The International Money Market, a futures exchange.

indenture The contract portion of a bond that specifies the terms and obligations of the debtor.

instrument A term synonymous with an investment security.

interest A payment made by a borrower to a lender for the use of money.

in-the-money option An option selling at a price such that it has intrinsic value.

investment company A company or trust that invests its capital in other companies. There are two principal types: closed-end and open-end, or mutual fund.

liquid Capable of being converted easily and rapidly into cash without a substantial loss of value. In money markets, a security is said to be liquid if the spread between bid and asked prices is narrow.

load A sales charge imposed by a mutual fund for buying or selling its shares.

long A position in which an investor owns debt securities, stocks, or futures contracts in anticipation of a price rise.

long bond A bond (usually a T-bond) with a long current maturity.

market value The price at which a security is trading and could presumably be purchased or sold.

maturity date The date on which a loan, such as a bond or a debenture, becomes due and is to be paid off.

money market A market in which short-term debt instruments (bills, commercial paper, banker's acceptances, etc.) are issued and traded.

money market funds Mutual funds that invest solely in money market instruments.

municipal bonds Bonds issued by state, city, other political subdivisions, or their agencies. In general, the interest paid is exempt from federal income taxes as well as state and local income taxes within the state of issue. Also called *municipals; munis; tax-exempt securities.*

municipal notes Short-term notes issued by municipalities in anticipation of tax receipts, proceeds from a bond issue, or other revenues.

municipals See *municipal bonds.*

munis See *municipal bonds.*

mutual funds Open-end investment companies or trusts that use their capital to invest in other companies.

naked option A call option in which the seller does not own the underlying security.

NASD The National Association of Securities Dealers.

NASDAQ The National Association of Securities Dealers Automated Quotations.

NAV See *net asset value.*

nearby contract A futures contract that is near its expiration date.

net asset value (NAV) The dollar price at which a fund will redeem shares from investors. The total assets divided by the number of shares issued. Also called *bid price.*

no-load mutual funds Mutual funds that do not impose a fee for buying or selling their shares.

noncompetitive bid In a Treasury auction, a bid for a specific amount of securities at the price, whatever it may turn out to be, equal to the average price of the accepted competitive bids.

notes Debt securities with relatively short original maturities.

NYFE The New York Futures Exchange, a futures exchange and a division of the New York Stock Exchange (NYSE).

NYMEX The New York Mercantile Exchange, a futures exchange.

NYSE The New York Stock Exchange. Also called the *Big Board.*

odd lot Less than a round lot (i.e., less than 100 shares).

offer The price asked by a seller of securities.

OID See *original issue discount.*

open-end funds Investment funds with an unlimited number of shares; mutual funds.

open interest In options and futures trading, the number of outstanding contracts at any point in time, which have not been exercised and have not yet reached their expiration dates.

option A contract for, but not the obligation to purchase or sell, an underlying security at a specified price by a specified date.

original issue discounts (OIDs) Fixed-income securities, such as zero coupon bonds, that are issued at a discount from par value.

original maturity Maturity at issue.

OTC markets See *over-the-counter markets.*

out-of-the-money option An option selling at a price such that it has no intrinsic value.

over-the-counter (OTC) markets Markets created by dealer trading, as opposed to the auction market prevailing on organized exchanges.

oversubscribed In a Treasury auction, the situation in which a greater amount is bid than is being offered.

par (1) A bond price of 100 percent. (2) The principal amount at which the issuer of a debt security contracts to redeem the security at maturity. Also called *face value.*

par bond A bond selling at par.

parity The conversion value of a convertible bond.

P/E (price/earnings) ratio The number times earnings that investors are willing to pay for a stock. The P/E ratio is equal to the market price of a stock times its earnings.

PHLX The Philadelphia Stock Exchange.

points (1) One hundred basis points = 1 percent. (2) One percent of the face value of a note or bond.

portfolio A collection of securities held by an investor.

preferred stock A class of stock with a claim on the company's earnings before payment of dividends may be made on the common stock; usually entitled to priority over common stock if the company liquidates.

premium (1) The amount by which the price of a security exceeds the issue's par value. (2) The cost of the option that a buyer pays to the option's seller (or writer); separate from any commissions, exchange fees, and taxes paid to the brokerage firm.

premium bonds Bonds selling above par.

principal The face amount or par value of a debt security.

prospectus A detailed statement prepared by an issuer and filed with the Securities and Exchange Commission (SEC) prior to the sale of a new issue. The prospectus gives detailed information on the issue and on the issuer's condition and prospects.

PSE The Pacific Stock Exchange.

puts Options that give the holder the right, but not the obligation, to sell underlying securities at a specified price during a fixed time period.

ratings Evaluations given by Moody's, Standard & Poor's, Duff & Phelps, Fitch, or other rating services of the credit-worthiness of securities.

redemption price The price at which bonds may be redeemed before maturity, at the option of the issuer.

refunding Redemption of securities by funds raised through the sale of a new issue.

registered bond A bond whose owner's name and address is registered with the issuer.

repos See *repurchase agreements*.

repurchase agreements (repos, RPs) Short-term instruments through which a buyer purchases an underlying security and, at the same time, the seller agrees to repurchase the security at the same price plus a specified amount of interest.

revenue bonds Municipal bonds secured by revenue from tolls, user charges, or rents derived from the facility financed.

rights Instruments issued to common stockholders when a corporation sells additional shares of common stock to the public. The purpose of rights is to permit common shareholders to buy additional shares in the company in order to maintain their proportionate ownership. In effect, a right is an option, but not the obligation to buy additional shares of common stock during a given time frame.

risk The degree of uncertainty of return on an asset.

round lot One hundred shares of stock.

RPs See *repurchase agreements.*

Sallie Mae The Student Loan Marketing Administration (SLMA).

secondary market A market in which previously issued securities are traded.

Securities and Exchange Commission (SEC) A federal regulatory agency created by Congress to protect investors in securities transactions. This however, does not include regulation of the trading of futures contracts.

senior securities Corporate bonds, which as debt, must be serviced to the bondholders before stockholders are entitled to any corporate profits.

settlement The date on which a trade is cleared by delivery of securities against funds. The settlement date may be the trade date or a later date.

shareholder's equity See *book value.*

short A position in which a market participant sells a security he or she does not own. The seller then makes delivery by borrowing the security sold or purchasing it on the open market.

SLMA See *Sallie Mae.*

spot price The cash price for immediate delivery of a commodity.

spread (1) The difference between bid and asked prices on a security. (2) The difference between yields on prices of two securities of differing sorts or with differing maturities.

standard deviation (SD or σ) The risk or short-term volatility of a mutual fund's total return.

straight bonds Nonconvertible bonds. See also *convertible bonds.*

STRIPS Separate Trading of Registered Interest and Principal of Securities. Zero coupon Treasury bond issues sold by the US Treasury.

stock An ownership in a company. There are two types of stock: common and preferred.

stop-out price The lowest price (highest yield) accepted by the Treasury in an auction of a new issue.

strike price See *exercise price.*

striking price See *exercise price.*

tail The spread between the average price and the stop-out price in Treasury auctions.

taxable equivalent yield The yield on a taxable security that would leave the investor with the same after-tax return as would be earned by holding a tax-exempt municipal bond.

tax-exempt securities See *municipal bonds.*

T-bills See *Treasury bills.*

T-bonds See *Treasury bonds.*

T-notes See *Treasury notes.*

tender A formal application offer to buy T-bills, T-notes, or T-bonds at auction.

term bonds A bond issue in which all bonds mature at the same time.

tick The minimum price movement on a futures contract.

ticker tape A record of the continuous trade-by-trade transactions of a stock exchange.

TIGRs Treasury Investment Growth Receipts. Zero coupon T-bond issues sold by Merrill Lynch.

Treasury bills Short-term discounted debt securities with maturities of 1 year or less. Also called *T-bills.*

Treasury bonds Long-term interest-bearing debt securities with maturities longer than 10 years. Also called *T-bonds.*

Treasury notes Interest-bearing debt securities with maturities longer than 1 year but no longer than 10 years. Also called *T-notes.*

underlying securities The actual securities on which an option is traded. Options that are traded can be based on common stocks, foreign currencies, or tradable stock indexes.

volume The number of shares, bonds, or contracts traded.

warrants Certificates giving the holder the right to purchase stocks at a stipulated price within a specified time limit. Warrants are frequently issued with stocks, as an inducement to buy.

when-issued (WI) trades Trades occurring during the lag between the time a new issue is announced and sold and the time it is actually issued. During this interval, the security trades WI—"when, as, and if issued."

WI See *when-issued trades.*

write (verb) To sell an option.

yield to maturity The rate of return yielded by a debt security held to maturity when interest payments and the investor's capital gain or loss on the security are taken into account.

zero coupon bonds Corporate bonds, municipal bonds, or T-bonds on which the owner separates the interest-bearing coupons and sells the remaining principal certificates at a discount.

Index